SIXTIES ROCK

A LISTENER'S GUIDE

ROBERT SANTELLI

CONTEMPORARY
BOOKS, INC.
CHICAGO

Library of Congress Cataloging in Publication Data

Santelli, Robert.
　　Sixties rock, a listener's guide.

　　Includes index.
　　1. Rock music—United States—History and criticism.
2. Rock musicians—United States.　　I. Title.
ML3534.S245　　1985　　784.5'4'009046　　85-4206
ISBN 0-8092-5439-5

Photography by Barry Goldenberg

Published by Contemporary Books, Inc.
180 North Michigan Avenue, Chicago, Illinois 60601
Manufactured in the United States of America
Library of Congress Catalog Card Number: 85-4206
International Standard Book Number: 0-8092-5439-5

Published simultaneously in Canada by Beaverbooks, Ltd.
195 Allstate Parkway, Valleywood Business Park
Markham, Ontario L3R 4T8 Canada

For Jaron

CONTENTS

ACKNOWLEDGMENTS

This book could not have been written without the generous assistance of Kenny Barr, Kathy Borkoski, George Brand, John Cinquegrana, Bob Dalley, Bruce Eder, Pete Fornatale, Sonny Kenn, August and Dorothea Kraft, Ben Liemer, Dave Marsh, Rhino Records, Wayne Stierle, Garry Tallent, Jeff Tamarkin, Dee Tango, Max Weinberg, and Tom Whalley. Thank you all.

A special thanks to Sandy Choron, the best friend any writer could ever have; to my sister, Jill Cucaz, who took care of the typing load down the stretch, and her husband, Marc, for his patience and genuine interest in the book; to Barry Goldenberg, a first-class photographer and a first-class friend; and to my editors, Patricia Romanowski and Kathy Willhoite.

Finally, a very special thanks to my wife, Cindy, who put up with me during all those trying moments and who never once complained about all the hours I spent with this book instead of her, and to our daughter Jaron, who thought her father and his typewriter were one and the same. I love you both.

INTRODUCTION

Sixties Rock: A Listener's Guide deals exclusively with the rock music created during the years 1960 through 1969. It is not intended to be the definitive book written about sixties rock. Nor is it specifically aimed at the overzealous record collector, who often is more concerned with the joy of collecting and accumulating than the music itself. Rather, *Sixties Rock* is meant to serve as a companion to one's discovery or rediscovery (whichever the case may be) of the truly great rock music recorded in that memorable decade.

The book consists of an overview of every major rock category that figured prominently in the sixties, plus brief biographical sketches of the decade's major rock artists and recommended album(s) for each. Every band and solo artist included in *Sixties Rock* is grouped in the genre that best represents them and their work. Virtually any attempt at such classification is risky business. But in a book like this, labels such as teen idol, girl group, and folk rock are necessary to preserve clarity and conciseness and help the reader appreciate the various rock offshoots that sprang up in the sixties.

I judged these albums with the following criteria in mind: one, the record's pure musical and artistic merit; two, its overall impact and influence on future artists and albums; and three, its relationship to the development of sixties rock in general and the artist or band who recorded it in particular. To minimize partiality, I researched what others in the field of rock criticism had to say about the music of the sixties. I weighed their comments against my own feelings and theories, and then made my final conclusions. Hopefully, what resulted is a set of albums that will provide one with a thorough and creditable sixties rock record collection and, most importantly, supply many of the answers to the hows and whys of the music made back then.

It's crucial to emphasize that the albums included in *Sixties Rock* represent only the best and most significant rock records made in the sixties. By no means do they reflect an artist's entire recording catalog, sixties or otherwise. Most of the albums selected are still in print and readily available. Nearly all of them were recorded and released in the sixties. Some, however, are greatest-hits and best-of packages released later. Still others are reissues of original sixties albums, many of which are British imports. In not all cases is the date given the date of an album's original release, since many of these LPs are available only as reissues. Finally, a limited number of records listed in *Sixties Rock* are out of print and, unfortunately, difficult to find. These are duly noted. But their inclusion was mandatory simply because they are so vital to the overall scheme and understanding of sixties rock. Many of these out-of-print records can be found in good used record shops, at record collector flea markets, garage sales, or through record collecting magazines such as *Goldmine* and *Record Auction Monthly* (see Appendix II).

You will find that many of the recommended albums for the artists popular in the early part of the decade are greatest-hits records. That's because in the years between 1960 and 1963, albums simply did not play the role in music that they do today. The primary way an artist got his or her music exposed was with the single. In addition, far too many of the albums recorded at that time contained mostly filler material. Usually rather pedestrian interpretations of standard rock & roll and rhythm & blues tunes made up most of the fodder. Therefore, the greatest-hits album is actually the best record to own in a number of cases, not to mention the fact that most of the LPs recorded in the early sixties have long been out of print.

· Like the records selected, the artists and bands also represent the decade's finest. Essentially, I followed the same standards in choosing them as I did the albums they recorded. The information contained in their biographical sketches is intended to shed enough light on their careers so the reader can easily and quickly understand their importance to sixties rock. Some artists' careers began in the fifties or continued into the seventies. In order to adhere to the general objective of the book, I dealt primarily with their accomplishments in the sixties. However, I also made an attempt to sum up anything of significance that occurred in their careers before or after the decade.

Admittedly, there are artists and bands that could have been included in *Sixties Rock* but for lack of space were not. Nevertheless, the book's essential quality, I believe, is firmly intact. By using *Sixties Rock* as a reference tool, a springboard for further study of sixties rock, a basic musical history of the decade, or all of the above, the reader will be able to make some sense as to why the sixties was indeed rock's golden era.

Robert Santelli
August 1984

Author's Note: All references to chart positions are based on *Billboard*'s pop charts and Joel Whitburn's *Top Pop Artists & Singles 1955-1978.*

1
TEENS IN LOVE
The Teen Idols

Of all the musical styles and developments that helped make sixties rock so exciting, the teen idol craze was the least significant. And for good reason. It was a craze, simply stated, in which good looks far outweighed good music. It was also deliberately reinforced by a music industry eager to make rock & roll more mainstream, more manageable, and, ultimately, more marketable than ever before.

Most of the teen idols who rose to stardom between 1959 and 1963 were ordinary kids with cute faces and beaming smiles. They were clean-cut, sprightly, and unquestionably wholesome. More a personality than a singer or rock & roll performer, the average teen idol had been sanitized to such a point that it often seemed he or she had no problems other than blind dates and pimples.

Though most of the teen idols were male, there were a few female teen idols. Brenda Lee, Connie Francis, and Annette Funicello topped the list. But because Lee and Francis appealed to older listeners as well as teens, they also regularly crossed over and recorded middle-of-the-road adult tunes.

Many of the big-name teen idols were discovered in the New York area (Paul Anka, Dion Di Mucci, Connie Francis, Bobby Darin),

Philadelphia (Fabian, Frankie Avalon, Bobby Rydell), and Southern California (Ricky Nelson, Annette Funicello). Nearly all of them, save Nelson, used Dick Clark's TV show, the Philly-based "American Bandstand," as a springboard to stardom. They also routinely appeared on the pages of *16 Magazine*, *Dig*, and *Teen*, photo-happy fanzines for dreamy-eyed girls.

On the whole, teen idol rock & roll was schmaltzy and innocuous, even sterile. Gone was the vivacity first heard from Elvis Presley in 1956. In its place were syrupy melodies, puppy-love lyrics, and arrangements without a driving backbeat.

Though far outnumbered by real rock & rollers, the teen idols got the most attention. Ever since Presley, rock & roll's very first teen dream, went to Hollywood to star in a motion picture, a number of teen idols—Frankie Avalon, Bobby Rydell, Bobby Darin, to name a few—sought to follow in his footsteps. Hollywood saw the pop star-movie star connection and lured many teen idols from the recording studio to the movie lot. Virtually all of the teen idols had a shot at Hollywood and films; all except Presley and Paul Anka came and went.

Traditionally, rock historians have viewed the teen idol phenomenon as nothing more than an embarrassing blemish. But though the bulk of the songs they recorded were indeed inane, not *every* teen idol deserved to be cast into the throwaway pile. Bobby Darin, Ricky Nelson, and Dion, for example, all considered teen idols at one point, made quite a few records that were surprisingly good. Nelson's "Travelin' Man" and "Hello Mary Lou" and Dion's "The Wanderer" and "Runaround Sue" are classic early-sixties rock & roll songs that hold up beautifully today. Over in England teen idol Billy Fury cut some of the best rock & roll/rockabilly heard in that country in the early sixties. What set these artists apart from their contemporaries was the notion that not all teen music necessarily be amorphous, vapid, or, at worst, insulting.

By 1964 when the Beatles fronted the first assault on America's rock & roll consciousness, the teen idols either had been forgotten or were working the supper-club circuit.

RECOMMENDED ARTISTS

Elvis Presley

In March 1958 Elvis Presley, early rock & roll's greatest singer and performer, became the property of Uncle Sam. Presley spent the next two years wearing a drab olive-green army uniform instead of a gold lamé suit, and toting a rifle instead of a guitar.

Prior to his induction, Presley *was* rock & roll. He set the standards by which virtually all the other artists were judged. He was the one who showed how easily a black man's music could transcend race barriers. He gave the music—and the performance of it—an undeniable spirit and power.

So much has been written about Presley, especially his early and most productive years as a rocker. And why not? There was much to say. But once he left the army, the King of Rock & Roll was a different man. As a person Presley had changed. He had mellowed considerably; some said he had simply grown up. Whatever it was, Presley's music reflected this change, this maturity. To be frank, it had lost much of its sparkle and ebullience.

Of the three Presley studio pop albums recorded and released between 1960 and 1963—*Elvis Is Back!* (1960); *Somethin' for Everybody* (1961); and *Pot Luck* (1962)—only *Elvis Is Back!* measures up to the material he had recorded before he went into the service. All three albums were recorded at the RCA studios in Nashville with the city's finest musicians: Scotty Moore on guitar and D. J. Fontana on drums (both of whom had been with Presley from the start; Bill Black, Presley's original bass player, left him to go solo in 1958), Hank Garland on guitar and bass, Floyd Cramer on piano, Buddy Harman on drums, Bob Moore on bass, and Presley's backup vocalists, the Jordanaires.

The problems with the albums stemmed not from the musicianship or from Presley's vocals; both were typically up to par. It was Presley's apparent lack of passion for the music that made many of the songs sound empty. With the notable exception of *Elvis Is Back!*, Presley never seemed able to inspire himself to rock as he used to.

Another element that sapped Presley's rock & roll inclinations was Hollywood. Throughout the sixties Presley spent a good portion of his time making lousy B movies and the ineffectual soundtrack LPs that accompanied them. Six soundtrack albums were released between 1960 and 1963: *G.I. Blues* (1960), *Blue Hawaii* (1961), *Girls! Girls! Girls!* (1962), *It Happened at the World's Fair* (1963), *Fun in Acapulco* (1963), and *Kissin' Cousins* (1963). Of these, only *G.I. Blues* and *Girls! Girls! Girls!* are worthwhile. The other four records contain two, perhaps three, decent tracks apiece. The remaining tracks were hopelessly insubstantial songs, their arrangements pure Hollywood. Yet Presley's fans made these LPs best-selling records.

Presley never again recaptured more than a passing glimpse of what he had accomplished in the fifties. There was only one strong flashback to the early days, a comeback TV special in 1968. Mostly, the sixties saw Elvis lose interest in rock & roll as he increasingly lost

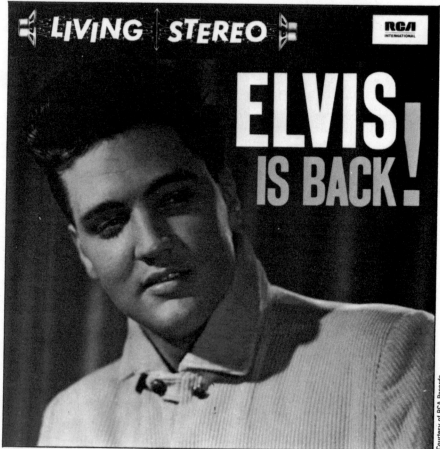

Courtesy of RCA Records

touch with the things that had made him and his music so special in 1956.

Elvis Is Back! / RCA / 1960

Presley's last great rock & roll studio album, this record has a terrific mixture of uptempo rockers ("Dirty Dirty Feeling," "Make Me Know It"), the blues ("Fever," "Reconsider Baby"), and ballads ("Soldier Boy," "I Will Be Home Again"). Presley's vocals aren't as raw or relentless as they were in the fifties. Instead, we hear a more polished singer with more control and composure.

G.I. Blues / RCA / 1960

G.I. Blues was Presley's first film after his discharge from the service. As is obvious from the title, the movie used Presley's army experience to fuel its story line, and, naturally, most of the songs deal with the "soldier in love" theme. Presley's rollicking version of "Blue Suede Shoes" shares the spotlight with one of his prettiest ballads, "Pocketful of Rainbows."

Girls! Girls! Girls! / RCA / 1962

With such songs as "Song of the Shrimp," "We're Coming in Loaded," and "The Walls Have Ears," *Girls!* appears suspect. But there's a certain subliminal quality to the songs that somehow makes them right. The best track is the classic "Return to Sender." True-blue Presley fans will want to have *Girls!* in their collections. Others might want to stick with just *G.I. Blues* and *Elvis Is Back!*

Two other albums Presley recorded later in the decade are worthy of note:

Spinout / RCA / 1966

The best soundtrack album from Presley's mid-sixties films, *Spinout* is quite similar in scope and musical content to *Girls!* but lacks a track with the immense appeal of "Return to Sender." What this LP does include, however, is Presley's magnificent interpretation of Bob Dylan's "Tomorrow Is a Long Time."

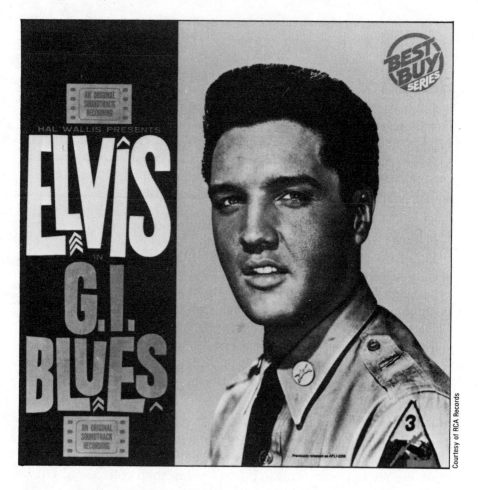

Courtesy of RCA Records

Elvis / RCA / 1968

This is the soundtrack album from Presley's 1968 Christmas TV special. The event initiated Presley's comeback, and it's easy to understand why. Elvis's performance was superb. Rather than merely going through the motions as he had done on the movie soundtrack LPs, Presley sang such songs as "Lawdy Miss Clawdy," "Jailhouse Rock," "All Shook Up," and "Heartbreak Hotel" with amazing energy. The show had even more significance because it included Presley's first performance before a live audience in years. *Elvis*, both the TV special and soundtrack album, proved beyond a doubt that when properly motivated, Presley could still rock with the best of them.

Elvis in Hollywood / Everest / 1980

This British import album is ideal for those who want a collection of Presley's best soundtrack songs without having to suffer through the original soundtrack LPs. The compilation includes "Jailhouse Rock," "Viva Las Vegas," "King Creole," "Blue Hawaii," and "Kissin' Cousins" among its twenty selections. Note the incredible difference in style and delivery between "Jailhouse Rock" recorded in 1957 and, say, "Charro" done in 1968.

Ricky Nelson

When it came to media visibility, Ricky Nelson was overshadowed only by Elvis Presley in rock & roll's early years. Throughout the fifties and early sixties, Ricky Nelson played himself on his parents' weekly television show, "The Adventures of Ozzie and Harriet." It was one of America's favorite TV programs, and Nelson used his cutesy mass appeal to launch a career in rock & roll.

Ricky Nelson was touted as a "tame" Elvis, one whom parents could trust and easily accept. And since he was a member of one of America's most popular families, his soft, safe demeanor made him a perfect alternative to the more raucous Presley. Ironically, Presley's influence on Nelson was unmistakable; it was Presley who inspired Nelson to become a rock & roll performer in the first place. And if you listen to Nelson's earliest recordings, selections from *Ricky*, Nelson's 1957 debut LP, or *Ricky Sings Again!*, released in 1958, the similarities to Presley's vocal style and rockabilly sound are obvious.

The fifties were undoubtedly Nelson's most productive years in terms of rockabilly and traditional rock & roll. Most of his recorded material from this era lacked the heavy pop edge that Nelson's songs would assume in the early sixties. Many of the better songs he recorded in 1957 and 1958 were written by the Burnette brothers—Dorsey and Johnny—either together or individually. "Believe What You Say," written by the Burnettes, was one of the best songs Nelson ever recorded. He also took numerous songs penned by Baker Knight ("Lonesome Town" and others), Jerry Fuller ("Travelin' Man"), and even Gene Pitney ("Hello Mary Lou").

Besides the use of first-rate composers Nelson had another advantage: his backing band was one of early rock & roll's tightest and most efficient units. The band consisted of the great James Burton on guitar, who, along with Scotty Moore and Carl Perkins, was one of rockabilly's most exciting and influential guitarists; James Kirkland and, a little later, Joe Osborn on bass; Butch White, then Richie Frost on drums; and Gene Garth and Ray Johnson on piano. Nelson and his band recorded some of the most convincing rockabilly outside the South.

Though two of his biggest songs of the sixties, "Travelin' Man" and its B side, "Hello Mary Lou," still had a rockabilly feel, more of his material—"Fools Rush In," "The Very Thought of You"—was limp compared to what he had cut five years earlier.

Nelson began to drop off the charts in 1964, due in part to his shift toward mopey ballads with incongruous arrangements. In 1972, after a disastrous appearance at a New York City rock & roll revival show, Nelson wrote and recorded "Garden Party," which expressed his frustrations over being an artist entrapped on the oldies circuit. Recorded with the Stone Canyon Band, another excellent backup group, the song was Nelson's last major hit, although he continues to record and perform.

Ricky Nelson / United Artists / 1971

This two-record set was released as part of United Artists' Legendary Master Series and is a grand collection of Nelson's greatest recordings. Of course, all Nelson's major hits are included here, but Ed Ward, who compiled the material and wrote the liner notes, included a number of truly excellent tracks from Nelson's out-of-print early albums. Songs like "If You Can't Rock Me," "Shirley Lee," and "Milkcow Blues" balance out biggies like "Poor Little Fool," "Teenage Idol," "Travelin' Man," and "Hello Mary Lou," and help depict Ricky Nelson as a serious, worthwhile rock & roller.

Ricky Nelson is also a fine introduction to the guitar genius of James Burton, especially on the set's first record. His lead work was always crisp and colorful, and it's easy to see Burton's contribution to Nelson's success.

Bobby Darin

Bobby Darin never really wanted to become a rock & roller. From the beginning of his career, he wanted to become an actor and, ultimately, a movie star. When singing brought him bigger rewards in the late fifties and early sixties, Darin modeled his style after that of Frank Sinatra and other supper-club entertainers rather than Presley.

Nevertheless, early on in his career Darin was a rock & roll singer. He could have been one of the very best had he not chosen to abandon rock & roll after the incredible success of "Mack the Knife" in 1959. He had a voice that was sharp and gritty in the right places and enough charisma to turn mediocre compositions into vocal triumphs.

Darin broke into the music business writing songs for Don Kirshner's Aldon Music. This led to a record deal with Decca and then with Atlantic and its subsidiary label, Atco. Darin's first hit, a novelty song called "Splish Splash," reached number three on *Billboard*'s chart in 1958. Next was "Dream Lover," a breezy, well-crafted teen ballad typical of the era.

It wasn't, however, until "Mack the Knife," which earned Darin two Grammies in 1959—one for Record of the Year and the other for Best New Artist of the Year—that Darin became a big star. It was a strange song for Darin to record. Not only was the song some thirty years old, and the first of his three hits not written by himself, but it came from Bertolt Brecht's *Threepenny Opera*. In addition, the song and its spicy delivery were a far cry from the lightweight "Splish Splash" or the tender "Dream Lover." Darin sang the tune with a cocky bravado that oozed macho charm, and the record-buying public went for it in a big way. It wasn't exactly rock & roll, but it was good enough to transcend virtually all barriers and tastes.

Darin didn't have the looks of Ricky Nelson or Fabian, but he was still categorized as a teen idol, and his numerous appearances on Dick Clark's "American Bandstand" only served to reinforce that image. But Darin realized that there was more money and fame for him in cabaret, and so he began performing regularly in Las Vegas and fashionable supper clubs like the Copacabana.

Darin, who had suffered heart damage after a childhood bout with rheumatic fever, died in 1973 during open-heart surgery.

The Bobby Darin Story / Atco / 1961

The most notable aspect of *The Bobby Darin Story* is how much Darin was influenced by the vocal style of Ray Charles and other black rhythm & blues singers of the fifties. The twelve tracks on this album provide an ample reflection of Darin's solid vocal talents, even if, as evidenced on certain selections, he did waste a fair portion of it on mundane middle-of-the-road songs.

Side one is the better side, representing Darin's rock & roll career with "Splish Splash," "Dream Lover," and "Early in the Morning," one of Darin's very best rock & roll efforts, both as a songwriter and singer. Side two presents Darin as the suave supper-club singer; "Beyond the Sea," "Artificial Flowers," and "Clementine" are hopelessly banal and whitewashed.

Dion

Like all the other teen idols, Dion Di Mucci sang about the pains and pleasures of being a teenager. But instead of crooning in candy-coated fashion, Dion came across a bit tougher, a whole lot sexier, and positively more streetwise than Frankie Avalon or Bobby Rydell. As a result, a number of Dion's records have surprising depth and more than a touch of soul, and so easily transcend the teen-idol era.

Dion, like Bobby Darin, wrote some of his own material. Two big hits for him in the early sixties, "Lovers Who Wander" and "Runaround Sue," were cowritten with friend Ernie Maresca. "Little Diane," another hit, was penned solely by Dion. His ability to write gave him more of a say as to how the songs should ultimately sound. This additional responsibility perhaps is what triggered the extra effort heard on so many Dion tracks.

Dion started his recording career fronting the Belmonts (Angelo D'Aleo, Carlo Mastrangelo, and Fred Milano), named after Belmont Avenue in their Bronx neighborhood. Though Dion and the Belmonts' first successful single was "I Wonder Why" in 1958, it wasn't until "A Teenager in Love" a year later that the group had its first big smash. The somewhat mushy ballad isn't the finest example of Dion's vocal charm, but the song addresses the problem of being in love in a rather unique way—*why* must I be a teenager in love? Dion really wanted to know the answer. It was a sincere enough performance to make the song a number-five hit in 1959.

Things looked good for Dion and the Belmonts until 1960 when D'Aleo was drafted. Then Dion decided to pursue a solo career, and Dion and the Belmonts went their separate ways. It was the right move for Dion. In the next three years he recorded "Runaround Sue," "The Wanderer," and "Ruby Baby" and outgrew his teen idol status. His vocals were sharper and more aggressive, and these records

RUNAROUND SUE

DION

LONELY WORLD
RUNAWAY GIRL
DREAM LOVER
TAKE GOOD CARE OF MY BABY
KANSAS CITY
LIFE IS BUT A DREAM
IN THE STILL OF THE NIGHT
THE WANDERER
LITTLE STAR
THE MAJESTIC
SOMEBODY NOBODY WANTS

helped further define the Italo-rock sound of the early sixties.

But around 1964 Dion's popularity began to fade. Although Dion had the vocal capacity and raw talent to survive the upcoming British Invasion, a heroin addiction sapped much of his artistic energy.

A brief 1967 reunion with the Belmonts failed, but in 1968 Dion won his bout with junk. That same year Dion reemerged with "Abraham, Martin and John." One of rock's most poignant social commentaries, the tune, penned by Dick Holler, dealt with the assassinations of Abraham Lincoln, Martin Luther King, Jr., and John and Robert Kennedy, and became one of 1968's biggest records. Dion got a new recording contract with Warner Brothers Records and a new lease on life as a folk singer.

None of Dion's seventies albums matched his earlier work, though

Sanctuary, a pleasant folk album with a wonderful live version of "Ruby Baby," and *Reunion*, recorded live in 1972 at Madison Square Garden with the Belmonts, came close.

Runaround Sue / Laurie / 1961

With "Runaround Sue" and "The Wanderer" on it, plus great covers of Darin's "Dream Lover" and the great Mike Stoller–Jerry Leiber song "Kansas City," this album rates as Dion's best early-sixties album. His voice exudes strength and amazing confidence and emphatically steers clear of teen-idol tackiness. *Runaround Sue* was rereleased by Collectible Records and is available at better record shops.

Everything You Always Wanted to Hear by Dion and the Belmonts / Laurie / 1973

The twenty tracks on this LP, part of the Laurie Limited Edition Series, include all the hits by Dion and the Belmonts *and* by Dion solo. The only problem with this outstanding compilation is that all but four tracks were electronically rechanneled for stereo, which gives the record an artificial sound.

Twenty-Four Original Classics / Arista / 1984

This two-record set chronicles Dion's full career and is especially valuable because it includes "Ruby Baby" (the albums mentioned above don't, for some reason), "Abraham, Martin and John," and the title tune from *Sanctuary*. It's also the best LP for its accurate, informative liner notes and packaging.

Bobby Vee

Bobby Vee was saddled with the teen-idol image mostly because of his appearances in the teen idol slot on Dick Clark's rock & roll tour, the Caravan of Stars. Vee was a handsome young man, and he played his part with little complaint. But unlike the other teen idols that Clark pushed, Vee was a capable musician; he belonged to a midwestern band, the Shadows, before he embarked on his solo career.

Vee got his big break in 1959, when the Shadows filled in for Buddy

Holly in Fargo, North Dakota (Vee's hometown), after Holly, Ritchie Valens, and the Big Bopper were killed in a plane crash. Immediately afterward, "Suzie Baby," a folky ballad that Vee wrote and recorded locally, was picked up by Liberty Records. Rereleased by Liberty, the song promptly stalled on the wrong end of the chart. But producer Snuff Garrett found better songs and developed a more commercial sound. "Devil or Angel," "Rubber Ball," "Run to Him," "Take Good Care of My Baby," and "The Night Has a Thousand Eyes" were early-sixties hits for Vee.

Garrett molded a sound around Vee that was cheery and pleasant. Vee's soft, easy-flowing voice matched up well against Garrett's backdrop of strings and female vocals. Because Vee didn't come across too syrupy, his songs have weathered time better than those of Frankie Avalon and Bobby Rydell. Vee's early-sixties accomplishments carried him through the teen-idol years and onto the supperclub circuit.

Bobby Vee's Golden Greats / United Artists / 1980

This compact album contains ten of Vee's top songs from the early sixties, the bare essentials necessary to understand and appreciate him. It's not difficult to notice more than a passing similarity to Buddy Holly on more than one track. Garrett attempted to capture the Holly sound on Vee's records, but he never quite pulled it off. Not all the selections on *Golden Greats* are chartbusters. "Someday," one of the best rock & roll songs Vee ever cut, is included here as are "How Many Tears" and "More Than I Can Say," two mildly successful singles. Noticeably absent is his biggest hit in 1963, "The Night Has a Thousand Eyes."

Those particularly interested in Vee's career will want to hunt down *Bobby Vee*, the most comprehensive collection of Bobby Vee material released in anthology form. Part of United Artists' Legendary Master Series of the early seventies, the record, unfortunately, is out of print and exceedingly difficult to find.

Cliff Richard

Cliff Richard was England's most popular singer in the late fifties and early sixties. A good-looking singer whose crisp, tidy vocals made him the clear-cut favorite over fellow teen idols Adam Faith and Billy Fury, Richard recorded a slew of hit songs beginning with the nifty rocker "Move It" in 1958.

For most of his early records Richard fronted the Shadows (*not* Bobby Vee's group). Originally named the Drifters, the group was led by guitarist Hank Marvin and was responsible for the punch in Richard's early rock & roll recordings. After the Shadows split from Richard in 1960, they went on to become England's most successful rock & roll group before the Beatles. (See Chapter 2, "Twangy Guitars: The Instrumental Groups.")

Richard continues to have hits. A self-proclaimed born-again Christian, Richard moved from rock & roll to easy-listening MOR. Despite his wide following in England, Canada, and parts of Europe, Richard never caught on in the States, although a couple of songs skirted the U.S. charts. In 1976, some seventeen years after the release of his first record in Britain, "Devil Woman" did break the U.S. top ten, followed in 1980 by "We Don't Talk Anymore."

Cliff / EMI / 1959

This hard-to-find British rerelease contains the best set of tracks recorded by Richard and the Shadows in the early stage of their careers. The LP also offers a pretty fair indication of the parasitic state of British rock & roll in the late fifties and early sixties. Most of the tracks on *Cliff* are fair interpretations of American rock & roll standards ("That'll Be the Day," "Whole Lotta Shakin' Going On," etc.). None of them is better than the originals, but they're interesting nevertheless.

Cliff Richard's Greatest Hits / EMI / 1981

Much of the material Richard recorded with the Shadows was pretty decent rock & roll considering Britain's pathetic music scene in the late fifties and early sixties. Unfortunately, the original albums that Richard recorded with the Shadows are nearly impossible to find in the States. This import contains the best tracks that Richard cut with the Shadows: "Move It," "Living Doll," "Travelin' Light," "The Young Ones," and "Do You Want to Dance." But there are also a few clunkers from the mid-seventies that the listener must endure in order to get a complete cross-section of Richard's career. Numerous Cliff Richard LPs recorded in the seventies are available in the United States. Be wary of these. Much of Richard's later work is simply dreadful.

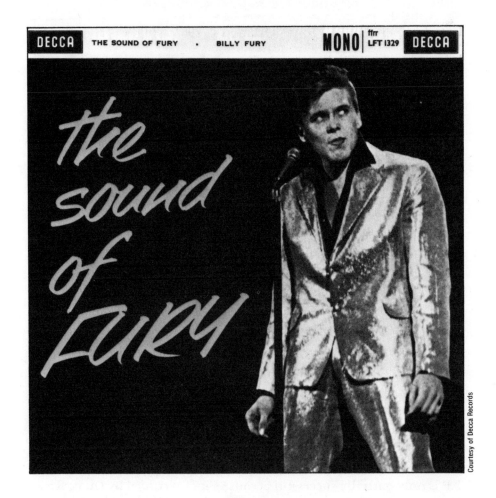

DECCA   THE SOUND OF FURY   ·   BILLY FURY   MONO | ffrr LFT 1329   DECCA

Courtesy of Decca Records

Billy Fury

Cliff Richard was England's biggest teen idol in the early sixties, but Billy Fury was its best. Fury's most memorable moments occurred when he took American rockabilly at face value and added just a touch of the English pop tradition. The result was some of the most convincing pre-Beatles rock & roll recorded by an Englishman.

Fury's voice was a cross between Ricky Nelson and Buddy Holly, and his main influences, it would seem, were Presley, Eddie Cochran, and Gene Vincent. Fury also penned many of his own tunes, four of which are found on the excellent rereleased mini-LP *The Sound of Fury*. As for singles, "Maybe Tomorrow" was his first hit; another was his version of Tony Orlando's 1961 single "Halfway to Paradise."

Fury remained popular until Beatlemania and the great English rock breakout of 1964. Although he continued to record and perform in England, his best days were behind him. Much of his later material is third-rate pop. Fury died in 1983 after a long struggle with heart disease.

The Sound of Fury / Decca / 1960

Though there's nothing exceptionally striking or innovative on *The Sound of Fury*, it's a good rockabilly/rock & roll album with hardly a weak track on it. *The Sound of Fury* represents Billy Fury at his peak: his vocal performance, while not overpowering, is more than adequate given his limited range, and his backup band seemed to have an unusually strong grasp of rockabilly. Joe Brown's guitar work accents most of the songs, while drummer Andy White anchors the bottom in fine rockabilly fashion. (White, by the way, was the drummer on the Beatles' "P.S. I Love You" after producer George Martin decided Ringo Starr couldn't cut it.)

OTHER RECOMMENDED ALBUMS

The Idols / Era / 1981

With sixteen tracks that attempt to recount the teen-idol era, the LP is only partially successful because songs recorded by Dion, Ricky Nelson, and Elvis are missing. *The Idols* is valuable, however, because selections such as "Venus" by Frankie Avalon, "Poetry in Motion" by Johnny Tillotson, "Tiger" by Fabian, and "The Wild One" by Bobby Rydell reveal what the other teen dreams were recording in the late fifties and early sixties.

2
TWANGY GUITARS
The Instrumental Groups

The proliferation of instrumental groups in the late fifties and early sixties was mainly a reaction to the gooey excess of the teen idol fad. In an era when pretty faces seemed to garner all the glory, such an overemphasis on cupcake smiles and pompadours was bound to alienate a large proportion of males, who, when they looked in the mirror, saw only a few zits and maybe a crooked nose.

Rock & roll has always remained close to its constituency; that's what makes it so special. You could feel the music, touch it, let its energy carry you away. It was real and it wasn't perfect. But as rock & roll in its most commercial form—pop—changed direction and moved toward the bright lights of Hollywood, it stranded its most basic level of popular support. The kid who enjoyed the music's visceral energy and excitement—and perhaps even had an idea or two of his own about playing rock & roll—felt somewhat abandoned. Forming a band, or listening to one that did without the white-bread looks and maudlin vocals, and just playing basic rock & roll was the solution to his problem. Any kid could buy a cheap guitar, learn a few chords and then a few songs, and start his own group—without having to worry about his tinny voice or his less than photogenic mug.

In the late forties and fifties, rhythm & blues dance bands filled

17

much of their repertoire with instrumentals. Then in 1956 Bill Doggett recorded rock & roll's first instrumental hit, "Honky Tonk (Parts 1 & 2)," which peaked at number two. Two years later the Champs' sassy rocker "Tequila" was a number one, and Duane Eddy's "Rebel-'Rouser" was also a big record. By the early sixties, instrumental groups had sprouted all over the place.

The basic difference between fifties-styled rock instrumentals and the early-sixties hits was the lead instruments. Fifties instrumentals generally featured a wailing saxophone or pounding keyboards, but after Eddy's twangy guitar sound and Link Wray's homemade fuzztone, sixties instrumentals were predominantly guitar-oriented.

Frankly, many of the popular instrumental groups between 1958 and 1963 weren't especially great. Stock riffs and elementary chord changes were the rule rather than the exception. There was also a simplistic approach to songwriting and arrangements, and tunes were often quickly recorded novelties that capitalized on a particular theme or a musical twist. Not surprisingly, listening to instrumentals got boring; the instrumental-group trend spawned more one-hit wonders than any other.

Despite all this, instrumental rock & roll played an important role in rock & roll's maturation. For one thing, while the teen dreams kept their smiles glowing, instrumental groups kept the energy flowing: Most of the instrumental hits were fast, fun to listen to, and easily digestible. For another, instrumental groups sparked a brand-new commitment to the guitar that wouldn't be fully realized until later in the decade. But with the Ventures making how-to-play records and artists like Duane Eddy selling millions of records on the strength of his guitar-playing abilities alone, some kids went beyond mastering a few chords and a couple of progressions. Finally, instrumental groups (particularly the Ventures and Dick Dale and His Del-Tones) opened the door for surf music, which led to the Beach Boys, who added a whole new element of their own to American pop music.

RECOMMENDED ARTISTS

Duane Eddy

Duane Eddy was the King of Twang, one of the biggest-selling instrumental artists of the late fifties and early sixties. Eddy's guitar sound was labeled "twang" because of its emphasis on a nasal resonance and steely tone. His approach was simple: Most of the time Eddy concentrated on the lower bass strings of his guitar and accented the notes with a tremelo effect. It was an appealing sound, and Eddy maximized its popularity by recording a number of twang instrumental hits.

Producer Lee Hazlewood played a significant role in developing Eddy's sound. Aside from working with him in the studio, Hazlewood contacted Dick Clark, whose Jamie Records signed Eddy. Eddy's second release on the label, "Rebel-'Rouser," was one of his biggest hits, staying on the charts for three months in 1958. Clark played Eddy's records on "American Bandstand," and he toured with Clark's Caravan of Stars. The exposure made Eddy instrumental rock's closest thing to a teen idol.

Duane Eddy's influence can be heard on records by the Ventures and the Shadows. One of the greatest rock & roll songs ever, Bruce Springsteen's "Born to Run," begins with a twangy guitar sound obviously influenced by Eddy.

The Greatest Hits of Duane Eddy / Line / 1983

This is a British rerelease of 1965's *Duane Eddy's Sixteen Greatest Hits* (Jamie Records). Unless you can find Sire Records' out-of-print *The Vintage Years*, a two-record set with comprehensive liner notes and the best anthology around, *The Greatest Hits* will have to do. It includes all the Eddy essentials: "Rebel-'Rouser," "Forty Miles of Bad Road," "Because They're Young," and "Peter Gunn."

Link Wray

Though Link Wray was never as popular as Duane Eddy in the United States, his importance as a rock & roll pioneer is undeniable. While both Wray and Eddy made it big on the charts in 1958—Eddy with "Rebel-'Rouser" and Wray with "Rumble"—their guitar styles were miles apart.

Wray's guitar sound was rough and raw; he created it by stressing fuzz-dominated power chords (the first to do so) against a simple background of drums and bass. Each chord had an arrogance that often made his songs sound downright threatening. (In 1958 "Rumble" was banned in New York City by radio people who believed it further aggravated an already tense local gang warfare problem.)

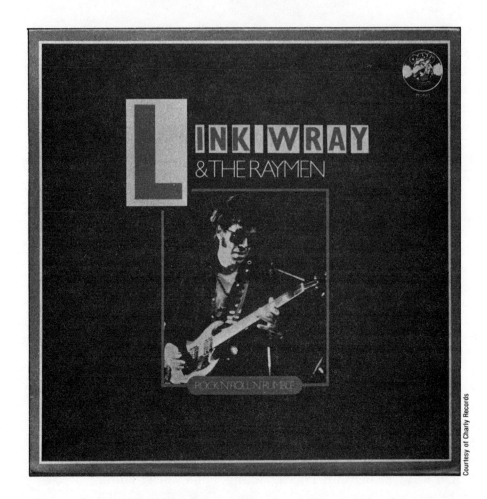

Those who bought "Rumble" and explored Wray's other instrumentals were not disappointed with what they heard if it was rock & roll they wanted. No one ever called Wray's guitar playing sugary or soft.

After "Rumble," Wray made his second of three appearances on the American charts with "Raw-Hide" in 1959. Even though there were no more hits, some of Wray's best work was done in the early sixties and can be heard on *There's Good Rockin' Tonite*. In the early seventies Wray made a few more records, none of which were even remotely successful. But in the late seventies Wray teamed up with rockabilly revivalist/singer Robert Gordon, and people who had never heard of Link Wray took notice of his guitar talents. For a short while there was even a rediscovery of and a demand for old Link Wray records.

Rock 'n' Roll 'n' Rumble / Charly / 1972

This album features seventeen tracks recorded from 1957 to 1965 and some of the most ripping guitar riffs of the era. The sound quality isn't very good, but it's authentic and apropos considering Wray's roughneck sound. Those interested in tracing the roots of rock guitar will find this record invaluable, for it includes riffs that later would become popular with Pete Townshend, Jeff Beck, and Marc Bolan. Also available on Union Pacific Records.

Johnny and the Hurricanes

Johnny and the Hurricanes emerged from Ohio in the late fifties. Led by tenor saxophonist Johnny Paris, the group had its first hit single with a sax-dominated tune called "Crossfire." It turned out to be one of the best-selling instrumentals of 1959. Paris and the Hurricanes followed it up with a novelty series of old standards to which the group gave a facelift and an energetic rock beat. "Red River Valley" became "Red River Rock," "Blue Tail Fly" was transformed into "Beatnik Fly," and the army's sunrise bugle call gave birth to "Reveille Rock." These were just a few short steps away from being novelty numbers. The *sound* of the band was what was most important about Johnny and the Hurricanes. Basically, each song they recorded was hard-driving with a thick bottom and charged with frequent short but colorful solos. Paris was a competent, if not outstanding, saxophonist, and guitarist David Yorko deserved more credit than he's received from rock historians.

Even though Johnny and the Hurricanes faded in America, they remained fairly big stars in Europe and England until about 1964. The group sold twice as many records abroad as it did at home. Paris and the Hurricanes even played the famous Star Club in Hamburg, Germany. Their opening act? Who else—the Beatles.

Johnny and the Hurricanes / Warwick / 1960

This LP is obviously long out of print, but if you can find it used, pick it up. Aside from "Red River Rock" and "Crossfire," *Johnny and the Hurricanes* contains a half-dozen or so fine instrumentals that do a better job defining the band's sound and capabilities than do the hits.

The Best of Johnny and the Hurricanes / Decca / 1981

There are a number of Johnny and the Hurricanes greatest-hits LPs around, but this one is special. A British import, this album not only contains eighteen tracks, including the band's biggest hits, but is nicely packaged and has well-written liner notes to boot. The tracks are all in mono, as they should be, and sound delightful.

Lonnie Mack

In 1963 Lonnie Mack, a country-blues guitarist who played juke joints and bars in Ohio and Indiana, cut an instrumental version of Chuck Berry's "Memphis." Mack's guitar interpretation of the tune refurbished it with a new coat of rock & roll excitement and sent it to number five on the pop charts. Mack then cut another single, "Wham!," a freight train of an instrumental complete with horns and a ripping R&B rhythm section that made it to number twenty-four. *The Wham of That Memphis Man* was the follow-up album.

Mack was also a blues- and gospel-influenced singer and a pretty good one at that. His next single was a vocal track called "Where There's a Will," but it was too rootsy and had too much gospel flair to make a dent in the charts, and Mack was forgotten about as quickly as he had been discovered. Mack's guitar licks were much more advanced than those that filled out the standard instrumentals of the day, because he used the melody of a song as a take-off point rather than a guiding force which dictated that the guitarist stick within a predetermined framework. The solos on *The Wham of That Memphis Man* cut a path for the guitar styles later heard from the Eric Clapton school of riffs.

After Mack's fling with stardom he returned to playing the club circuit in the Midwest and the South, cutting a few more albums along the way, none of which was as striking or innovative as *The Wham of That Memphis Man*.

The Wham of That Memphis Man / Fraternity / 1963

It's a pity this record hasn't been rereleased. Even worse is that there are no retrospective LPs or anthologies either. The album contains both Lonnie Macks—the vocalist and the guitarist—and they're both good. The inclusion of "Wham!" is reason enough to search out this out-of-print record.

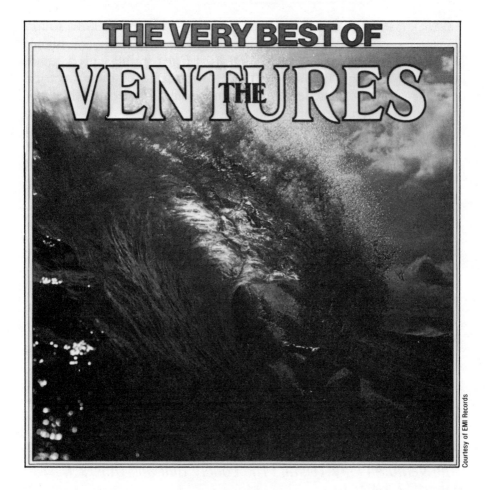

Courtesy of EMI Records

The Ventures

In terms of overall significance to the development of sixties rock & roll the Ventures rank as the greatest contributors in the instrumental category. Nokie Edwards (lead guitar), Don Wilson (rhythm guitar), Bob Bogle (bass), and drummer Howie Johnston (later replaced by Mel Taylor) hailed from Washington and were part of a pretty decent Pacific Northwest rock & roll scene that favored instrumental rock. Other instrumental outfits from the region included the Wailers, the Kingsmen, and—before they added vocals—Paul Revere and the Raiders.

The Ventures were a guitar-dominated group in classic instrumental rock fashion. They shied away from the hard and reckless sound of, say, Link Wray but never were their songs wimpy or bland. Instead, the Ventures delivered a clean, refined sound with a subtle but firm rock edge. Because their appeal crossed over and attracted a broad spectrum of listeners, the Ventures sold more records than any other instrumental group.

Edwards, Wilson, and Bogle were heavily influenced by Les Paul and Chet Atkins. It was Atkins's interpretation of Johnny Smith's "Walk—Don't Run" that first introduced the group to the song that became their first smash. After it came "Perfidia," "Ram-Bunk-Shush," and "Walk—Don't Run '64," released in 1964 to capitalize on the instrumental surf craze. The Ventures had their share of hit singles, but what the group sold most were albums. They became the first rock & roll group to be considered LP-oriented artists. In all, the Ventures recorded more than thirty albums in the sixties.

When the instrumental era ended in 1963, the Ventures moved on to the surf music scene. Much of what was passing for surf music imitated what the Ventures had done before. All the group had to do was shift to surf themes.

Rock & roll guitar owes much to the Ventures. Their success prompted thousands of kids to pick up guitars and learn how to play them. By the end of the decade the glowing results of their influence were being heard loud and clear.

The Ventures / Liberty / 1960

The Ventures Play Telstar, The Lonely Bull and Others / Liberty / 1963

Both of these early Ventures albums have been rereleased by Liberty. Listen for the precision in the guitar playing and the fine balance of the instruments with the rhythm section. Neither the reverb nor the subtle twang of the guitars is ever excessive or untempered. If there's one thread that winds its way through most of the early Ventures, it's consistency.

The Very Best of the Ventures / Liberty / 1975

This is a basic ten-tune glance back at some of the Ventures' biggest singles: "Walk—Don't Run," "Ram-Bunk-Shush," "Telstar," "Perfidia," and the Ventures' 1969 hit "Hawaii Five-O" as well as the group's version of Duane Eddy's "Rebel-'Rouser," the Surfaris' "Wipe Out," and three others. As the Ventures became more popular they recorded more cover tunes, but their earliest material is by far their best, and this LP has a fair sampling of it.

The Ventures / United Artists / 1973

This two-record set is another in United Artists' excellent Legendary Masters Series. It is the definitive Ventures anthology and contains *all* of their most important recordings. A thorough discography of all American singles and LPs made by the group, plus those LPs specifically marketed in Japan and the United Kingdom, comprise the inner sleeve of the album. A rather difficult album to find (a British import), but a critical one for understanding the Ventures' importance.

Sandy Nelson

Sandy Nelson was the first rock & roll drummer to step into the limelight and become a successful solo recording artist. Borrowing from such Big Band and jazz drummers as Cozy Cole and his hit "Topsy II," Nelson was able to score big with rock & roll instrumentals that featured drums. Bringing the drums out in front, Nelson had hits with "Teen Beat" (1959), "Let There Be Drums" (1961), and a slew of less than memorable records in the early sixties.

The Very Best of Sandy Nelson / Liberty / 1975

There aren't too many who would consider Sandy Nelson an exceptional drummer or even an above-average one. But Nelson's reworking of such standards as "Honky Tonk" and "The Stripper" plus his own compositions, "Teen Beat" and "Let There Be Drums," set the stage for the more illustrious rock drumming that came along later in the decade.

The Shadows

What the Ventures were to American rock & roll in the early sixties the Shadows were to the English scene, plus a bit more. The Shadows never had a hit single in the States, but in England, where they had more than thirty of them, they were the most popular band before the Beatles. Many rock historians on this side of the Atlantic have unjustly ignored their accomplishments.

The Shadows, who were first known as the Drifters, formed in 1958. The group consisted of bass player Jet Harris, drummer Tony Meehan, and guitarists Hank B. Marvin and Bruce Welsh. Both Marvin and Welch were attuned to American R&B by way of the imported records they heard on British jukeboxes.

As Cliff Richard's backup band, the Drifters played a significant role in Richard's rise to the top, giving his early recordings much of their drive. In 1960 Marvin and the others decided to strike out on their own. Changing the name of the group to the Shadows to avoid confusion with the American vocal group the Drifters, they recorded and released "Apache." The instrumental consisted of a rich, thick layer of acoustic rhythm guitar (Welch) and a tight, trebly lead (Marvin) with elements of Duane Eddy's and Nokie Edwards's styles in it. The song went to number one on the British charts.

Marvin went on to become England's first star rock & roll guitarist, and he influenced many later musicians. Marvin's guitar playing wasn't exceptionally innovative, but it was clean and beautifully fluid. In terms of importance, he ranks almost as high as his early-sixties American counterparts Duane Eddy, Link Wray, Nokie Edwards, and Steve Cropper.

Throughout most of the sixties the Shadows had two careers: They continued to back up Cliff Richard even though by 1963 Richard's rockin' days were over; and they recorded on their own, releasing a slew of albums, many of which were best-sellers. The Shadows finally broke up in 1969 only to re-form and break up again a couple more times in the seventies.

The Shadows / Fame / 1961

This is a British import rerelease of the Shadows' first LP, which had been released on the heels of their hit single, "Apache." For some strange reason, though, "Apache" was not included. Still, these songs give a wonderful indication of how good the group was. Marvin's lead work is as good as anything coming out of the States during the early sixties, and it's way better than what any other English guitarist was playing then.

THE BEST OF
BOOKER T.
& THE
MG'S

STEREO

HIP HUG-HER.
SLIM JENKINS' PLACE
GREEN ONIONS
SOUL DRESSING
JELLYBREAD
GROOVIN'
MO'ONIONS
SUMMERTIME
BOOT-LEG
CAN'T BE STILL
TIC-TAC-TOE
RED BEANS & RICE

SD 8202

ATLANTIC

Courtesy of Atlantic Records

The Mar-Keys

The Mar-Keys and Booker T. and the MG's created the durably
textured soul signature that would in the mid-sixties become known
as the Memphis or Stax-Volt Sound. The Mar-Keys consisted of the
venerable Steve Cropper on guitar, Donald "Duck" Dunn on bass,
Terry Johnston on drums, Jerry Lee Smith on piano, Charles Axton
and Don Nix on saxophones, and Wayne Jackson on trumpet. When
it came down to raw talent and proficiency, the Mar-Keys had few, if
any, peers. Although there were no black musicians in the band, the
inherent feel of their music was undoubtedly black. They played
rhythm & blues rather than rock & roll, but it was a sound that rock

listeners could appreciate. With nearly flawless deliveries and neatly refined layers of instrumentation that were more clever than bold, it was apparent from the band's one and only hit, "Last Night," that the Mar-Keys would outlast the instrumental band craze.

Because of the Mar-Keys' initial recording success and their obvious musical talent, Jim Stewart, head of Stax Records in Memphis, made them the label's house band. Thus began a relationship that spurred years of great music. The Mar-Keys played behind some of soul's earliest vocalists—Rufus and Carla Thomas, Eddie Floyd, Sam and Dave, Otis Redding, and many others—and in the process cultivated the sharp, trim style known as the Memphis Sound.

Last Night / Atlantic / 1961

There aren't any greatest-hits albums or rereleases that cover only the Mar-Keys around the time of "Last Night." However, there are numerous anthologies from the mid- and late sixties that will give a pretty good idea of what the band sounded like in its earlier days. Still, if *Last Night* can be found (it is out of print), do pick it up. Those interested in the late-sixties Stax-Volt Memphis Sound can hear the instrumental roots of it here. The playing is exquisite, the arrangements challenging, and the title song, Cannonball Adderley's "Sack O Woe," and an instrumental version of Paul Anka's "Diana" are still rewarding. (See Chapter 14, "The Soul Sound.")

Booker T. and the MG's

Booker T. and the MG's grew out of the Mar-Keys. The initial lineup was Booker T. Jones on organ, Steve Cropper on guitar, Al Jackson, Jr., on drums, and Louis Steinberg on bass. Duck Dunn, however, replaced Steinberg shortly after the group was formed.

The MG's (MG stood for Memphis Group) were one of the first successful integrated pop groups to come out of the South. Despite the difference in skin color (Jones and Jackson were black; Cropper and Dunn, white), their musical roots were identical. All four grew up listening to country & western swing, R&B, blues, and lots of gospel, and they incorporated these musical forms into their sound. In a way, Booker T. and the MG's was soul music's first superstar unit, although none of its members played the role or even knew what that role entailed. Each player was an excellent musician. Cropper's guitar work, simple and curt, punctuated records with grace and style. Dunn's playing inspired a whole generation of bass players with his steady, unshakable riffs. Jones was an accomplished musician who could play a number of instruments but whose biggest gift seemed to be his sharp ear for splicing the right riffs in the right places. Jackson's trademark was his incredible sense of timing, which was as close to perfect as any human drummer ever got. Some swear he *never* missed a beat in his life.

"Green Onions," a cool, calculated instrumental that showcased the band's restraint, was the group's first hit, in 1962. But like the Mar-Keys before them, the MG's wound up doing session work more than promoting themselves as a separate recording act.

The early Memphis scene was tightly knit and an open-door policy existed between the Mar-Keys and the MG's. At times it was hard to tell them apart. Members of one group would sit in on the other's session until, stylistically, there was little difference between the two. After Cropper and Dunn joined the MG's, the Mar-Keys continued, but with a more loosely structured format. Members came and went and came back again. The bonds among Memphis musicians created a precious studio intimacy that's rare in pop music today. In interviews members of the MG's warmly recollect memories of the "sixth sense" that tied the band together in the studio.

The reign of Booker T. and the MG's and the Mar-Keys faded by decade's end. But the two groups left behind a bright legacy and a long list of recording accomplishments.

The Best of Booker T. and the MG's / Atlantic / 1968

This LP is a basic history of the MG's and includes the hit "Green Onions" as well as "Mo-Onions" from the early years and an instrumental version of the Rascals' "Groovin' " plus "Hip Hug-Her" from 1967. The rest of the tracks fall somewhere in between. For a more precise view of the early-sixties period of the MG's, try to track down *Green Onions*. Long out of print in this country, the record was rereleased in England and occasionally turns up.

3
EARLY SIXTIES POP

A big part of the story of pop music in the early sixties revolved around the Brill Building in New York City. It was there that pop music's best songwriters went to work each day, sat in tiny rooms with pianos, and pumped out light, mostly sweet melodies and clever teen-slanted lyrics to be recorded by the best pop artists of the day.

One of the men behind the Brill Building songwriters and pop style was Don Kirshner, who, along with Al Nevins, formed Aldon Music. Kirshner was responsible for harnessing the talents of a number of songwriters and songwriting teams who turned out songs—hit songs—that were special. Writing for Kirshner was the talented husband-and-wife songwriting team of Gerry Goffin and Carole King (King wrote the melodies, Goffin the lyrics). The duo turned out almost two hundred songs in the early sixties, more than twenty of which were huge hits: the Cookies' "Don't Say Nothin' Bad (About My Baby)," Little Eva's "The Loco-Motion," the Drifters' "Up on the Roof," the Shirelles' "Will You Love Me Tomorrow," and "It Might as Well Rain until September," sung by Carole King herself.

Another husband-and-wife team, Barry Mann and Cynthia Weil, wrote pop tunes that were a bit more sophisticated, especially in the lyrics department. Rather than dwell solely on teen love and broken hearts, Mann sought to insert a bit of social commentary into his words. "We Gotta Get Out of This Place," a big hit for the British Invasion group the Animals, dealt with the inner city. "Uptown," which the Crystals recorded, was about retaining one's dignity in an oppressive urban environment. But, ironically, the best song the two ever wrote together was a love song, "You've Lost That Lovin' Feelin'," done by the Righteous Brothers.

Howard Greenfield and Neil Sedaka didn't have quite as many hits as Mann-Weil or Goffin-King, but their "Stupid Cupid" helped get Aldon Music rolling in 1958. Many of the pair's best tunes were recorded by Sedaka in the early sixties: "Calendar Girl," "Happy Birthday, Sweet Sixteen," and "Breaking Up Is Hard to Do."

Besides Kirshner's writers, a number of others contributed to the Brill Building Sound and the richness of pop music in the early sixties. Other songwriting teams such as Jeff Barry and Ellie Greenwich (husband and wife), Doc Pomus and Mort Shuman, Burt Bacharach and Hal David, and, of course, the greatest team of all, Jerry Leiber and Mike Stoller, wrote an incredible number of pop classics.

Leiber and Stoller's story begins in the fifties. The two were responsible for Elvis Presley's "Hound Dog" and "Jailhouse Rock," the Coasters' "Charlie Brown," "Poison Ivy," and "Yakety Yak," Dion's "Ruby Baby," Peggy Lee's "I'm a Woman," the Drifters' "On Broadway," and Wilbert Harrison's "Kansas City," among many others. Also, Phil Spector apprenticed with them (Leiber and Spector wrote "Spanish Harlem" for Ben E. King) and influenced countless other aspiring songwriters and producers. Without Leiber and Stoller's uncanny ability to merge black musical attitudes with white tastes, R&B, rock & roll, and pop might have taken much different courses.

Not all the great pop music filling the charts in the early sixties came out of New York. In Detroit, Chicago, Memphis, Los Angeles, Philadelphia, and elsewhere such artists as Del Shannon, the Everly Brothers, Roy Orbison, and the Four Seasons were contributing to pop's wealth.

The early sixties were also the golden age of the dance craze. There had been dance records and dance fads before Chubby Checker's "The Twist" came along in 1960, but none were as big or as influential. The song unleashed a flood of dance and dance-related tunes. Artists rose and fell as the hot dances they promoted suddenly went cold and another new dance and song came to the fore. There were dozens of Twist spin-offs; Sam Cooke's "Twistin' the Night Away," the Isley Brothers' "Twist and Shout," and Joey Dee's "Peppermint Twist—Part 1" were three of the best. But there was also the Mashed Potato made popular by Dee Dee Sharp's "Mashed Potato Time" and the Bristol Stomp promoted in the Dovells' song of the same name. The Orlons scored with "Wah-Watusi" and the dance, the Watusi, became the rage. Little Eva's "The Loco-Motion," which spurred the Locomotion, was one of the most exciting songs of the dance-craze era. There were also the Monkey (Major Lance's "Monkey Time"), the Pony, the Jerk, the Swim, and the Hully Gully.

The dance craze was really the culmination of the black-white cultural consolidation that Leiber and Stoller helped to create displayed in physical terms. But it was also simply an expression of rock & roll fervor. The original idea of rock & roll was to get people up on their feet and moving. Whether it was shaking and shimmying or dancing to a specified pattern, rock & roll was supposed to be energy in motion. The early-sixties dance craze, despite the triteness of many of the songs that fueled it, was just that.

RECOMMENDED ARTISTS

The Everly Brothers

Don and Phil Everly were the most popular duo in all of rock & roll during the late fifties and early sixties. Raised in a musical home, the Everly Brothers grew up with country music, and their music reveals those roots. Their sound was simple and straightforward, the focus being their impeccable voices and silky smooth harmonies sung against the vigorous strumming of acoustic guitars.

A bulk of the Everly Brothers' best material belongs to the fifties. "Bye Bye Love," "Wake Up Little Susie," the brilliant ballad "All I Have to Do Is Dream," "Bird Dog," and "Devoted to You" had gone to the top of the charts before the decade ended. Thanks to songwriter Boudleaux Bryant and the warm relationship the brothers had with

INCLUDING
BYE BYE LOVE
WAKE UP LITTLE SUSIE
CATHY'S CLOWN
ALL I HAVE TO DO IS DREAM
BIRD DOG
WALK RIGHT BACK
LET IT BE ME
WHEN WILL I BE LOVED
A N D   M O R E

Courtesy of Arista Records

such Nashville stalwarts as Chet Atkins, Wesley Rose, and Archie Bleyer, all of whom contributed something to the Everly Brothers' success, six of the earliest singles recorded by the Everlys broke the Top Ten. Three of them—"Wake Up Little Susie," "Bird Dog," and "All I Have to Do Is Dream"—went to number one.

The Everlys' Nashville connection was strained in 1960 when contract problems caused the duo to cut their ties with Cadence Records and its president, Archie Bleyer. Warner Bros. Records offered them a million dollars and a ten-year contract, the biggest contract in the business at the time. The Everly Brothers packed up and went West.

Financially, it was a terrific move, but musically it was wrong.

Boudleaux Bryant's tunes were perfect for the Everly Brothers, and the Nashville production strategy had few, if any, flaws. At first the change was hardly evident. Phil and Don wrote "Cathy's Clown," their biggest-selling single of all time. The future looked bright indeed, especially when "When Will I Be Loved?" and "So Sad (To Watch a Good Love Go Bad)" reached number eight and seven, respectively.

But the hit songs eventually stopped. The Everly Brothers had not drastically changed the way they recorded or sang their songs. It was the songs that had changed. The Everlys had turned to pop songwriters for their material, but none of them were as consistently good as Boudleaux Bryant. The catchy hooks and irresistible melodies were gone.

Years of intense and bitter sibling rivalry, marital problems, and drugs caused the brothers to part in 1973. Ten years later, when Phil and Don Everly reunited and performed together at London's Albert Hall, the live two-record set *The Everly Brothers Reunion Concert* (Passport Records) was recorded. Their album *EB84* (Polygram Records) the following year was a critical success.

The Golden Hits of the Everly Brothers / Warner Bros. / 1962

This collection contains most of the best material recorded with Warner Bros. Although few of the tracks are exceptional, save "Cathy's Clown" and "Crying in the Rain," they're certainly listenable.

The Very Best of the Everly Brothers / Warner Bros. / 1964

For this LP, the Everlys returned to Nashville, where they searched out their old buddies and rerecorded six of their Cadence hits and six of their Warner hits. Both Warner Bros. and the Everly Brothers realized that they should have stayed in Nashville in the first place.

Twenty-Four Original Classics / Arista / 1984

This is the most comprehensive Everly Brothers anthology available and the most highly recommended. This two-record set spans the duo's entire career before their 1983 reunion, is attractively presented with excellent liner notes and photos, and has a sound that's cleaner and crisper than that of any other collection.

The Drifters

Despite possessing solid ties to fifties-style gospel and rhythm & blues, the Drifters made the transition from these predominantly black music forms to white pop in the early sixties with astonishing success. The typical Drifters record was essentially R&B in style and in interplay between the lead and backing vocals. But most of the songs the Drifters recorded from 1959 through 1964 were produced by the Brill Building's Leiber and Stoller, written by Brill Building composers, including Doc Pomus and Mort Shuman, Gerry Goffin and Carole King, and Barry Mann and Cynthia Weil, and made accessible with orchestrated strings in the background. It was a wonderfully fine formula and accounted for such Drifters classics as "There Goes My Baby," "This Magic Moment," "Up on the Roof," "On Broadway," and "Under the Boardwalk."

The Drifters' history is long and often confusing. Incredibly enough, the group has endured in one form or another for over thirty years now despite more than fifty different members. The group's history can be broken down into three separate eras.

The first era was dominated by the vocal genius of Clyde McPhatter. This period stretched from 1953, when the group was first formed, until 1958. Basically an R&B outfit with heavy gospel undertones, the early Drifters were regulars on the R&B charts and occasionally crossed over into pop ("Fools Fall in Love," "Hypnotized").

When McPhatter quit the Drifters to pursue a solo career in 1958 the group broke up. Manager George Treadwell took Ben E. King and his group, the Five Crowns, rechristened them the Drifters, and so the group, or rather its name, began its most successful period.

Atlantic Records' Jerry Wexler and Ahmet Ertegun had produced the original Drifters, but they let Jerry Leiber and Mike Stoller take on the new lineup. Leiber and Stoller cut through the heavy R&B/gospel roots and diluted the "blackness" of the Drifters' sound by incorporating strings, a first in rhythm & blues. "There Goes My Baby" sold a million units and peaked at number two. King was a superb vocalist; his careful blend of gospel resonance and soul-sanctifying notes of passion paved the way for a slew of soul singers to come on the music scene in the mid-sixties. Like McPhatter before him, King also had the urge to strike out on his own and after cutting "Save the Last Dance for Me," a number one song in 1960, he left the group.

Courtesy of Atlantic Records

Lead singer Rudy Lewis performed admirably in his new role, but King and McPhatter have always overshadowed Lewis and his successor, Johnny Moore (Lewis died of a drug overdose in 1964), though both Lewis and Moore were excellent vocalists. "Up on the Roof," "On Broadway," "Sweets for My Sweet," "Under the Board-walk," and "Saturday Night at the Movies" are firm testaments to their talent.

By this time Bert Berns had assumed production responsibilities (Leiber and Stoller turned their attention to other artists) and proved he was as adept as Leiber and Stoller when it came to making hit songs. When he died of a heart attack in 1967, the Drifters' second era came to a close.

From 1967 to the present there have been so many personnel changes that it is impossible to keep track of them. It really doesn't matter, though, because after "Saturday Night at the Movies," the Drifters recorded little of importance. Today various past and current members of the group make the rounds as an oldies outfit.

The Drifters' Golden Hits / Atlantic / 1968

The worst thing about *The Drifters' Golden Hits* is that it includes only twelve tracks. The nicest thing about the record is that the songs selected adequately depict the Drifters' golden years, 1959 to 1964. With the exception of "Under the Boardwalk," "I've Got Sand in My Shoes," and "Saturday Night at the Movies" (produced by Berns), all the songs were Leiber-Stoller productions.

As for the Drifters' three lead vocalists, "There Goes My Baby" is King's masterpiece, while Lewis is best represented by the brilliant "I Count the Tears" and "On Broadway," and Moore with "Under the Boardwalk" and "Saturday Night at the Movies."

The Drifters Twenty-Four Original Hits / WEA / 1975

This is a British import that's not always easy to locate. It includes not only most of the classic Drifters' hits but material from their post-1967 era, none of which really deserves to be on the record. Hardcore Drifters fans might see it differently, however.

The Early Years / Atco / 1971

Those interested in the Drifters during Clyde McPhatter's tenure will find *The Early Years* an important record. Notice the differences in sound, production, and material. It is an entirely different group from the one on *Golden Hits*.

Ben E. King

When Ben E. King left the Drifters in 1960, some in the music industry thought it was a foolish move, but King was confident he'd succeed as a solo artist.

His first single was one of his best. Written by Jerry Leiber and an up and coming talent named Phil Spector, "Spanish Harlem" easily could have been a Drifters song. Although Spector produced the

BEN E. KING'S
★★★★★★★★★★★★★★★★★★★★★★★★★
GREATEST HITS

THAT'S WHEN IT HURTS
AROUND THE CORNER
WHAT NOW MY LOVE
I (WHO HAVE NOTHING)
AUF WIEDERSEHEN, MY DEAR
I COULD HAVE DANCED ALL NIGHT
HOW CAN I FORGET
YOUNG BOY BLUES
SPANISH HARLEM
STAND BY ME
DON'T PLAY THAT SONG
AMOR

song, he basically used Leiber and Stoller's production techniques and came up with a sound not at all different from what King had been used to as a Drifter. A few months after "Spanish Harlem" came "Stand by Me." King cowrote the song and, in terms of vocal performance, production, instrumentation, arrangement, and overall delivery, the record ranks as one of the greatest and the most influential of the era. Later in the decade, soul singers would listen to "Stand by Me" not only for guidance but for inspiration.

King broke into the Top Forty three more times with "Amor" (also a hit in 1961), "Don't Play That Song" (1962), and "I (Who Have Nothing)" (1963). Things dried up after that until 1975, when he struck back with "Supernatural Thing—Part 1."

Ben E. King's Greatest Hits / Atco / 1966

King's vocals helped lay the foundation for the mid-sixties soul explosion. Yet many songs King interpreted were middle-of-the-road pop and the arrangements were closer in style to the Brill Building formula or Leiber and Stoller's than to what his contemporaries, like the Impressions, were recording. *Greatest Hits* reflects this quite well. "Stand by Me" and "Spanish Harlem" are obviously highlights; right behind them are "Young Boy Blues" (another song Spector helped write) and "Don't Play That Song." But then there's "Auf Wiedersehen, My Dear," "Amor," and "I Could Have Danced All Night"—pop schmaltz. King probably would have been much bigger had he recorded better material or written more songs of the caliber of "Stand by Me."

Roy Orbison

Roy Orbison began recording in the mid-fifties for Sam Phillips and Sun Records, the producer and the Memphis record label responsible for the initial success of Elvis Presley, Jerry Lee Lewis, and Carl Perkins. But the Sun formula that made the latter three stars—the fusing of blues, rockabilly, and country into a particularly potent and volatile hybrid called rock & roll—didn't work for Orbison. That's not to say that Orbison couldn't rock. On the contrary. One listen to his "Oh, Pretty Woman" or, better yet, "Mean Woman Blues" quickly puts that notion to rest. But Orbison wasn't a rocker in the sense the others were, although Presley's influence on him was large and unmistakable. Instead, Orbison's calling was mainly to write, arrange, and sing ballads—romanticized rock & roll ballads—often with vocal climaxes virtually unmatched to this day. Though it took Orbison until 1960 to find his niche, he became one of rock & roll's most deeply respected and most passionate singers ever.

Born and raised in Texas, Orbison's earliest musical influences were those of western swing and country. The Wink Westerners, his first group, became the Teen Kings after Orbison changed the band's format from country to rock & roll with a country feel. The Teen Kings' recording debut, produced by Norman Petty (Buddy Holly's producer), was the unsuccessful "Ooby Dooby." Orbison later rerecorded it for Sam Phillips and Sun, adding some new touches. This version went to number fifty-nine.

That song, however, was the only one of note that Orbison cut for Sun; he left the label in 1958, drifted to Nashville and began a career as a songwriter for Acuff-Rose, country music's biggest music publishing company. Orbison got a recording contract with Monument Records, a new independent label in Nashville. His third single, "Only the Lonely (Know How I Feel)," was the hit that Orbison and Monument were both hoping for, and from 1960 to 1964 Orbison was a constant presence on the charts.

As a songwriter Roy Orbison was deeply introspective. He wrote a great deal about the insecurity that seems to haunt love and the agonizing loneliness and self-pity that frequently results from it. This was heavy stuff for hit records.

As a vocalist Orbison sometimes sounded more like an opera singer than a rock & roll balladeer. His beautifully textured voice was striking in its range and ability to explode with emotion. Songs such as "Only the Lonely," "Running Scared," and especially "It's Over" are vocal masterpieces.

Even as an arranger, Roy Orbison was in a class by himself. Most of his ballads were lavishly delivered, complete with background vocals, and ended with stunning crescendos. Along with Leiber and Stoller and Phil Spector, Orbison helped legitimize the use of strings on rock & roll records.

From 1960 to 1964 Roy Orbison had nine Top Ten hits. But there were none in 1965 or 1966, the year his wife Claudette was killed in a motorcycle mishap. Her death deeply affected Orbison. Two years later he lost two of his children in a fire. Although he continued to tour (he was a huge star in England), Orbison's later recordings never quite matched those of his heyday.

The All-Time Greatest Hits of Roy Orbison / Monument / 1972

Monument has released a number of Roy Orbison greatest-hits records, but this one stands out above all the others. It is a superb two-record set that includes each of Orbison's biggest singles as well as some choice extras like "Blue Bayou," which Linda Ronstadt made a hit in 1977, the rocker "Candy Man," and "Leah." Other greatest-hits packages released by Monument are *Greatest Hits* (1963), *More of Roy Orbison's Greatest Hits* (1964), and *Very Best of*

Roy Orbison (1966). His original studio LPs are out of print and difficult to come by.

Gene Pitney

Gene Pitney was another great ballad singer who surfaced in the early sixties, recording such hits as "Only Love Can Break a Heart," "(The Man Who Shot) Liberty Valance," and "It Hurts to Be in Love." His strong, soaring voice, which at times peaked in a sort of falsetto shrill, was dramatic and easily broke through the mesh of orchestration that usually filled out his records.

Pitney began his career with a rock & roll song called "(I Wanna) Love My Life Away" on which he played all the instruments and overdubbed all the vocals. But he quickly abandoned that route to record the theme to the movie *Town Without Pity*. From then on he relied principally on the hit-making machinery of Hal David and Burt Bacharach for his success as a recording artist. This was an ironic twist since Pitney was a fine songwriter himself, having penned "(I Wanna) Love My Life Away" as well as "Hello Mary Lou" for Ricky Nelson and "He's a Rebel" for the Crystals.

Pitney's importance diminished as he turned increasingly toward the role of Italian love-song singer and country-styled crooner, and the hits stopped coming.

Anthology: 1961–1968 / Rhino / 1984

This is by far the most comprehensive and complete Gene Pitney retrospective available. A double-record set lovingly compiled by the folks at Rhino, its songs such as "It Hurts to Be in Love," "Town without Pity," and "Mecca" reveal Pitney's best moments.

The Righteous Brothers

Not all of what Phil Spector accomplished in the early and mid-sixties came from girl groups like the Ronettes and Crystals (see Chapter 4, "The Girls Groups"). In 1964 he took the Righteous Brothers, Bill Medley and Bobby Hatfield, into the studio to cut a Barry Mann and Cynthia Weil song called "You've Lost That Lovin' Feelin'." Using the same elements that bulked up records by the

Ronettes—layer upon layer of strings, background vocals, percussion, and a lush, responsive feel that made all this come together into a Wall of Sound—Spector created the first—and greatest—blue-eyed soul record.

Medley and Hatfield had been together for two years but had never experienced the success that "You've Lost That Lovin' Feelin' " brought them. The song went to number one in late 1964. Spector played Medley's black-sounding baritone against Hatfield's rangy tenor and scored with "Just Once in My Life," "Unchained Melody," and "Ebb Tide" before the relationship ended in 1966. Switching from Spector's Philles label to Verve resulted in the duo's first million-seller and second number-one hit, "(You're My) Soul and Inspiration." The song, another Mann–Weil number, was produced by Medley, who simply imitated Spector. The following year, though, the duo split, only to reunite in 1974 for another big hit, "Rock and Roll Heaven." The Righteous Brothers continue to perform today.

You've Lost That Lovin' Feelin' / Philles / 1964

This album is out of print but worth picking up used. Not only does it contain the title song (the only one on the LP that Spector produced), but Medley and Hatfield perform all the other tracks with the same gusto and emotion. "Old Man River," "Summertime," and "Soul City" are top tracks.

Soul and Inspiration / Verve / 1966

This LP is also out of print but essential, particularly since "Soul and Inspiration" doesn't appear on the greatest-hits LP listed below. The album's powerhouse versions of "Turn on Your Love Lights," "Bring It On Home," and "In the Midnight Hour" make other white soul acts sound tepid by comparison.

The Righteous Brothers Greatest Hits / Verve / 1967

This one *is* in print, although it's now manufactured by Polygram Records. It contains all of the Righteous Brothers' main charttoppers with the exception of "Soul and Inspiration." A must record if you can't find the other two.

Neil Sedaka

Although Neil Sedaka had a string of bubbly early-sixties hits—
"Oh Carol," "Stairway to Heaven," "Calendar Girl," "Happy
Birthday, Sweet Sixteen," and "Breaking Up Is Hard to Do," among
others—and was RCA's biggest-selling artist after Elvis Presley, his
importance lies in his songwriting. With lyricist Howie Greenfield,
Sedaka wrote some of the most finely crafted pop songs of the era, not
just for himself, but for many other artists (Connie Francis, the
Shirelles, Bobby Vee, the Tokens, LaVerne Baker). Sedaka and
Greenfield made up the first successful songwriting team at Aldon
Music Company and were important links to the Brill Building
Sound.

Sedaka had received classical training on the piano since childhood. He later attended the prestigious Juilliard School on a
scholarship. Sedaka's instrumental talent may have been in the
classics, but his ability to compose a melody was definitely in the pop
vein. He and Greenfield penned Connie Francis's 1958 Top Twenty
hit, "Stupid Cupid." Sedaka then signed a recording contract with
RCA. His first big hit was "Oh! Carol" in 1959; his last hit of the era
was "Next Door to an Angel" in 1962.

Neil Sedaka Sings His Greatest Hits / RCA / 1962

There are a few Sedaka greatest-hits collections still in print. This
one deals with only his late-fifties/early-sixties material. For a wider
overview of Sedaka's career, which includes a comeback in the mid-
seventies ("Laughter in the Rain," "Bad Blood"), check also *Neil
Sedaka Sings His Greatest Hits* (RCA, 1975) or *Neil Sedaka's Greatest
Hits* (RCA, 1977), which is out of print but still around in cutout
bins.

Del Shannon

The unique thing about Del Shannon is that he wrote most of his
songs. He had considerable success from 1961 to 1964. Beginning
with his very first recording, "Runaway," which went straight to
number one, many of Shannon's songs possessed quick-tempo,
impatient melodies which often made them sound as if they were in

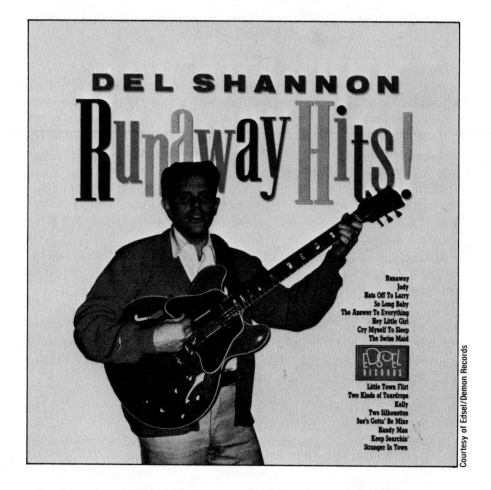

DEL SHANNON
Runaway Hits!

Runaway
Jody
Hats Off To Larry
So Long Baby
The Answer To Everything
Hey Little Girl
Cry Myself To Sleep
The Swiss Maid

Little Town Flirt
Two Kinds of Teardrops
Kelly
Two Silhouettes
Sue's Gotta' Be Mine
Handy Man
Keep Searchin'
Stranger In Town

a hurry to end. But these tunes were honest and interesting and sounded remarkably strong on Top Forty radio. Coupled with his fast-paced falsetto on one end and an equally speedy Musitron on the other, Shannon's tunes usually swelled with infectious energy. Shannon's three Top Ten hits were "Runaway" and "Hats Off to Larry" (1961) and "Keep Searchin' (We'll Follow the Sun)" (1965). "Handy Man," "Little Town Flirt," and "So Long Baby" were also big sellers in the early sixties.

Runaway Hits / Edsel / 1983

Del Shannon was always big in England. (During a 1963 tour of the country, Shannon was on a package tour that included the

Beatles—who got bottom billing.) This handsome British import contains sixteen of Shannon's most memorable tracks: "Little Town Flirt," "Runaway," "Hats Off to Larry," "Keep Searchin'," and "Two Kinds of Teardrops," each either written or cowritten by him.

Chubby Checker

Ernest Evans became Chubby Checker when Dick Clark's wife suggested the name because he resembled a younger Fats Domino. Checker then went on to record the most popular dance record of all time, "The Twist," and launch the early-sixties dancemania.

Checker came from the same South Philly area as Frankie Avalon and Fabian. Had he not been black, he would most certainly have been promoted as another of Cameo-Parkway's teen idols, since he also had the good looks to go with the role. Checker began his recording career doing imitations; the novelty record "The Class" was his first single to enter the charts. Then, on the advice of Dick Clark, Cameo-Parkway's Bernie Lowe took "The Twist," the B side of Hank Ballard's "Teardrops on Your Letter," and recorded it with Checker. The record raced up the charts to number one in 1960 and, incredibly, repeated the feat a year later when the Twist got its second wind.

Checker's interpretation of "The Twist" was neither different nor better than Ballard's; it was a near-perfect copy of the song. But Checker got something that Ballard didn't: full-blown exposure, and lots of it, on "American Bandstand." That more than anything else made Chubby Checker and "The Twist" a phenomenon.

Checker went on to record a number of dance tunes, including "The Hucklebuck," "Limbo Rock," "Pony Time," and "Let's Twist Again." Although there were better dance songs—Little Eva's "The Loco-Motion," Major Lance's "Monkey Time," and "The Wah-Watusi" by the Orlons—no artist better captured the spirit of early-sixties dance music than Chubby Checker.

Chubby Checker's Greatest Hits / Abkco / 1972

None of Checker's early Cameo-Parkway albums released at the height of his popularity contain enough worthwhile material to be considered here. However, a compilation of Checker's biggest dance tunes, which is what essentially makes up *Greatest Hits*, is indeed interesting and all the average listener needs. *Greatest Hits* has them all with the exception of "Popeye the Hitchhiker." One of the best tracks on the album is "Slow Twistin'," recorded with Dee Dee Sharp. Never a distinctive vocalist, Checker still turned in his best vocal performance on vinyl here.

Joey Dee and the Starliters

Joey Dee was one of many artists and songwriters to exploit the Twist craze. It was Dee and his group, the Starliters, who were most responsible for reviving Twist fanaticism in late 1961 and 1962 after they recorded "The Peppermint Twist." The song, written by Dee and producer Henry Glover, was penned with the Peppermint Lounge in mind, an ordinary New York City bar that was instantly transformed into the hottest dance club in America.

"The Peppermint Twist" made it to number one in 1961. Dee and the Starliters recorded a few other dance songs (most notably "Shout" in 1962), but, for the most part, they were one-hit wonders. A later edition of the Starliters included Felix Cavaliere, Gene Cornish, and Eddie Brigati, who quit the Starliters to team up with drummer Dino Danelli in 1964. Together they became the Young Rascals, one of America's best mid-sixties rock 'n' soul bands.

Doin' the Twist at the Peppermint Lounge / Roulette / 1962

Recorded live at the Peppermint Lounge, this out-of-print LP includes Parts I and II of "The Peppermint Twist" as well as Dee and the Starliters' other hit, "Shout." The Starliters were one of the first white rock & roll bands to make heavy use of the organ as a lead instrument. Listen to Carlton Latimor on "Ram-Bunk-Shush." Much of what Felix Cavaliere would do with keyboards in the Young Rascals has its roots in the Starliters' work.

The Four Seasons

Although the Four Seasons sold tens of millions of records in the early sixties and were among the few major American pop stars to survive the British Invasion, their place in rock & roll history isn't as prestigious as one might expect. The Four Seasons did not break new ground or set any influential vocal or stylistic trends.

Featuring lead singer Frankie Valli's piping falsetto illuminated against a backdrop of doo-wop-style harmonies, the Four Seasons' sound was unquestionably linked to the fifties at a time when rock & roll was moving away from its fifties roots. Theoretically, the immense popularity of the Four Seasons should not have occurred when it did. But the Four Seasons not only endured, they prospered.

The real driving forces of the group were songwriter/Season Bob Gaudio and producer Bob Crewe. Gaudio was originally with the Royal Teens and had written "Short Shorts," a number-three hit in 1958. When he became one of the Four Seasons in 1960, he assumed the group's songwriting chores and, with the production acumen of Crewe, vastly changed the group's sound and direction. It was Crewe who recognized the marketability and uniqueness of Valli's falsetto, and he who encouraged and worked with Gaudio to pen songs that would accent it.

What followed was a remarkable string of hits: "Sherry" and "Big Girls Don't Cry," both number ones in 1962; "Walk Like a Man" and "Candy Girl" in 1963; "Dawn (Go Away)," "Ronnie," "Rag Doll," "Alone," "Save It for Me," and "Big Man in Town" in 1964. And there were others later on, like "Let's Hang On" and "Working My Way Back to You."

Gaudio was a superb tunesmith. His simple, identifiable songs with irresistible hooks paired with Valli's distinctive vocals provided the hit power. There's no question that he and Crewe as well as Valli, and Nick Massi and Tommy DeVito, the two other Seasons during the group's heyday (there were other personnel changes both before and after this period) borrowed considerably from such fifties groups as the Diamonds ("Why Do Fools Fall in Love," "Silhouettes," "Little Darlin'," "The Stroll"). But Gaudio and Crewe contemporized the doo-wop sound and stocked it with enough song ideas to keep the Four Seasons in high gear for five years.

Success faded quickly when Gaudio and the group strayed from their success-proven formula and tried to force their way into the psychedelic era with a disastrous LP in 1969 called *Genuine Imitation Gazette*. By the time the sixties ended, the group had folded and Frankie Valli was pursuing his solo career.

Then, almost as if to prove that great groups never really die, Gaudio, Valli, and Crewe joined together and scored big with two terrific songs, "Who Loves You" (1975) and "December, 1963 (Oh, What a Night)" (1976). The latter hit number one and is one of Gaudio's finest compositions.

The Four Seasons Story / Private Stock / 1975

This two-record, twenty-eight song set is undoubtedly the best Four Seasons compilation LP. Every major hit from the sixties is included as well as some of the not-so-major hits that are great songs nevertheless: tunes like "Big Man in Town," "Marlena," "Silence Is Golden," "Opus 17 (Don't Worry 'Bout Me)," and a pleasant rendition of the Goffin–King classic "Will You Love Me Tomorrow," released by the group in 1968. Out of print, but still around.

4
THE GIRL GROUPS

The early-sixties girl groups owed much of their success to the same people and factors that contributed to the popularity of the teen idols. The upper echelon of the record business (and rock & roll was always a business)—those most removed from rock & roll's grass roots—sought a bigger say in the direction of the music since artistic control, through the manipulation of sound and style, could reap greater financial rewards. And what better way to achieve that control than taking kids barely out of high school who would jump at the chance to make a record and building a pop music trend around them?

Most of the girls in the groups were very young; some were as young as fourteen or fifteen. Very often they were city kids, middle or lower class, completely malleable, totally inexperienced in the rigmarole of the recording business, and wonderfully talented.

Producers gave these girls an identity. Then they were given songs, taken to the recording studio, and told how to sing them. If all went right, they would then have a song on the charts—maybe even a hit song. Profits were usually pocketed by the producer and the record company, and performers received little more than a pittance for their efforts.

Very few girl groups wrote their own songs. The tunes the girls sang were written by the same songwriters and songwriting teams that supplied material to the other pop stars of the day. The best songs usually came out of the Brill Building (see Chapter 3, "Early Sixties Pop"). Jeff Barry, Ellie Greenwich, Barry Mann, Cynthia Weil, Gerry Goffin, and Carole King wrote many of the biggest girl-group singles. These songs were simple but carefully crafted, with clever hooks, unforgettable melodies, and lyrics aimed directly at teen-agers.

But the girl groups' success hinged on more than teen-age girls with bright, innocent voices and professionally composed songs. There was a special girl-group sound, and the producers were responsible for it. No one girl-group producer was more successful or instrumental in the development of that sound than Phil Spector. Without question he made the best girl-group records and did more to make record production an art form than anyone else. Records by the Crystals, Bob B. Soxx and the Blue Jeans, Darlene Love, and the Ronettes sparkled because of Spector and his multilayered, multitextured Wall of Sound. He might have been arrogant, reclusive, even ruthless at times, but he was a brilliant technician in the recording studio.

The Spector Wall of Sound was a complex, multitextured one. It consisted of layer upon layer of guitars, drums, keyboards, percussion, strings, background vocals, and, every now and then, special effects (such as the thunder on the Ronettes' "Walking in the Rain"). Spector would stuff too many musicians into too small a room, and the sound that came out of it would be simply overwhelming.

Of all the instruments Spector used in the recording process, none seemed as important as the drums. Session drummer Hal Blaine's famous "boom ba boom BANG!" was the heartbeat of the Ronettes' "Be My Baby" and became a Spector trademark. The use of castinets and other percussive instruments accented the song's rhythm. Finally, the adroit use of strings gave the records their fullness, filling as they did every single niche.

Ironically, Spector's production process contradicted what he was producing. The songs were basic pop songs with a streetcorner simplicity that was a throwback to the doo-wop days of the fifties, but they were recorded with this complicated, meticulous sound. On paper it didn't make much sense, but it worked because each note, each drumbeat sounded like the only one that could ever have been hit.

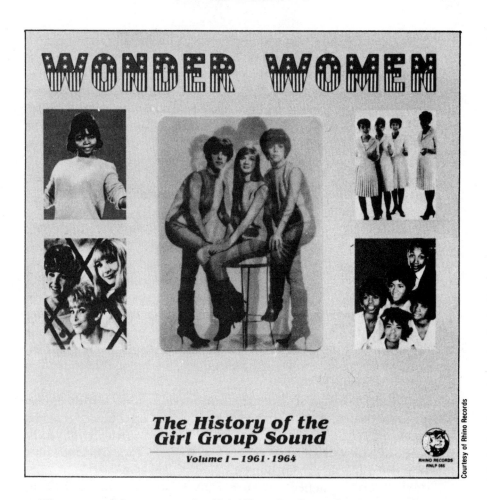

The great girl groups—the Shirelles, the Crystals, the Ronettes, the Shangri-Las—cut some of the most exciting records of the early sixties. They provided rock & roll with a rich legacy of songs that never seem to lose their vitality or bubbly enthusiasm. Interest in the girl groups faded in the wake of the British Invasion, and by 1966 the girl groups were rock & roll history.

RECOMMENDED ARTISTS

The Chantels

Two years after the Chantels began recording in 1957, Arlene Smith, lead singer and composer of some of their songs, left the group to go solo. Only two Chantels records broke into the Top Ten. Yet the Chantels are important because they did much to inspire the girl-group sound.

Prior to the Chantels, few female rock & roll vocal groups were recording, let alone scoring hit records. But that didn't deter Richard Barrett, a New York City songwriter/producer who discovered the girls. The Chantels had a strong rhythm & blues vocal style tempered with gospel and black doo-wop. Barrett was convinced that with Arlene Smith singing lead he could make records that would sell in not only the R&B market but the pop market too.

The Chantels consisted of Smith, Lois Harris, Sonia Goring, Jackie Landry, and Rene Minus. At the time their first single was released, a song written by Smith called "He's Gone," the girls ranged in age from thirteen to sixteen. The single was not a success, but Barrett brought the girls back into the studio, this time to sing his song "Maybe."

With sixteen-year-old Arlene Smith delivering like a singer twice her age and with twice her experience, "Maybe" turned out to be one of the most memorable songs of 1958. Smith's singing was magnificent; her voice, brimming with a passion and intensity, could not have sounded better.

In addition, many of Barrett's production ideas—full, lavish backdrops accenting Smith's lead vocals—would later be perfected by Phil Spector. One only has to compare "Maybe" with the Crystals' first hit, "There's No Other (Like My Baby)," to appreciate how much Spector learned from Barrett.

"Maybe" only reached number fifteen on the charts, but its significance as the record responsible for sowing the seeds of the girl-group sound cannot be overstated. Unfortunately for the Chantels, Arlene Smith's departure virtually ended their chances to cross into the sixties and fully capitalize on the sound they played such a large part in creating. Even more of a loss was Arlene Smith's swing away from pop music. With the determination and the proper songs, Smith could have rivaled the very best vocalists of the girl-group era.

The Chantels / Roulette / 1984

This is a rerelease of the only girl-group album not recorded in the sixties that's worth owning, since the roots of the girl-group sound are plainly evident here. Be advised, though, that the recording quality is barely acceptable. For a laugh, read the original liner notes that Roulette reprinted on the back of the LP.

The Shirelles

If the Chantels initiated the girl-group sound, the Shirelles shifted it into full gear. They were the first girl group to have a number one record: "Will You Love Me Tomorrow" in 1960. They also were the first to have two records in the Top Ten at the same time. These feats inspired a flurry of girl-group activity in the early sixties, especially in the New York area, as producers there searched out budding talent to capitalize on rock & roll's newest trend.

The Shirelles were Shirley (Owens) Alston; Doris (Coley) Kenner (maiden names in parentheses); Miki Harris, and Beverley Lee. The four became a group after hearing the Chantels and began singing at school dances and parties in and around Passaic, New Jersey. They were signed to Tiara Records, a small label begun by a friend's mother, Florence Greenberg. The Shirelles' first two singles, "I Met Him on a Sunday" and a cover version of the "5" Royales' "Dedicated to the One I Love," had moderate sales. But "Tonight's the Night," released in 1960, peaked at number thirty-nine, while "Will You Love Me Tomorrow," released two months later, went all the way to number one. A rerelease of "Dedicated to the One I Love" landed in the Top Ten as well.

There was one other Top Ten hit in 1961 ("Mama Said"), two in 1962 ("Baby It's You" and "Soldier Boy"), and one in 1963 ("Foolish Little Girl"); in between were a slew of minor hits.

Doris Kenner and Shirley Alston shared the role of lead singer. Alston, for example, can be heard on "Will You Love Me Tomorrow," and Kenner sang lead on "Tonight's the Night." Both sang well enough, even if their voices weren't as powerful or as compelling as, say, Darlenee Love's or Ronnie Spector's. Alston had a bit of songwriting talent as well: She and the rest of the group composed "I Met Him on a Sunday," and Alston shared the songwriting credits with producer/songwriter Luther Dixon on "Tonight's the Night" and a couple of album tracks. Many of their other songs came from Brill Building writers.

Producer/arranger Luther Dixon developed the Shirelles' sound: a calculated lead vocal, not too pushy or sexy, but not too soft either, fortified with backup vocals and mixed in with a light pop rhythm that worked marvelously for the group. But once Dixon quit working with the Shirelles, they eventually slipped off the charts.

The Shirelles continue to perform as a trio (Harris died in 1983) mostly at New Jersey/New York supper clubs and on the rock & roll revival circuit.

Tonight's the Night / Scepter / 1961

With "Tonight's the Night," "Will You Love Me Tomorrow," "Dedicated to the One I Love," and "Boys" on it, this is the first great girl-group LP. The production is fairly sparse and low-key, especially when compared to Spector's work with the Crystals and the Ronettes. But the songs are enjoyable and the girls' voices youthful and naive in a positive way. Unfortunately, it's out of print.

Anthology: 1959–1967 / Rhino / 1984

Ten of the Shirelles' greatest songs make this two-record set a must to own. The additional eighteen tracks included here complete the story of the group's recording history. All of the Shirelles' Top Ten hits can be found here, plus the always irresistible "Sha-La-La" (which Manfred Mann had a big hit with in 1964), "Tonight's the Night," and many others.

The Marvelettes

The Marvelettes—Gladys Horton, Katherine Anderson, Georgia Dobbins, Juanita Cowart, and Wanda Young—were still in high school when Berry Gordy, Jr., signed them to Tamla Records. The group's first single, "Please Mr. Postman," went to number one and stayed on the charts for more than twenty weeks in 1961 and early 1962. The Marvelettes' second record, "Twistin' Postman," Gordy's attempt to cash in on the Twist craze, didn't fare as well, stalling at number thirty-four. But the Marvelettes rebounded with "Playboy" and "Beechwood 4-5789," both Top Twenty hits. By year's end, the Marvelettes were one of Gordy's top acts.

It didn't last long, however. The Marvelettes had a dry year in 1963, around the time Gordy began working more closely with Martha and the Vandellas and the Supremes. Both groups showed much promise, and when Martha and the Vandellas struck gold with "Heat Wave" and "Quicksand" and the Supremes finally hit with their seventh single, "Where Did Our Love Go," Gordy forgot the Marvelettes.

The biggest strike against the Marvelettes was that they were more of a girl-group than a Motown group. They were directly influenced by the Chantels and succeeded on the charts with a typical girl-group sound. "Please Mr. Postman," for instance, could easily have been written by a Brill Building writer, and recorded by a girl-group producer.

The Marvelettes did hang on longer than other girl groups. "Don't Mess with Bill," which went to number seven in 1966, was written and produced by Smokey Robinson, as was "The Hunter Gets Captured by the Game" and "My Baby Must Be a Magician." But these fine records, even though they had a Motown feel to them, weren't enough, especially when other Motown artists were scoring two and three number-one singles a year. The Marvelettes were shoved aside; they broke up in 1969.

Anthology / Motown / 1975

In the early and mid-seventies, Motown began releasing double- and triple-record anthology sets of its great artists. Like the other Motown anthologies (see Chapter 9, "Motown"), this is a full and comprehensive recording history of the group. Chronologically presented, the two-record set contains all the Marvelettes' major hits, not-so-major hits, and even a couple of tunes cut in 1970 and 1971 by a revived but short-lived version of the group featuring Anne Bogan in place of Gladys Horton.

The Crystals

With the Crystals, Phil Spector made his first grand attempt at developing his Wall of Sound. The group's first single, "There's No Other (Like My Baby)," with Barbara Alston singing lead, was a Top Twenty hit. It was followed by "Uptown," which peaked at number thirteen. Neither song, though, displayed Spector's genius, only his potential. "There's No Other (Like My Baby)" was an unabashed imitation of the Chantels' "Maybe," while "Uptown" courted many of the stylistic gracings—namely the orchestrated strings and city theme—heard on Ben E. King's "Spanish Harlem."

It was with the 1962 number-one hit "He's a Rebel" that Spector finally began to focus on his soon-to-be supreme mastery of the girl-group sound. The song, written by Gene Pitney, was about a tough guy who had a big heart for his girlfriend. Strangely, however, it was a Crystals record in name only. Spector owned the name of the group and could do with it whatever he pleased, including using outside singers when necessary. To record the song he brought in West Coast vocalist Darlene Love and her group, the Blossoms. Love was a terrific singer: Her voice had a wide range, plenty of charisma, and was ideally suited to Spector's production style. Her performance was good enough that Spector recorded her again and again, as a Crystal, as a member of Bob B. Soxx and the Blue Jeans, and as a solo artist.

Spector had some real momentum going now, and the following year he cut "Da Doo Ron Ron" and "Then He Kissed Me," two big girl-group records, in 1963. Increasingly, Spector was packing his records with layers of instrumentation, driven by his belief that *anything* and *everything* that might work had to be included. "Da Doo Ron Ron" stands out as his Crystals' masterpiece with its nonsensical chorus hook, remarkable rhythm, and rich sound.

It was pretty much downhill for the Crystals after "Then He Kissed Me." Two other 1964 singles bombed. What Spector accomplished with the Crystals helped him to perfect the records he subsequently made with the Ronettes.

The Crystals Sing Their Greatest Hits / Phil Spector International / 1975

This British import, Volume 3 of the Phil Spector Wall of Sound collection, includes all anyone would want to hear by the Crystals. Aside from the group's major hits, there are versions of "Mashed Potato Time" and "On Broadway" from the Crystals' two early-sixties studio LPs, *Uptown Twist* and *He's a Rebel*—both of which are long out of print and not worth searching for. Also included is the Crystals' controversial "He Hit Me (And It Felt like a Kiss)," which was widely banned and withdrawn because of its masochistic lyrics.

The Chiffons

The Chiffons had two major hits in 1963: "He's So Fine," which stayed at number one for nearly a month, and "One Fine Day," which fell just short of its predecessor, peaking at number five. The success of the two records made the Chiffons one of the year's top girl groups.

The potential of the Chiffons' vibrant, peppy vocals and smooth delivery was never realized. From the beginning the group endured managers and producers who sought only to exploit the girls' singing talent. Their story is a perfect example of what happened to so many one-hit acts who had little or no knowledge of the record business and were prime targets for eager managers looking to make a fast buck.

Only "Sailor Boy" made the charts in 1964, at a disappointing eighty-one. In 1965 "Nobody Knows What's Goin' On (In My Mind But Me)" stalled at number forty-nine. The Chiffon's final Top Ten hit, "Sweet Talkin' Guy," came in 1966. Its success was due to its Motown sound and lead singer Judy Craig's fine singing. But it was too late for the group to reestablish its career. Management problems continued to complicate things for the Chiffons, and they soon disappeared only to resurface in the seventies at rock & roll revival shows.

Everything You Ever Wanted to Hear . . . But Couldn't Get / Laurie / 1973

A very nicely packaged British import, this LP includes sixteen tracks and a complete Laurie/Rush Records discography. In the early and mid-sixties Laurie released three Chiffons studio albums: *He's So Fine, One Fine Day,* and *Sweet Talkin' Guy.* Because each focused on the title hit single and was stuffed with hastily recorded filler tracks, none has any redeeming value today. *Everything You Ever Wanted to Hear,* then, is the wisest choice. Widely available, it has all the hits plus the best LP tracks from the sixties studio albums.

The Ronettes

The Ronettes were the greatest of all the girl groups and the one that best exemplified Phil Spector's Wall of Sound. The trio consisted of sisters Veronica (Ronnie) and Estelle Bennett and their cousin Nedra Talley. They lived in New York and had been dancers at the Peppermint Lounge during the Twist craze, occasionally had sung backup harmonies on records, and had gone on the road with Joey Dee.

From the start, Spector had a special interest in the Ronettes. Part of it was his instant affection for Ronnie Bennett, the group's lead singer. But he also realized the extraordinary quality of her vocals;

she had the sexiest voice in rock & roll. There was a foxy, honey-dipped seductiveness in her voice; most important, it was a voice that wasn't far removed from the average kid listening in on his transistor. Unlike the fabricated vocals of sexy Hollywood crooners, Ronnie Spector's voice was *real*.

Add to this the Ronettes' look and it's easy to see why no other girl group could touch them. The Ronettes simply *looked* like they sang rock & roll. Their slender bodies, beehive hairdos, and tight skirts slit up the leg only enhanced the way they sounded. There was nothing wimpy about them, and that's what turned Spector on.

The Ronettes' first hit was also their biggest. "Be My Baby," which is right up there with the greatest rock & roll records ever made, peaked at number three in 1963. The sound of the record is, in a word, spectacular. It's big, bold, and full-bodied in grand Spectorian fashion and sounds three-dimensional with Ronnie Spector's voice out front, the voices of the other two Ronettes behind her, and an entourage of musicians strumming, drumming, clicking, and constructing the most solid Wall of Sound yet. "Walking in the Rain," the Ronettes' last chart single (1964), was done the same way. In between these two songs were "Baby, I Love You," "(The Best Part of) Breakin' Up," and "Do I Love You," each tenderly produced and beautifully sung, but inexplicably, none became Top Ten hits.

The Ronettes were on the charts only in 1963 and 1964; their recorded output for Spector was represented on only one album, *Presenting the Fabulous Ronettes Featuring Veronica*. Yet they toured with the Beatles and the Rolling Stones and were the princesses of rock & roll in the mid-sixties. But when Phil Spector realized he could get no more out of his records, or himself—that the sound he'd captured was the best he could possibly get—the Ronettes simply slipped out of the limelight. Ronnie married Phil in 1968; the two divorced in 1973. Estelle Bennett and Nedra Talley eventually returned to a more normal life.

Presenting the Fabulous Ronettes Featuring Veronica / Philles / 1964

This is the only album the Ronettes ever recorded and it is extremely rare. It's been out of print for a long time, and due to a continued fascination with the Ronettes collectors have already picked up any available copies. In mint condition, this LP can cost upwards of one hundred dollars. The album includes all the Ronettes' hits, which sound every bit as exciting today as they did back in 1964. It's Phil Spector's brightest moment and the best girl-group album of the early sixties.

The Ronettes Sing Their Greatest Hits /
Phil Spector International / 1975

This is part of the Phil Spector Wall of Sound collection (see the Crystals) and contains the same material as *Presenting the Fabulous Ronettes*. Unfortunately, this album is also hard to come by. Track it down anyway. The sound quality is excellent (it is available as both a British and a Japanese import), and the Ronettes' version of Ray Charles's "What'd I Say" as well as an interpretation of the Dixie Cups' "Chapel of Love" round the album out just splendidly. Music this good should be widely available. Either this LP has to be rereleased one more time or a new Ronettes anthology is in order.

The Shangri-Las

The Shangri-Las were rock & roll's first bad girls, girl group greasers; they dressed in knee-high black boots, short leather skirts, and skin-tight blouses. Annette Funicello was *not* one of their early influences. The truth was that the Weiss sisters, Mary and Betty, and the Ganser twins, Marge and Mary Anne, were New York City street kids and their tough, hard-girl stance was usually authentic. It provided the inspiration for later tough girls like Suzi Quatro and Joan Jett.

The Shangri-Las were produced by George "Shadow" Morton. Working with sound-effects gimmickry (motorcycle revs, squawking seagulls, breaking glass, etc.), which he spliced into a series of teen melodramas, Morton took the Shangri-Las' brazen qualities and turned their records into hits.

"Remember (Walkin' in the Sand)" was the group's first hit. Its haunting, isolated tone sounded detached yet exciting when it came out in 1964. Morton wrote that song, but then got help from Ellie Greenwich and Jeff Barry with the number-one hit "Leader of the Pack," the Shangri-Las' most noted tune and one of the best teen-rebel songs of the early sixties. Using dialogue and, of course, sound effects to unfurl the narrative, Morton achieved his brightest mo-

ment. The song consisted of: girl meets biker, parents disapprove of biker, biker speeds off, biker gets killed in crash. The Shangri-Las made the lyrics sound autobiographical. The song also spawned a couple of spin-offs, including the Detergents' parody hit, "Leader of the Laundromat." "Leader of the Pack" was also a big smash in England, where its popularity never quite disappeared. The song was rereleased twice in the seventies and was a hit all over again both times.

The Shangri-Las had four more songs on the charts before they faded. Two of these, "Give Him a Great Big Kiss" (with its tough-sounding spoken line "When I say I'm in love, you best believe I'm in love, l-u-v") and "I Can Never Go Home Anymore," are outstanding. The former, bright and upbeat rather than somber like other Shangri-Las tunes, also used dialogue and a sharp sense of sexuality.

"I Can Never Go Home Anymore" lacked the rebellious spirit of previous songs; condescending in theme, it was another case of a broken love done in teentalk, only this time Mom and Dad were right.

Leader of the Pack / Red Bird / 1964

There are only three members of the Shangri-Las on the cover of *Leader of the Pack* because Betty Weiss left the group after the success of "Remember (Walkin' in the Sand)." This is the Shangri-Las' first LP; it's also their best. Three of their hits—"Remember," "Leader of the Pack," and "Give Him a Great Big Kiss"—make side one excellent. Side two was recorded live and consists of all cover material. But with Mary Weiss singing lead, the group's version of "Twist and Shout" is titillating, as is a truncated version of "Shout" with "Good Night, My Love" slapped in the middle. Rereleased and widely available.

Shangri-Las 65 / Red Bird / 1965
I Can Never Go Home Anymore / Red Bird / 1965

The *Shangri-Las 65* album was released before the success of "I Can Never Go Home Anymore." But after the song broke into the Top Ten, a new version of the LP, which included the hit and used its title as the title for the album, was released.

Teen Anguish, Vol. 2 (The Shangri-Las) / Charley / 1981

Teen Anguish, Vol. 2 is the best Shangri-Las greatest-hits record. It's a British import with liner notes by Englishman John Tobler, all the hits, and "Past, Present and Future," which some believe is the group's best vocal effort on vinyl. That's debatable, but the song is very well done and possesses a unique production angle, courtesy of Shadow Morton.

OTHER RECOMMENDED ALBUMS

Wonder Women / Rhino / 1982

Wonder Women purports to be "the history of the girl group sound," but any record dealing with girl groups that doesn't include

tracks by the Crystals or the Ronettes is not complete. Despite this weakness, *Wonder Women* is valuable, for many of its tracks are by such one-hit wonders as the Ad-Libs ("The Boy from New York City") and the Jaynetts ("Sally Go 'Round the Roses"), among others, which are either difficult to find or from original LPs not worth searching out. Also, girl-group expert Alan Betrock's liner notes are superb.

Wonder Women, Vol. 2 / Rhino / 1984

More one-hit girl groups and singers like the Butterflies and Roddie Joy, plus unjustly forgotten outfits like the Dixie Cups and the Angels. Volume 2 also includes two classic Shirelle songs, "Will

You Love Me Tomorrow" and "Baby It's You," in addition to the Shangri-Las' "I Can Never Go Home Anymore." Still no Crystals or Ronettes, though.

Girl Groups (The Story of a Sound) / Motown / 1983

This LP is the companion record to Betrock's book, *Girl Groups: The Story of a Sound*. This compilation is understandably a bit heavy on Motown artists (the Marvelettes, the Supremes, Mary Wells, Martha and the Vandellas) and, like *Wonder Women*, contains no Phil Spector tracks. In any case, *Girl Groups* and *Wonder Women* provide a fairly comprehensive overview of the girl-group era and would round out any girl-group record collection quite nicely.

5
EARLY SIXTIES
R&B
The Roots of Soul

The rhythm & blues heard in the early sixties wasn't a distinctive or short-lived musical trend like instrumental rock or girl groups. R&B was part of an ongoing process that originated in the forties and fifties. Many of the major R&B artists had careers with roots firmly embedded in the fifties. However, in the early sixties black artists such as Sam Cooke, Jackie Wilson, and Ray Charles were more able to cross over to the pop charts.

After World War II, Southern blacks migrated to Northern cities because urban industries offered employment and a higher standard of living than the rural South. They brought with them a rich musical heritage that got richer when immersed in the sounds and excitement of cities like New York, Philadelphia, Detroit, and Chicago.

For the most part, the music that originated from these cities was a jumpy, blues-oriented sound that, while not yet popular with whites, could sell enough records to keep such small independent labels as Okeh of Chicago in business. The Chicago blues scene was dominated by Muddy Waters, Little Walter, Howlin' Wolf, and John Lee Hooker. Their style—at least in the early sixties—was too rough, too bluesy, and too raw to attract more than a handful of serious white listeners. What was needed, and indeed what evolved, was a more mainstream, slicker sound that retained the basics of the blues but was lightened up with a pop delivery.

Artists such as Curtis Mayfield, Jerry Butler, Gene Chandler, and Major Lance made great strides with pop audiences with their Chicago-style brand of rhythm & blues. Other black singers, like Little Willie John, Gary "U.S." Bonds, and Solomon Burke, along with Sam Cooke, Jackie Wilson, and James Brown, cut through with their own interpretations of R&B that projected them into pop territory.

The blues, however, wasn't the only black musical form from which early-sixties R&B borrowed. There were very definite and very strong elements of gospel that could be heard in the music of *all* the artists mentioned above. Many of them began their careers in gospel groups and church choirs. There were also elements of doo-wop and even rock & roll à la Little Richard and Screamin' Jay Hawkins.

During the sixties blacks were asserting themselves politically. The civil rights movement and later the black power movement helped blacks realize their political power and inspired changes in laws and social attitudes. More blacks were stepping out of the white man's shadow and aiming for a better life, and the music that was being made reflected this.

Because of the shifting nature of rock & roll in the early sixties and the manufacture of teen idols and lightweight pop stars, an increasing number of disenchanted whites looked to black R&B for fulfillment—and found it. Much of the era's memorable music was R&B, and the influence its artists exerted over the decade's future rockers was substantial.

Finally, late-fifties and early-sixties R&B and its antecedents, especially gospel, helped define soul music, black popular music's crowning achievement. Atlantic Records' Jerry Wexler and Motown's Berry Gordy, Jr., were among those who laid the foundation for the great music and great artists to come.

RECOMMENDED ARTISTS

Sam Cooke

Today most people know Sam Cooke from the many interpretations of his songs by white rockers from Rod Stewart ("Twistin' the Night Away") to Southside Johnny and the Asbury Jukes ("Having a Party"). Cooke was an excellent songwriter who could mix pop and R&B to create a melody so delectable it transcended all musical preferences. Yet too many people fail to recall his cool, velvety voice, one of the purest and prettiest to come out of the early sixties, and his graceful, composed demeanor, both in the recording studio and onstage. Cooke didn't pack the passion of James Brown or the exhilaration of Jackie Wilson. Instead, he concentrated on romantic balladeering and sang each tune with unusual articulation and charm. Even though he was very popular with blacks—he was their first real pop star—he seemed to cater to white tastes. The sexuality so prominently heard in the vocal styles of other black R&B artists was strictly controlled, even smothered, whenever Cooke opened his mouth to sing.

Cooke was still in his teens when he became lead vocalist in the Soul Stirrers, a popular gospel group. Cooke eventually found gospel a bit too stifling (not to mention unprofitable), and in 1956 he released a secular tune called "Lovable" before leaving the group. One year later he had his first number-one record, "You Send Me." An easy, relaxed ballad written by his brother, it displayed to the pop world his magnificent vocal talent.

It was, however, three years before Cooke repeated that success. In 1960 "Chain Gang" reached number two, and from 1960 to 1965 Cooke placed twenty songs in the Top Forty, among them "Cupid," "Twistin' the Night Away," "Bring It on Home to Me," "Another Saturday Night," "Frankie and Johnny," and "Shake." "Having a Party" and "Bring It on Home to Me" was a double-sided hit in 1962. The former was a joyous, finger-popping tune, complete with a perfect pop hook, a rechargeable melody, and lyrics that were light and easily remembered. Cooke sang the song with an upbeat yet typically controlled tone. "Bring It on Home to Me," on the other hand, was gospel-influenced soul. Its call-and-response vocal pattern was performed in the best gospel tradition and featured another ex-Soul Stirrer, Lou Rawls, on the response.

The details surrounding Cooke's untimely death in 1964 have been questioned. But the facts are that Los Angeles motel manager Bertha Franklin shot Cooke to death after he attacked her. Franklin had come to the aid of Cooke's female companion after she ran screaming from Cooke's room.

Frankie and Johony
You Send Me
Sad Mood
Summertime (from "Porgy and Bess")
Chain Gang
Little Red Rooster
Cupid
Sugar Dumpling
Send Me Some Lovin'
Everybody Loves to Cha Cha Cha
Feel It
(I Love You) For Sentimental Reasons
Another Saturday Night
Wonderful World
Having a Party
Baby, Baby, Baby
Only Sixteen
Love Will Find a Way
Bring It On Home to Me
Twistin' the Night Away

Courtesy of RCA Records

This Is Sam Cooke / RCA / 1970

Sam Cooke's early-sixties pop albums are out of print and difficult to find but occasionally show up in import racks. *This Is Sam Cooke,* a two-record set containing twenty tracks, fills the void rather well. With the exception of "Shake," all of Cooke's major hits are included. "Twistin' the Night Away," "Bring It on Home to Me," and "Having a Party" stand out because Cooke's vocal *and* songwriting gifts are clearly evident.

The Best of Sam Cooke / RCA / 1965

This is the more popular of the two albums mentioned here; it's a single record of Cooke's most memorable songs. But because everything here is on *This Is Sam Cooke*, those seriously interested in Cooke's contribution to early soul and pop (beyond his hits) would be better off with the double album. With an artist of Cooke's caliber, it pays to own as much of his material as possible.

Little Willie John

Little Willie John is the most underrated and the least known of the great black R&B singers of the late fifties and early sixties. John sang—and truly lived—the blues, and his influence on artists including James Brown and Al Green is substantial.

John's voice, sort of a cross between Jackie Wilson's and Smokey Robinson's, was, despite his size, powerful. At five feet four inches, Little Willie John cloaked his vocals with a bluesy, emotional drive that gave new breath to early-sixties rhythm & blues. A voice as pure and convincing as his rarely failed to strike its target; regardless of how history has treated him, few of his contemporaries could match his vocal delivery.

Born in Arkansas and raised in Detroit, Little Willie John learned his craft on the street. By the time he was in his late teens, he had a recording deal with King Records. Most of Willie John's early recordings made impressive showings on the R&B chart. His pop chart debut was in 1956 with "Fever," and from then on he had several more hits, including "Sleep" in 1960.

Paranoid and acutely aware of his height (or lack of height), John was also a hot-tempered drinker who carried a weapon. In 1966 he killed a person in a Seattle bar. He was convicted of manslaughter, and two years later he died of pneumonia in a Washington state prison.

Free At Last / Gusto / 1976

This two-record anthology contains more than enough top-notch material to demonstrate Little Willie John's special talent as a vocalist. Twenty-three tracks from the fifties and sixties cover his complete recording career on King Records. Top tracks include "Fever," "Sleep," "I'm Shakin'," "Letter from My Darling," "Leave My Kitten Alone," and "Sufferin' with the Blues."

Jackie Wilson

If there ever was a performer blessed with a tremendous vocal talent *and* the sex appeal to electrify an audience, it was Jackie Wilson. With a voice that could exceed Sam Cooke's in smoothness, Wilson could also rival James Brown when it came to vocal projection, dancing, and rock & roll shaking. Jackie Wilson could have—and should have—been the greatest black rock & roller in history.

But Wilson never quite achieved such fame, although he did leave behind a legacy that was far from ordinary. Three obstacles stood in Wilson's way. First, he didn't have enough first-rate material. "Baby Workout" and "(Your Love Keeps Lifting Me) Higher and Higher" proved what Wilson could do with really good songs. These are two of the best songs to come out of sixties R&B. But Wilson usually had to wade through mediocre material. Second, like many other black artists, Wilson did not control his career. He flirted too much with the supper-club circuit (listen to "Night") and success with that style left him unsure about which direction to pursue. Third, Wilson was a victim of circumstance. Berry Gordy, for instance, wrote a few of Wilson's early hits before he founded Motown. As Joe McEwen wrote in his excellent chapter on Wilson in *The Rolling Stone Illustrated History of Rock & Roll*, "Wilson would have been a logical choice to head the Motown roster, but instead he remained at Brunswick, a label with a dubious reputation and few facilities for promoting his career."

Yet from the start it was apparent that Jackie Wilson was special. He began his career as lead singer for Billy Ward and the Dominoes when Clyde McPhatter departed in 1953. He was cocky, but he was good. The Dominoes never got over McPhatter's departure from the group, but they did score a Top Twenty hit with Wilson in 1956, "St. Therese of the Roses." Wilson, though, had bigger ambitions. He left the group in 1957, and in the late fifties hit with "To Be Loved," "Lonely Teardrops," "That's Why," and "I'll Be Satisfied." His momentum was slowed a bit in 1961 after a crazed female fan shot him. But Wilson recovered and went on to record a bunch of hit records in the early sixties, including "Baby Workout."

Released in 1967, "Higher and Higher" was Wilson's last big hit, and it remains his most fondly recalled song. It has bright lyrics, a catchy guitar riff, a hook-laden melody, and Wilson's spirited, soaring vocals. Of all the many renditions of the song over the years, none comes close to the original.

After 1967 Wilson's hits came no more. Though he kept recording, Wilson never quite adapted to the late-sixties soul sound and survived by doing oldies shows, mostly with Dick Clark. Wilson suffered a massive heart attack onstage in 1975 and remained in a coma until his death in 1984.

The Jackie Wilson Story / Epic / 1983

There are many Wilson anthologies and greatest-hits packages around, but none comes close to this one. This double-record set's jacket is attractively designed and contains some interesting photos and Joe McEwen's fine liner notes. Major hits as well as tracks never released as singles make up the compilation. With Wilson's Brunswick LPs long since out of circulation, *The Jackie Wilson Story* becomes even more valuable.

Solomon Burke

Though Solomon Burke never had a monster pop hit, his presence high on the R&B charts throughout the sixties was constant. Burke's material, delivered in his gospel, preachy vocals, was often a bit too strong for pop tastes. Though his forte was R&B—the earliest component of pure soul—he experimented with country & western and did pretty well with the tune "Just Out of Reach (Of My Two Open Arms)" in 1966. Rarely, if ever, did Burke compromise his music for the payoff that middle-of-the-road hits might have brought him. Because of this, whenever other soul singers and rock singers like Mick Jagger later went searching for inspiration, they usually stumbled on Solomon Burke somewhere along the line.

Burke's two biggest hits were "Got to Get You Off My Mind," a bouncy soul tune, and "Just Out of Reach," the quirky country & western and pop hit that he sang beautifully. Other soul songs include "Cry to Me," "If You Need Me" (one of his very best), and "Tonight's the Night." Burke never abandoned his strong Philadelphia gospel roots. On these songs and the many others he recorded between 1960 and 1968 for Atlantic Records, the gospel overtones are heard time and time again.

The Best of Solomon Burke / Atlantic / 1966

A decent twelve-track greatest-hits album that barely reflects Burke's finer moments, *The Best of Solomon Burke* is, unfortunately, all there is from Burke's early-sixties period. Most of the songs are soul ballads and all are sung with an explicit attempt at elaborating on the best elements of preacher-style emotionalism. Top selections: "Got to Get You Off My Mind," "If You Need Me," "Cry to Me," and "Tonight's the Night." Solomon Burke fans are still waiting for the definitive Solomon Burke anthology.

James Brown (Part I)

No R&B artist in the early sixties took the emotional force of gospel music and stretched it as far as James Brown did. Brown's vocal dynamics were such that he could extract every last ounce of sexuality out of any song he sang. He'd work both himself and his audience into a veritable frenzy: When he and his band climaxed, it seemed as if the whole world was gasping for air.

James Brown still ranks among the greatest performers in the history of rock & roll. Billed as The Hardest Working Man in Show Business and Mr. Dynamite, Brown easily lived up to the hype he built around himself. The collapse/revival scenario of "Please, Please, Please" that ends his shows is legendary. Many of his moves, mannerisms, and dance steps have been widely imitated. And only a handful of live acts have ever performed with the precision he demanded from his backup band, night after night.

Few of Brown's studio albums from the sixties come close to capturing what he achieved live, but at least two albums he made for Federal in the late fifties and early sixties (see below) capture some of his onstage power. It was during this period of his career that he developed his vocal intensity; certainly what he recorded in the early sixties proved that James Brown either was going to forge a brand new path in rhythm & blues or else burn up like a comet trying.

Before James Brown signed on with Syd Nathan's Federal Records, he'd been part of a Georgia gospel group called the Swanees. In time they became the Famous Flames, then James Brown and the Famous Flames. As popular as Brown and his group were with blacks in the early sixties, they lacked the pop appeal of Sam Cooke and Jackie Wilson. But even while Brown was too threatening, too scary, too dangerous for most whites, five of his tunes did cross over onto the pop Top Forty between 1960 and 1964: "Think," "Bewildered," the instrumental "Night Train," "Oh Baby Don't You Weep (Part I)," and "Out of Sight." A sixth, "Prisoner of Love," made it into the Top Twenty. In 1965, however, Brown lodged two monster songs in the Top Ten ("Papa's Got a Brand New Bag [Part I]" and "I Got You [I Feel Good]") and became Soul Brother Number One. (See Chapter 14, "The Soul Sound.")

Live and Lowdown at the Apollo, Vol. 1 / Solid Smoke / 1980

This is a reissue of the original King LP, *Live at the Apollo, Vol.*

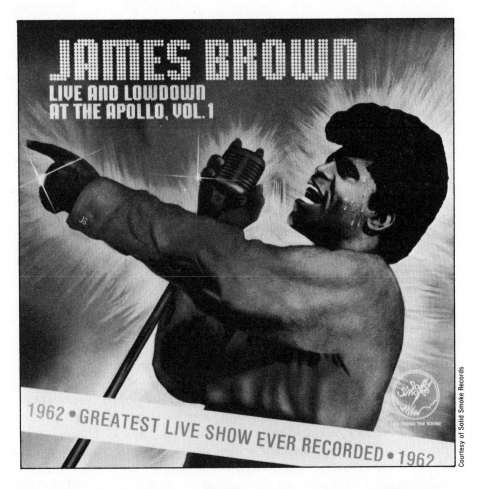

1, recorded in 1962 at New York's Apollo Theatre. One of the greatest live records ever made, the LP is Brown in full swing, tearing up tunes like "Please, Please, Please," "Think," and "Try Me." James Brown's best moments have always been on a stage, and this album is the ultimate proof of that. Backed by the Famous Flames and complete with audience hysteria, this record is a downright necessity for those interested not only in James Brown and the advent of soul, but live recordings. Few can match this one.

Prisoner of Love / King / 1963

In the early eighties Polydor bought the rights to Brown's King catalog and rereleased eight of the best albums he recorded between 1962 and 1967. *Prisoner of Love* was originally recorded in 1963 and includes some of Brown's best early-sixties studio tracks. Listen closely: Here are the roots of soul.

Gary "U.S." Bonds

Gary "U.S." Bonds (born Gary Anderson) made some of the worst-sounding records of the early sixties: thin, full of distortion, and often muddy beyond the point of toleration. Producer Frank Guida's studio methods were a far cry from state-of-the-art production techniques of the day.

Gary "U.S." Bonds was nevertheless a big recording star in the early sixties because his records were party records, full of good-time flavor. The records sound as if they were recorded in the middle of a drunken celebration. A typical Bonds record background consisted of people shouting, screaming, clapping their hands, and generally having a ball. Just above all this chaos was Bonds, singing as if the party depended on him.

The records were made in Norfolk, Virginia, where Guida had his skimpy studio and where he had discovered Bonds. Their first song together was "New Orleans," an uptempo rocker and Top Ten hit that introduced Guida's unorthodox production ideas and Bond's wild enthusiasm. A follow-up single, "Not Me," flopped, but "Quarter to Three," Bonds's third single, went to number one. One of Guida's promotional gimmicks was to print "Buy U.S. Bonds" on the record jacket and call the singer of the tune U.S. Bonds (as in Ulysses Samuel). This was done without Bonds's knowledge, but due to the success of the record, he had no choice but to be called Gary "U.S." Bonds from then on.

Not wishing to tamper with a hot formula, Guida and Bonds continued making records that sounded horrible but were a whole lot of fun to listen and dance to. Between Bonds, Guida, and saxman Gene "Daddy G" Barge, enough tunes were written to keep Bonds on the charts in 1961 and 1962. After "Quarter to Three" came two songs with a school theme, "School Is Out" and "School Is In." Then came Twist records, but instead of recording "Dear Lady Twist" and "Twist, Twist Senora" with a Twist beat, Guida used calypso rhythms. Incredibly, both tunes broke into the Top Ten.

"Twist, Twist Senora" was Bonds's last hit of the sixties. For the rest of the decade he continued to record and perform but didn't have another hit until after he was rediscovered by Bruce Springsteen in a

New Jersey nightclub in 1980. Springsteen was a big fan of Bonds, and he and Steve Van Zandt produced Bonds's 1981 comeback LP, *Dedication.* "This Little Girl," a Springsteen tune, reached number eleven on the charts, and suddenly, after nineteen years, Gary "U.S." Bonds was again a star. A second LP, *On the Line,* yielded another hit, "Out of Work."

Dance 'till Quarter to Three / Legrand / 1961

This LP, Bonds's debut, is available as a German import. As expected, the sound is horrid yet authentic. Daddy G Barge's roaring saxophone is heard on every cut and gives each song color and focus amid all that riotous background noise. This includes "Quarter to Three," "New Orleans," and "School Is Out" and remains the best album Bonds ever made before the Springsteen-produced LP.

Twist Up Calypso / Legrand / 1962

More party music from Bonds and Frank Guida, but this time it's calypso instead of rock & roll. "Naughty Little Flea," "Twist, Twist Senora," and "Day-O" provide plenty of bounce despite poor sound quality. A German import and not an essential album, but one Bonds fans will find delightful.

Greatest Hits / Ensign / 1981

All the hits are here with some interesting B sides: "Havin' So Much Fun" and "Mixed Up Faculty," another school number. Listen, though, to "Quarter to Three" and "Twist, Twist Senora" in particular, and it's no wonder why Springsteen wanted to revive Bonds's career. Many of Springsteen's vocal mannerisms and live intonations were influenced by Bonds.

Ray Charles

There's never been a recording artist quite like Ray Charles. No one has absorbed so much American music—jazz, blues, gospel, rhythm & blues, rock & roll, pop, and country & western—as he has. No one else has ever possessed his immense versatility. The Genius, as he's affectionately called, had a major impact on each of these musical forms. No one else can boast of that achievement.

Blind since childhood, Charles first recorded in 1949 with Swing Time Records. Many of Charles's earliest recordings were ballads that bear Nat "King" Cole's influence. In the fifties Charles signed on with Atlantic Records and began working with Ahmet Ertegun and Jerry Wexler, two of R&B and, later, soul's greatest producers. Under their supervision, Charles revealed his unique talent and recorded some of the decade's finest records. Working with such R&B stars as Ruth Brown and Guitar Slim, Charles was further exposed to the various musical ideas and influences that would later appear on his albums. Charles discovered the keys to the successful marriages of blues and gospel; rhythm & blues and rock & roll; and even country & western and blues, and created a catalog of music so extensive and profound in its conviction and inspiration that there are few sixties artists—white or black—who weren't moved by him.

Despite what some may claim, Charles wasn't a true originator; he didn't invent anything. Charles was like a wise chef who instinctively knew what ingredients went together to make the best soup. In that sense, Charles was indeed an original. His perfect blend of gospel emotion, R&B's romp, and the blues forged a sound that dominated musical tastes in the fifties.

"What'd I Say" was the ideal record to culminate a decade's worth of great music. Released in 1959, the song went to number six on the pop charts and revealed Charles's talent, both as a pianist and a singer, to a wider audience. There was no getting around the record. The rhythmic base of the song was a typical blues riff, but Charles's passionate, gospel-styled delivery that went back and forth and up and down was spectacular.

Charles left Atlantic in 1960 for ABC-Paramount (whose most notable R&B artist was Lloyd Price of "Stagger Lee" fame) for more money. Charles had three excellent years with ABC, recording such classics as Hoagy Carmichael's "Georgia on My Mind," his first number one pop hit; "Hit the Road Jack," his second; "One Mint Julep"; and "Unchain My Heart." In 1962 came "I Can't Stop Loving You," which settled at number one for five weeks and sold more than three million copies. The song and the album from which it came, *Modern Sounds in Country and Western Music*, announced a new direction for Charles.

It was a direction that had less to do with R&B or rock & roll and more to do with country & western. But Charles explored new horizons and, later in the sixties he embraced pop music. If chart success was any indication of whether or not his move to country was the right one, Charles never had a bigger record than the 1962 Grammy winner "I Can't Stop Loving You."

Because Charles drifted away from R&B, his influence on rock & roll in the early sixties grew less noticeable. Critically speaking, his albums suffered from a benign quality that often resulted in ineffectual tracks. As Charlie Gillett wrote in his book *The Sound of the City*, "From 1962, Ray Charles degenerated, a musical decline closely matching that of Elvis Presley. Charles applied his style to anything, inevitably adjusting himself to awkward material, losing contact with the cultural roots that had inspired his style."

The Greatest Ray Charles / Atlantic / 1963

For those just interested in the R&B Charles and how this period of his career influenced sixties rock & roll, *The Greatest Ray Charles* is the best choice. There are only nine tracks on the record, but they're all monsters. A quick sampling: "What'd I Say," "I'm Movin' On," "I Got a Woman," "Talkin' 'Bout You." This record is easily found.

A Life in Music / Atlantic / 1982

For understanding Ray Charles's accomplishments in the early sixties—before he went country—an ABC-Paramount compilation album would do. Unfortunately, no such album exists, and all the original early-sixties R&B/rock & roll albums that Charles recorded on the label are no longer in print. The best way to take in the genius of Ray Charles, then, is to purchase *A Life in Music*, a boxed set of four records that covers all of Charles's illustrious career. It's expensive and may include some material not absolutely satisfying, but most of the tracks help to sum up clearly his contribution to contemporary music.

The Impressions

The Impressions helped shape the sounds of R&B and soul, Chicago-style. Theirs was a smooth, silky sound, always well-crafted and superbly executed. The group's two main members were Jerry Butler and Curtis Mayfield. (Other members were Richard and Arthur Brooks, Sam Gooden, and, for a short spell, Fred Cash). It was

Butler's inviting baritone that was heard on the group's first hit, "Your Precious Love." Released in 1958 on the tiny Abner/Falcon label, the song made it to number eleven. But when the Impressions couldn't muster a successful follow-up, Butler left the group to pursue a solo career. Happily, the split didn't stop Butler and Mayfield from writing and recording together in the early sixties.

When Butler left, Mayfield became the group's principal vocalist. (Cash, who was brought in to replace Butler, didn't work out.) Mayfield's tenor was in direct contrast to Butler's heavier delivery, and the group's sound changed. Mayfield was also the Impressions' producer and chief songwriter. "Gypsy Woman" (1961) and especially "It's All Right" (1963), both hits, were proof of his abilities.

Mayfield was among the most important and influential singer/ songwriter/producers in black music in the sixties. Mayfield cultivated his strong gospel roots on originals like the poignant "Amen" and, to a lesser extent, on "I'm So Proud" and "Keep On Pushing," two brilliant compositions. He was also responsible for socially conscious songs like "People Get Ready" and "Keep On Pushing." They paved the way for other black songwriters to make political statements. Finally, Mayfield was as good a producer as he was a singer or songwriter. Not only did he handle production chores for the Impressions' and Jerry Butler's early solo recordings, he also was responsible for the success of Major Lance, Gene Chandler, and others. In short, Mayfield did for Chicago soul what Smokey Robinson did for Motown.

The Impressions, Curtis Mayfield (as a solo act), and Jerry Butler all continued to record into the seventies. Butler's best years were still ahead, and although Mayfield's heyday was in the years 1961 through 1965 he later scored a couple of best-sellers, most notably the soundtrack for the black exploitation movie *Superfly* (1972).

Keep on Pushing / Kent / 1964

A British import reissue, *Keep on Pushing* highlights the Impressions' soothing harmonies and Mayfield's penchant for writing songs that accent them. With arrangements by Johnny Pate, the tracks, especially the title song, flow gracefully. Mayfield's behind-the-scenes effort to make his sound firm yet subtle is evident here. Also available as an import is *The Never Ending Impressions*, another fine early-sixties Impressions LP, but for some reason it is slightly more difficult to come by in the United States.

The Vintage Years / Sire / 1976

A full, comprehensive anthology of the Impressions, featuring Jerry Butler and Curtis Mayfield, is what you'll find on *The Vintage Years*. Complete with thorough and informative liner notes by Joe McEwen, the double-record set begins with "Your Precious Love" and ends with Mayfield's "Superfly." In between are twenty-six tracks, none of which has been enhanced or rechanneled for stereo and all of which reveal Mayfield's brilliance. All anthologies should be this good. May be hard to locate as it is out of print.

Jerry Butler

Even though Jerry Butler left the Impressions for his solo career, he returned to cohort and close friend Mayfield to get it properly tracked. Together they penned the 1960 hit "He Will Break Your Heart." The song, which made it to number seven, was the first of Butler's early-sixties hits and established him as a crooning, soul-satisfying artist.

Butler's early-sixties vocal style was settling and mature. He opted for a more conservative pace (as did many early-sixties Chicago soul singers) and concentrated on love ballads with relaxed deliveries. Much of the material he recorded in these years has been overshadowed by Mayfield's records with the Impressions, even though "Find Another Girl," "I'm a Telling You," and "Need to Belong" were all Top Forty hits.

Jerry Butler didn't mind straying into the MOR market where he felt his chances for a hit were better. He did this most noticeably with a swooning rendition of "Moon River" in 1961 which, ironically, came the closest in commercial success to "He Will Break Your Heart." It peaked at number eleven and stayed in the Top Forty for almost three months.

Up on Love / Charly / 1980

There are few Jerry Butler LPs that deal exclusively with his early-sixties output save this greatest-hits package. (Actually, there are few Jerry Butler LPs available, period.) An English import, *Up on Love* includes the best of Butler's Vee Jay recordings from 1960 to 1962. Of the sixteen tracks, three were recorded with Curtis Mayfield ("I'm a Telling You," "Find Another Girl," and "He Will Break Your

Heart'') and one with the Impressions ("For Your Precious Love").
Most of the songs are easy-listening soul ballads.

Major Lance

It isn't because Major Lance's influence was widespread or that his
recording catalog is thick with hits that he's included here. Lance, a
Chicago-based singer with strong gospel roots and a protégé of
Curtis Mayfield, did have a few hits in 1963 and 1964. Two of them,
"The Monkey Time" and "Um, Um, Um, Um, Um, Um," were Top
Ten entries. It's just that the records he made with Mayfield were
effectively postured, full of endearing vocals, and simply too good
not to mention. At his best, Major Lance was as good an example of
the Mayfield–Chicago soul sound as anyone.

"The Monkey Time," written and produced by Curtis Mayfield,
launched the Monkey dance craze. It's a fun, happy record, as is
"Um, Um, Um, Um, Um, Um." Without Mayfield, Lance probably
would have turned out to be just another struggling Chicago singer
on the local club circuit. With him, Lance made a bunch of solid, if
not spectacular, records to be remembered by.

Monkey Time / Edsel / 1983

This British import best-of LP is not to be confused with Lance's
debut album of the same name released on Okeh in 1963. (Both of
Lance's early-sixties studio LPs—*Monkey Time* and *Um, Um, Um,
Um, Um, Um*—are long out of print.) This record is similar to
Major's Greatest Hits, an Okeh record from 1965. Both contain
Lance's best songs: "The Monkey Time," "Um, Um, Um, Um, Um,
Um," "Hey Little Girl," "The Matador," and "Rhythm." The
British *Monkey Time* is smartly packaged and contains a thorough
biography and discography on the back.

Gene Chandler

Although Gene Chandler was one of the better singers to come out
of the Chicago–Curtis Mayfield school of soul in the early sixties,
he's best known for his gigantic 1962 hit, "Duke of Earl"—the one
tune that least represents his style. The song was a million-seller, but
it was a one-shot throwback to the doo-wop days of the fifties.

Like Major Lance, Gene Chandler relied heavily on Curtis Mayfield for material and guidance. Mayfield took a particular interest in Chandler because his easy crooning qualities were similar to his own.

Perhaps the best Chandler records that Mayfield penned and produced were a pair of Top Twenty hits: "Just Be True," with its startling Impressions-like production (1964), and "Nothing Can Stop Me" (1965). Chandler recorded a number of other songs under Mayfield's supervision, but none was as successful.

Just Be True / Charly / 1980

This sixteen-track anthology from England is chock-full of Chicago soul and rarely fails to impress. Mayfield wrote and produced half of the songs, and all Chandler's best records are here, including "Duke of Earl."

Stroll on with the Duke / Solid Smoke / 1984

For serious Chandler fans. *Stroll on with the Duke* contains six great Chandler cuts not found on *Just Be True*: "I'll Follow You," "Bless Our Love," "I Wake Up Crying," "Rainbow '65" (the complete version—recorded live in 1965), "If You Can't Be True," and "Walk on with the Duke." Since it's an American LP, *Stroll On* might be a bit easier to find than *Just Be True*.

6
THE SOUNDS OF SURF

It was Dick Dale, a frustrated country singer, who first came up with the idea of surf music. In the summer of 1961 Dale and his band, the Del-Tones, began playing the Rendezvous Ballroom in Southern California's Newport Beach. What they played wasn't all that different from what other instrumental bands were playing at the time. Most of the songs were coarse instrumental rockers with lots of raw energy and localized fervor.

But two elements would ultimately separate surf bands from all others, and Dale was responsible for both. With the help of Leo Fender of Fender Instruments, who later became the godfather of the rock guitar (Telecaster and Stratocaster are two classic Fender guitars), Dale hooked up a reverb unit to his guitar. This gave the instrument a snarly, echoey tone that Dale claimed was intense and real enough to vividly portray the thrill of surfing, both Dale's and Southern California's favorite sport.

Secondly, though he didn't know it at the time, the alliance Dale forged between instrumental rock and surfing would soon result in a whole new trend in pop music. Rare was a rock & roll song that dealt with sport. What was even more fascinating was that the sport was surfing, something then done only in California and Hawaii, with tiny pockets of surfers on the East Coast in New Jersey and Florida.

In the beginning surf music consisted of only surf instrumentals fueled with tireless teen energy. But when Brian Wilson and the Beach Boys began writing and singing lyrics to surf songs, surf music took on a bigger, more encompassing role in pop. Surf music wasn't just about surfing or capturing the sound of surf on a guitar. Through Brian Wilson's vision, surf music came to epitomize eternal youth. Surf music dealt with innocence, freedom, good health, and opportunity, all intricately connected with the worship of sun, sand, and surf. The early sixties was a great time to be seventeen or eighteen years old and living in Southern California. There was a sense of idealism and even euphoria that hovered over L.A. and the Orange County beach towns to the south of the city. All things were possible there; all things were fun.

Surf-rock groups sprang up in Denver (the Astronauts), Minneapolis (the Trashmen), and Texas (the Fireballs). Other more established instrumental groups like the Ventures (from Washington) began recording records with surf themes. It didn't matter that some of these kids in surf bands outside California couldn't even swim, let alone surf.

Musically, surf music borrowed considerably from rockabilly, rhythm & blues, and traditional rock & roll. The surf beat was a basic rock beat, although Dale undoubtedly accentuated its primal qualities. You can also hear the stylistic influences of Duane Eddy and Link Wray on Dale and other surf guitarists, and Chuck Berry, Bo Diddley, the Everly Brothers, and Eddie Cochran figured heavily in Brian Wilson's outlook on songwriting.

Surf music also encompassed hot-rod music. The music and the sound were the same, and while one glorified beach and surf themes and the other cars and drag strips, both celebrated freedom. The Beach Boys, among others, moved comfortably from the beach to the street.

Surf music climaxed in 1963 and 1964 when the genre's two biggest groups, the Beach Boys and Jan and Dean, had a slew of songs high on the charts. From the Beach Boys came hits like "Surfin' U.S.A.," "Surfer Girl," "Little Deuce Coupe," "Fun, Fun, Fun," and "I Get Around." Jan and Dean had "Surf City," "Drag City," "The Little Old Lady (From Pasadena)," and "Ride the Wild Surf."

It's easy enough to say that the Beatles and the other British Invasion groups stifled surf music as effectively as they did all the other early-sixties rock & roll trends. But more important, it was the tainting of innocence and youthful scampers in the sun that stopped surf music from spreading further. President John F. Kennedy had been assassinated, stories about some country called Vietnam began appearing in newspapers, and civil rights marchers were beaten up in the South. Folk singers with acoustic guitars were singing about issues that had nothing to do with baggies, woodies, and Waimea Bay. Suddenly there seemed more to life than "tryin' to keep the summer alive."

RECOMMENDED ARTISTS

Dick Dale

Even though the Beach Boys and Jan and Dean had great national and international success with surf music, its founding father Dick Dale never broke out of Southern California. His domination there, however, was complete and enabled him to sell out the fifteen thousand-seat L.A. Sports Arena and to sell thousands of records in L.A. and Orange Counties. His first surf single (and surf music's first) was "Let's Go Trippin'," recorded and released independently on Deltone Records in 1961. But the song that best displays Dale's surf-sound guitar was "Misirlou," released a year later. The success of these two singles and others, plus an LP called *Surfer's Choice*, resulted in a recording deal with Capitol Records. Capitol promptly rereleased *Surfer's Choice* in 1963.

Much has been made of Dale's guitar style; he was known as King of the Surf Guitar. His staccato licks were undoubtedly influenced by Duane Eddy. Dale, a lefty, played a right-handed guitar upside down, and so the bottom bass strings yielded a thicker, more sinewy sound. Also, the use of Leo Fender's reverb unit and the Fender Showman amplifier made Dale's guitar sound even more emphatic.

With the popularity of the Beach Boys and Jan and Dean and Dale's reluctance to tour after a disappointing set of gigs on the East Coast, his chances of becoming a major national act all but disappeared. As far as Capitol was concerned, the commercial fate of surf music rested with the Beach Boys, and even then the label was doubtful of the music's appeal outside California. Dale recorded with Capitol until his contract expired, appeared in a couple of surf movies, and performed in Southern California with the Del-Tones until it was discovered he had cancer. Doctors gave Dale little hope of recovering, but he did, and has since launched a comeback amid the surf-music revival of the early eighties.

Surf-music fanatic Bob Dalley publishes a catalog of available surf albums and singles called *Surf Wax*. Old surf records, including Dick Dale's *Surfer's Choice*, can usually be found for sale in it. *Surf Wax*'s address is 6209 Oakbank Drive, Azusa, California, 91702.

Surfer's Choice / Capitol / 1963

This is Dale's first and best album, for it contains the earliest examples of surf instrumentals. Dale's guitar playing is loud and wildly aggressive, but a lot of the primal energy he unleashed live simply didn't translate onto vinyl. Both the Deltone and Capitol editions of *Surfer's Choice* are out of print. But surf-music fans can find copies of the record at record collectors' conventions or swap meets.

Greatest Hits / Crescendo / 1975

This is a fine collection of Dale's top hits, including "Misirlou," "King of the Surf Guitar," and "Let's Go Trippin'," but they are not the original recordings. Producer Jim Pewter, members of the Del-Tones, and Dick Dale recut some of his best tunes. The deliveries are authentic and interesting and give a good account of the original surf-music sound. Also contained on the record are a couple of less interesting, previously unrecorded tunes.

The Challengers

The Challengers were one of surf music's most prolific instrumental bands; they released more than nine albums and singles. But despite such an impressive recording output, the band never had much of an impact outside Southern California.

The roots of the Challengers can be found in the Belairs, an early South Bay band. Both drummer Richard Delvy and pianist Jim Roberts were members of the group before they became Challengers. The Challengers' sound was neither as raw nor as primitive as Dale's. Instead the Challengers strove for a more patient, steady sound, one

built on mature musicianship rather than unfocused energy. Three elements characterized the group's approach to surf music: Nick Hefner's grumbling sax, Art Fisher's smooth guitar leads, and Richard Delvy's busy and powerful drumming. Delvy, in fact, was perhaps the very best drummer to come out of the early-sixties surf scene. *Surfbeat*, the Challengers' first LP, was released in early 1963 on a local label and included a remake of the Belair's single "Mr. Moto," plus Johnny and the Hurricanes' "Red River Rock" and interpretations of Dick Dale's "Misirlou" and "Let's Go Trippin'."

Few surf instrumental bands possessed the tightness and flexibility of the Challengers. Virtually all of their LPs were solid endeavors even if they included too many cover tunes. "Apache," "Wipe Out," "Telstar," and "Pipeline"—all great instrumentals—were also recorded by the Challengers.

The Best of the Challengers / Rhino / 1982

All the original Challengers' albums are currently out of print. *The Best of the Challengers* is the only record that's widely accessible. And it's a good one, too, complete with liner notes by Bob Dalley. The LP begins with "K-39," one of the Challengers' best songs, and continues with some of the best-*played* surf music recorded in the early sixties. Top tracks include "Tidal Wave," "Mr. Rebel," and an interesting version of "Wipe Out," done in especially good taste.

The Chantays

The Chantays were only one of two surf instrumental bands that scored a Top Ten hit during the surf-music era. "Pipeline," undoubtedly one of the best surf instrumentals ever recorded, is their claim to fame.

From Southern California, the Chantays were much influenced by Dick Dale and his Del-Tones. "Pipeline" was originally the B side to a tune called "Move It." Named after Hawaii's ultimate—and most dangerous—surf spot, which the Chantays claimed to have surfed during a tour of Hawaii in 1964, the song begins with a plummeting bass run that is the aural equivalent of riding a twenty-foot Pipeline wave. From there, Chantays guitarist Bob Spickard breaks in with a simple but effective lead and takes the song to its conclusion.

Pipeline / Dot / 1963

Long out of print, *Pipeline* was obviously quickly recorded and released to take advantage of the title track's success. There's another version of this album on Downey Records, but that's even more difficult to find than this one. Fortunately, the song "Pipeline" can be found on Rhino Records' *The History of Surf Music, Volume One*. (See "Other Recommended Albums" at the end of this chapter.)

The Surfaris

The Surfaris had a Top Ten hit in 1963 with "Wipe Out," the quintessential surf instrumental. The Surfaris were a high-school band that made a record so that they could promote themselves at local dances. But unlike so many other young surf groups who made amateur recordings, the Surfaris had created a gem. "Wipe Out" was supposed to be the flip side to "Surfer Joe," but the incredible response to the instrumental changed that. The tune has a torrid drum riff woven through the melody and is carried by some nice guitar work (even if it is out of tune). The song had all the right surf-inspired ingredients: lots of energy, a reverberating lead guitar, and an action-packed bottom, thanks to Ron Wilson's drumming. His riff is perhaps the most popular drum riff in rock history.

Because of the commercial success of "Wipe Out," Dot Records released an LP titled *Wipe Out*, but according to surf-music expert Bob Dalley, only the title song and "Surfer Joe" were recorded by the Surfaris. In its haste to capitalize on the single's popularity (it had gone to number two), Dot released an album of tracks recorded by the Challengers. Since the Surfaris had recorded the same songs knowing that additional work would be done on them, it took them a while to realize that the group on the record wasn't them. After a couple of lawsuits, future editions of the LP were called *The Surfaris, the Original Hit Version of "Wipe Out" and "Surfer Joe" and Other Popular Selections by Other Instrumental Groups.*

Although "Wipe Out" was their only hit, the Surfaris released other singles and toured California, Hawaii, Australia, and New Zealand, all places where surf music was extremely popular. They also continued to play locally in Southern California until 1966. Various editions of the Surfaris, however, continued to perform in the seventies but included only a couple of the original members.

The Surfaris Play / Dot / 1963

This was the second Surfaris LP on Dot, and this time all of the tracks were recorded by the group. Both "Wipe Out" and "Surfer Joe" are included, as is a decent version of "Misirlou." It's now out of print, but "Wipe Out" can be found on Rhino Records' *The History of Surf Music, Volume One.* (See "Other Recommended Albums" at the end of this chapter.)

The Beach Boys (Part I)

The one group that completely manifested the full spirit of surf music was the Beach Boys. Dick Dale and the instrumental groups went far in capturing the genre's unchecked excitement, but the Beach Boys added lyrics and vocals. Most important, the Beach Boys also portrayed a fresh, sun-kissed romanticism that went beyond California. With the Beach Boys, surfing and surf music became more than a sport and a regional music form; combined, they became a state of mind, and the Beach Boys became one of America's greatest pop groups.

The Beach Boys originated in Hawthorne, California, in 1961. Managed by their father, the Wilson boys—Brian, Carl, and Dennis—formed the group's nucleus, with cousin Mike Love and friend Al Jardine rounding out the outfit. In the beginning they went by such names as Kenny and the Cadets, Carl and the Passions, and the Pendletones. But by the time their first single, "Surfin'," was released in 1962 they were the Beach Boys.

The group's relationship with surf music and surfing began with Dennis's enthusiasm for the sport. Being the only surfer in the group, Dennis suggested that Brian and Mike Love write a song about it. Since surfing was beyond fad status in Southern California, and since a number of local groups had used the surfing theme with some success, they penned "Surfin'."

Released on two local labels, X and Candix, "Surfin'" became a big hit in Southern California, and so Brian Wilson wrote "Surfin' Safari" with Mike Love, and then a hot-rod song, "409," with friend Gary Usher. Seeking a better recording deal for his sons, Murry Wilson took the songs to Capitol Records. Capitol liked what it heard but wasn't so sure that the rest of the country would be interested in a song about surfing. Thus they released both songs, but made "409" the A side and "Surfin' Safari" the flip.

As it turned out "Surfin' Safari" got the most attention and hit the Top Twenty in late 1962. The song was a simple celebration of the surf craze and featured Mike Love's nasal lead vocals and Carl Wilson's short but colorful lead guitar.

Capitol still wasn't sure that surfing songs would continue to sell, so it released "Ten Little Indians," a dumb song based on the nursery rhyme. When that bombed, Capitol put out "Surfin' U.S.A." with a hot-rod B side, "Shut Down." Next came "Surfer Girl" backed with yet another car number, "Little Deuce Coupe." "Surfin' U.S.A." reached number three and "Surfer Girl," number seven. Surf music ruled.

Many of the early Beach Boys songs remained true to their early influences. The clear, remarkably smooth harmonies that filled out just about all of their songs, and which became their trademark, were easily traced to the Everly Brothers, the Four Preps, the Four Freshmen, and the Hi-Lo's. Melodically, Chuck Berry was the main inspiration. "Surfin' U.S.A.," for instance, was an obvious imitation of Berry's "Sweet Little Sixteen." A number of Beach Boys hits would contain that driving rhythm so familiar in Berry's songs, and Brian Wilson was usually the first to admit the impact Berry had on him and the group.

By the time 1963 was over the Beach Boys had released six singles and four albums. *Surfin' Safari* came first, then *Surfin' U.S.A.* and *Surfer Girl*. Then, to take advantage of the airplay "Little Deuce Coupe" was getting, Capitol rushed out *Little Deuce Coupe*. A concept album of sorts, it contained mostly car songs and helped unleash a slew of hot-rod songs on the charts.

During the Beach Boys' reign as the undisputed kings of surf music, they raised surfing to the level of a cultural phenomenon. Because of the Beach Boys, kids in Iowa and Chicago were ordering surfboards from factories in California and picking up on surf lingo and style. Even Hollywood got in on the action with grade-B surf 'n' sand movies starring teen idols like Annette Funicello and Frankie Avalon.

Interest in surf music, however, began to ebb in 1964. Brian Wilson broadened his songwriting horizons with such songs as "Be True to Your School," "Don't Worry Baby," and "When I Grow Up (To Be a Man)." In these songs Wilson dealt with the more mature themes of loyalty, security, and adulthood. Wilson's songs became more personal but retained a universal spirit. The melodies also became more complex and advanced as Wilson experimented with more innovative arrangements and instrumentation.

It was at this time that Wilson began to get involved with production. An admirer of Phil Spector, Wilson was a perfectionist in the studio, working on a tune, or even a piece of a tune, tirelessly until it was absolutely right. He produced *Surfer Girl* in 1963, and from then on spent even more time in the studio. Although Wilson's production masterpiece was still a couple of years away, his early Beach Boys albums were masterfully done and Brian Wilson became rock & roll's first bandleader/songwriter/musician/producer.

Such success, though, had its price. The pressure to write, record, produce, and tour became too much for Brian Wilson and in late

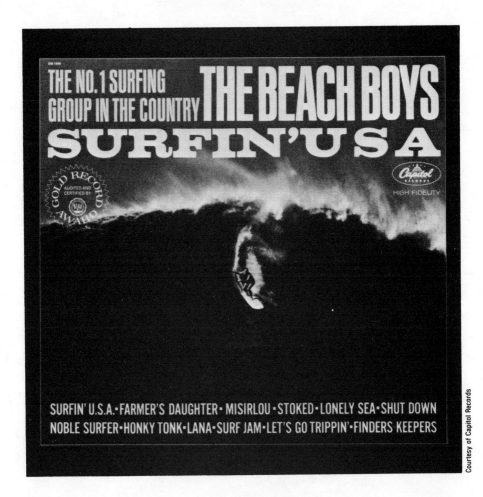

SURFIN' U.S.A.•FARMER'S DAUGHTER • MISIRLOU •STOKED•LONELY SEA•SHUT DOWN
NOBLE SURFER•HONKY TONK•LANA•SURF JAM•LET'S GO TRIPPIN'•FINDERS KEEPERS

Courtesy of Capitol Records

1964, en route to Australia, he suffered a nervous breakdown. After that, he ceased performing and confined his musical activities to writing and producing. Thus ended the Beach Boys' first phase. (See also Chapter 8, "The American Response.")

Surfin' U.S.A. / Capitol / 1963

Surfin' U.S.A. was one of the best-selling rock & roll albums of the early sixties. In addition to the hit title single, the LP also included five instrumentals. Granted, "Honky Tonk" and "Surf Jam" are weak, mostly because they sound rushed. But the Beach Boys provide capable, polished versions of Dick Dale's "Misirlou" and "Let's Go Trippin'," and "Stoked" revealed that if Brian Wilson *really* had

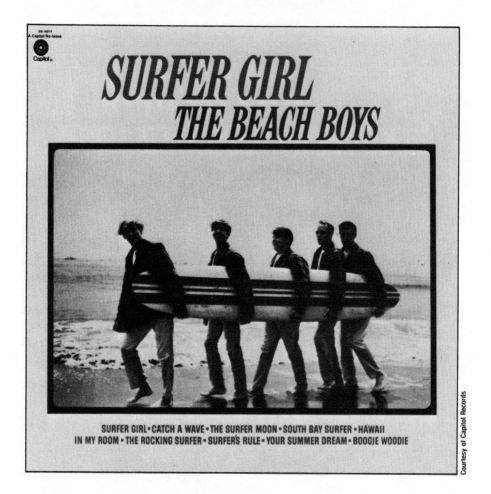

SURFER GIRL · CATCH A WAVE · THE SURFER MOON · SOUTH BAY SURFER · HAWAII
IN MY ROOM · THE ROCKING SURFER · SURFER'S RULE · YOUR SUMMER DREAM · BOOGIE WOODIE

wanted to write instrumentals, he could have turned out some memorable ones.

Surfer Girl / Capitol / 1963

As is the case with just about all the early Beach Boys albums, *Surfer Girl* is widely available as a Capitol rerelease. But for some odd reason, these LPs are usually missing two tracks. *Surfer Girl* deletions are "Little Deuce Coupe" and "Our Car Club." Fortunately, both of these can be found on *Little Deuce Coupe*.

Surfer Girl contains the best of the early Beach Boys ballads. "Surfer Girl," a cuddly, intimate gem, proved surfers were interested in more than waves and woodies. On "In My Room," Brian Wilson revealed himself in a way few songwriters did before the late sixties. The ballads "The Surfer Moon" and "Your Summer Dream" were tributes to the Four Freshmen.

Little Deuce Coupe / Capitol / 1963

Little Deuce Coupe is the best of the Beach Boys' car song albums. There are some great rockers here—the title song, "Shut Down," "409," and "Be True to Your School." The Beach Boys' hot-rod songs featured the same near-perfect harmonies and bright arrangements that their surf records had.

Endless Summer / Capitol / 1974

This double-record compilation of the Beach Boys' early hits sparked a renewed interest in the group. All the hits are here, from "Surfin' Safari" to "All Summer Long." For those not interested in collecting the LPs mentioned above, this album is a must. Twenty tracks in all, and each is excellent.

Jan and Dean

When it came to vocal surf groups, only the Beach Boys and Jan and Dean mattered. Although the Beach Boys had launched the trend—that is, *singing* about surfing rather than merely recording instrumentals with surfing themes—Jan and Dean notched surf music's first number-one record. The song was "Surf City," its writer none other than their friend Brian Wilson.

Jan Berry and Dean Torrence were high-school pals when they began recording. In 1958 their first record, "Baby Talk," a sprightly doo-wop-influenced tune sung with a sunny California style, made it all the way to number ten. The duo's next few singles barely charted. After recording a song called "Linda," a takeoff on the Four Seasons, the duo's producer/manager Lou Adler suggested they record a surfing song because of the Beach Boys' considerable success with "Surfin' Safari." The Beach Boys had recently backed up Jan and Dean at a local dance where everyone met for the first time. Berry and Torrence had been particularly impressed with Brian Wilson's songs, and a couple of weeks later, they asked Wilson if they could record a couple of his surf tunes for an album that would be titled *Jan and Dean Take Linda Surfing*. Wilson was honored, and when the duo asked him if he had any new songs he might consider giving them, Wilson responded with a partially completed "Surf City." Together Berry and Wilson finished the song. In the summer of 1963 it hit number one and became Jan and Dean's biggest seller.

Berry and Wilson collaborated on a number of surfing and hot-rod songs: "Drag City," "Surfin' Wild," and "The New Girl in School," to name three. The Beach Boys often backed up the duo during their recording sessions, and Jan and Dean would occasionally sing on Beach Boys records. Torrence, for instance, sang lead on the Beach Boys' hit version of "Barbara Ann," although he couldn't be credited because of contractual complications. It was like one big happy family, and Jan and Dean benefited considerably from the relationship.

Jan and Dean fit the surfer image quite well. Both were handsome, healthy, athletic types, well-tanned, with bright smiles. They personified youth and zest. As purveyors of surf music their contribution was substantial even though they broke no new ground. In the years 1963 and 1964, nine of their singles made it into the Top Forty. Their career, however, came to an abrupt halt in April 1966 when Berry demolished his Corvette and nearly killed himself in an automobile crash that left three other people dead. Berry suffered total paralysis and brain damage; for years he was confined to a bed. But, incredibly, he eventually recovered to the point where the duo was able to once again perform together in the seventies.

Ride the Wild Surf / Liberty / 1976

Of the numerous Jan and Dean compilation and greatest-hits packages available, this British import rates as the best. (Although the now hard-to-find Jan and Dean *Anthology*, released by United Artists, is a classic.) *Ride the Wild Surf*'s twenty tracks include everything anyone would want from the duo's 1963–64 period.

The Best of Jan and Dean / Liberty / 1976

The tracks on this best-of LP are those recorded prior to "Surf City." "Jennie Lee," "Baby Talk," and "Barbara Ann" are pre-surf music and give a good idea of the duo's accomplishments before they got involved with Brian Wilson and the Beach Boys.

OTHER RECOMMENDED ALBUMS

The History of Surf Music, Volume One
(Instrumental Surf Hits 1961–1963) / Rhino / 1982
The History of Surf Music, Volume Two
(Original Vocal Hits 1961–1964) / Rhino / 1982

Superbly presented, these two records depict surf music—both instrumentals and vocals—and do so with annotations, photos, and Rhino Records' typical high quality. Volume One contains one track each from the most important instrumental bands: Dick Dale and the Del-Tones, the Surfaris, the Challengers, the Chantays, the Pyramids, and the Crossfires (who later evolved into the Turtles). Volume Two has three Beach Boys tracks, the most important being "Surfin'," the very first surf tune with a vocal track. There are also two tracks by Jan and Dean and two classic surf songs from one-hit wonder groups: "New York's a Lonely Town" by the Trade Winds and "Surfin' Bird" by the Trashmen.

Surfin' U.S.A. / Capitol / 1978

A double-record Swedish import that contains a random selection of surf tunes from the Capitol catalog. Not surprisingly, most of the tracks are from the Beach Boys and Dick Dale, the label's two top surf acts. Other artists included here—John Severson, the Super Stocks, and Jerry Cole—are only mildly interesting. However, surf-music fanatics will get some joy out of this, especially since some of the Dick Dale tracks are otherwise hard to come by.

Golden Summer / United Artists / 1976

This two-record anthology gives a broad overview of surf and surf-related tunes. The tracks from Frankie Avalon, Annette Funicello, and the Ventures are interesting from a historical standpoint. The better tracks are by the Beach Boys, Jan and Dean, the Surfaris, and Dick Dale.

7
THE FIRST BRITISH INVASION

The year 1964 was a big one for rock & roll. Prior to that year pop music on both sides of the Atlantic was fairly predictable. With the exception of the arrival of Elvis Presley in 1956 there really had been nothing to shock pop music or catch it off guard in the late fifties and early sixties. *Good* music was indeed being made; the girl groups, the Beach Boys, the black R&B singers made sure of that. But there was nothing to jolt rock & roll in a powerful and lasting way.

In Britain things were even more static. Since the mid-fifties American artists dominated the British pop charts. The slots they didn't control were taken by British acts who imitated American acts. Cliff Richard, Billy Fury, and Adam Faith were teen idols; the Shadows were inspired by the Ventures. The British music scene—at least on the surface—was more than predictable. It was dull.

Then came the Beatles. And the Rolling Stones. And the Animals, the Kinks, and the Searchers. And Manfred Mann, the Dave Clark Five, Gerry and the Pacemakers, the Hollies, and the Who. And so on. Things would never be the same. The impact these bands and others had on pop music was enormous, and affected rock for the rest of the sixties and beyond.

The funny thing is that, with the exception of the Beatles, the

Rolling Stones, and one or two other groups, much of the music from the British Invasion was all but forgotten a couple of years later—and with good reason. A lot of it was mediocre pop music but in all the excitement sounded like much more than that. Also, much of it was essentially rehashed American music with a British accent. It was the same music we had known about but had forgotten or simply ignored. If nothing else, the British Invasion bands helped us to rediscover our rock & roll heritage: the work of Chuck Berry, Buddy Holly, Bo Diddley, and Little Richard. The British also taught us about our own rhythm & blues and blues artists. Solomon Burke, Muddy Waters, and John Lee Hooker were introduced to many white American record buyers by their British admirers.

The 1964 British Invasion also affected the way the music was made. The Beatles, the Rolling Stones, and the Kinks were among the first successful self-contained groups. With the exception of the instrumental bands that flourished in the late fifties and early sixties, very few American acts wrote and performed their own songs. In the States, the studio musician had an important and comfortable role in pop music. After the British Invasion, he was scratching for work.

The amount of music that came from England, its chart success, and the social implications of phenomena like Beatlemania prompted an upsurge in American rock & roll, the likes of which hadn't been seen since the mid-fifties. Bands sprouted all over the States in response to the flood of British bands (see Chapter 8, "The American Response"), particularly the Beatles. All the excitement pumped new blood into American rock & roll, gave it a new energy, and pushed it to new levels of quantity and quality.

But how and why did all this come out of England? How did a music scene so dependent on America give birth to the Beatles? First, in a country where the accessibility of rock & roll was minimal, teenagers were often forced to create their own music and stars. Second, English pop fans had a genuine interest in the traditional rock & roll of Bill Haley, Eddie Cochran, Gene Vincent, Little Richard, Elvis Presley, Buddy Holly, and Chuck Berry. Even though Britain had its share of teen idols and a fascination for American pop stars like Del Shannon, Gene Pitney, and Roy Orbison, such artists weren't as much a part of the scene as it might have seemed. Third, an appreciation of black blues and rhythm & blues music was considered quite adventurous and chic among England's young musicians, especially in London, where there was a small but healthy blues scene led by Alexis Korner, Cyril Davies, and Chris Barber.

There was one other thing—timing. Both America and England were ripe for a change, and in 1964, with unprecedented millions of baby-boomers coming of age, the Beatles gave pop music more than that. John Lennon, Paul McCartney, George Harrison, and Ringo Starr landed a knockout punch that put pop on the canvas for a ten count. When it finally came to, the whole world had changed.

RECOMMENDED ARTISTS

The Beatles (Part I)

The advent of the Beatles was the single most important event in sixties rock history. Actually, it's not inconceivable to consider their impact the most significant in *all* of rock's history, with all due respect, of course, to Elvis Presley. The truth is that in the years between 1964 and 1966 the Beatles' sound, their faces, their hair, their photos, their presence were felt in virtually every nook and cranny of popular culture.

It wasn't that the Beatles' music was so incredibly unique or that their image was so compelling. Musically, the Beatles borrowed from American rock & roll and rhythm & blues, as all the other British groups of the day did. Listen to the Beatles' early LPs and you can't miss hearing bits of Presley, Buddy Holly, Chuck Berry, Carl Perkins, Little Richard, the Everly Brothers, and even the Shirelles. And as for their image, the beats or beatniks in the fifties had worn their hair in a similar fashion, but few took notice. And before the Beatles put on suits, they wore black leather jackets just like a good many American rockers and greasers did in the fifties and early sixties. What the Beatles gave us didn't all of a sudden simply *appear*.

Again we go back to timing. In 1964 America was on the verge of a nervous collapse. Consider the facts: John F. Kennedy, America's most popular president since Franklin Roosevelt, had been assassinated. Racial tension was beginning to boil. The Cuban Missile Crisis had revealed just how perilously close we were to annihilation. The world seemed destined to blow any second.

We needed a break, a diversion. Beatlemania was it. Since its inception, rock & roll had only one superstar: Presley. There was no one else big enough to help us while away our troubles and make us feel better than we really should. Except the Beatles. They were fresh and new. They weren't American. They had cute faces, English accents, and an odd sense of humor. They were great musicians and performers. Whether they liked it or not, the Beatles were thrust into the spotlight—thanks to the smitten media—and made to provide us with a sense of relief. And they did just that.

Along the way, they also changed the way millions of people would view and listen to pop music. Before the Beatles it was rock & roll; after their arrival it was rock. As composers, Lennon and McCartney permanently upgraded the standards of pop and rock songwriting. Later they would permanently upgrade the art of recording. As John Swenson wrote in *The New Rolling Stone Record Guide*, the Beatles "created the line between fifties and sixties rock." After the Beatles, new areas of music were explored, new genres and offshoots of rock sprouted like flowers after a fresh rain.

The Beatles legitimized rock. Their impact and talent were such that the musical form could no longer be denied even by those who detested it. In February 1964 they made their first of three historic appearances on "The Ed Sullivan Show." In April the Beatles owned the top five positions on the American pop charts: "Can't Buy Me Love," "Twist and Shout," "She Loves You," "I Want to Hold Your Hand," and "Please Please Me" were almost all you heard on the radio. With the Beatles, rock became more than a business; it became an industry. With the Beatles, rock's future was guaranteed.

So much has been written about the Beatles, that merely recapitulating the story of Beatlemania in its early years serves no purpose here. (For a comprehensive biography of the Beatles, and an extremely well-written one at that, check *Shout!* by Philip Norman, Fireside, 1981.) Yet it's important to at least mention the major events that led to the group's domination of sixties rock.

From 1963 to 1965, the Beatles wavered between being a pop group with lots of rock undertones and being a rock group with lots of pop undertones. During this time Lennon and McCartney wrote such pure pop dandies as "She Loves You," "All My Loving," "And I Love Her," "If I Fell," and "This Boy." Yet they balanced them out with the rockers "I Want to Hold Your Hand," "Please Please Me," and perhaps the best rock & roll song they *ever* wrote, "I Saw Her Standing There." And when they weren't writing great rockers, they were covering someone else's. On *The Beatles' Second Album* were Chuck Berry's "Roll Over Beethoven," the Marvelettes' "Please Mister Postman," and Little Richard's "Long Tall Sally."

Prior to this, however, the Beatles were nothing *but* a hard-edged rock & roll band, as evidenced by the LP *Live at the Star Club*, recorded in Hamburg, Germany, in 1962. Performing as much as they did in Hamburg—several sets every single night—gave the band polish and tightness and made their later performances at the Cavern in Liverpool some of their very best.

Brian Epstein became interested in the band after customers at his father's record store requested the Beatles' "My Bonnie." Epstein became the Beatles' manager and set out to "sell" the group to the public and the press and to secure them a recording contract. He made them dress in suits, tone down the rock & roll—at least the hard, raunchy stuff—and write songs that were commercially viable. It is incredible that the Beatles complied without sacrificing their rock & roll spirit or drive.

Although the degree of producer George Martin's influence and direction in the studio is still in question, he brought stability to the group and created a marketable sound. Soon after the first couple of albums, Lennon and McCartney became more involved in the production and recording of their albums. But, like Epstein's, Martin's early presence was crucial to the Beatles' initial success.

In August 1966—after two and a half years of sold-out tours and hit records—the Beatles announced that they were through touring. This decision effectively ended the hysteria surrounding the Beatles and gave them more time to write and record. The retirement paid off. A year later the world would behold the brilliant *Sgt. Pepper's Lonely Hearts Club Band.* (See Chapter 15, "The Second British Invasion.")

Live! At the Star Club in Hamburg, Germany, 1962 / Lingasong / 1977

The sound of this two-record set is raw and amateurish (it was recorded on an ordinary tape recorder with one microphone), but it is an invaluable historical document of the Beatles' earliest days. There are twenty-six tracks here, most of them speeded-up rockers, full of energy and excitement. Although Ringo was not yet a member of the band, he just happened to be sitting in on drums for Pete Best the night this tape was made. Ignore your standards for sound quality. This is a first-class live rock & roll album that proves that the Beatles were great even before they became superstars.

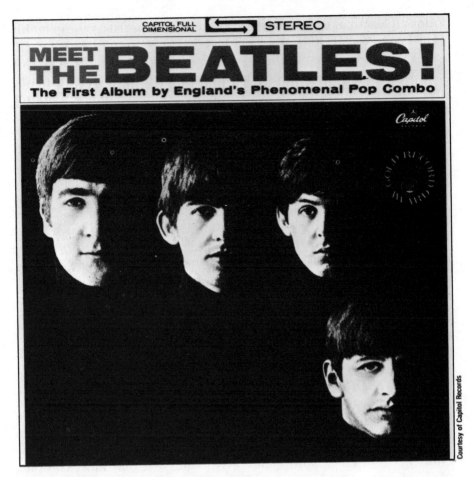

Courtesy of Capitol Records

Meet the Beatles / Capitol / 1964

Prior to this album it was common practice to make a rock & roll album out of one or two hits and lots of filler material. The twelve songs on *Meet the Beatles* are anything but filler. Beginning with "I Want to Hold Your Hand," the LP includes the hard-driving "I Saw Her Standing There," Paul's picture-perfect "All My Loving," and Ringo's "I Wanna Be Your Man." A beautifully crafted LP in every way, *Meet the Beatles* was an instant classic.

The Beatles' Second Album / Capitol / 1964

The year 1964 was indeed a big one, album-wise, for the Beatles. *Meet the Beatles* was released in January; *The Beatles' Second Album* followed less than three months later. It was anchored by the great hit "She Loves You" but mostly includes cover versions of the rock & roll songs the band played at the Star Club and the Cavern. A remake of Chuck Berry's "Roll Over Beethoven" was yet another Beatles smash, and don't overlook the excellent interpretations of Smokey Robinson's "You Really Got a Hold on Me," Little Richard's "Long Tall Sally," and the group's rendition of Barrett Strong's "Money (That's What I Want)."

A Hard Day's Night / Capitol / 1964

Four of the twelve selections on this soundtrack from the Beatles' first movie are pretty instrumentals but don't amount to much in the long run. But "A Hard Day's Night," "Tell Me Why," and the pleasing pop ballad "And I Love Her" make this record a good one. Especially considering the hectic production and songwriting schedules the Beatles were on, their deliveries and output were simply amazing. Some of the tracks found on *A Hard Day's Night* also were included on *Something New*, released in July 1964, one month after this LP.

Beatles '65 / Capitol / 1964

Beatles '65, the sixth album the group released in 1964, is an especially interesting record because it signals the start of a new era for the Beatles. "I'm a Loser," "Baby's in Black," "I'll Follow the Sun," "I Feel Fine," and "She's a Woman" are a bit more complex than what came before them and reveal the group going beyond basic pop structures. Unlike the previous albums, which are primarily collections of hit singles, *Beatles '65* combines a selection of songs that work together and make the album an entity in its own right. The songs here hint of things to come.

The Early Beatles / Capitol / 1965

This record doesn't shed any light on the Beatles' progression because the material was well over a year old when it was released. But it's an interesting and enjoyable record nevertheless. Many of the songs were originally released in the States on Vee Jay (*Introducing the Beatles*).

Help! / Capitol / 1965

Soundtrack number two in as many years. The title song plus "Ticket to Ride" and the brilliant, moody ballad "You've Got to Hide Your Love Away" are standouts. Once again a couple of instrumental fillers are included.

Rubber Soul / Capitol / 1965

Rubber Soul reveals what *Beatles '65* suggested. Along with its "companion," *Revolver*, this LP defines the group's new direction, its new outlook on stardom, and a new seriousness that begins with the Beatles' somewhat solemn expressions in the album-cover photograph. New musical elements include increased use of the acoustic guitar, introduction of the sitar to Western pop music, and a more basic approach to sound and instrumentation. Lyrically, the songs veer away from pure pop, offering instead more introspective glimpses into Lennon and McCartney as individuals rather than as Beatles. Top tracks include "Norwegian Wood," stark, simple, and beautiful; and "Michelle," the first of McCartney's masterpiece ballads. The sound of *Rubber Soul* is soft, the touch light, almost folkish, but its impact was substantial.

Yesterday . . . and Today / Capitol / 1966

Released after *Rubber Soul* but before *Revolver, Yesterday . . . and Today* interrupts the conceptual flow between the two. Nevertheless, it is an excellent album and includes four big hit singles: "Nowhere Man," "Yesterday," "We Can Work It Out," and "Day Tripper." Harrison's "If I Needed Someone" is another of the LP's gems. *Yesterday . . . and Today* was originally released with the controversial "butchered baby" cover. If you have a copy with this cover, you've got something a lot of Beatle fanatics would love to own.

Revolver / Capitol / 1966

Revolver might be *Rubber Soul's* sister album, but there's more electric rock than acoustic strumming here. Harrison's "Taxman" opens the LP, followed by the classic "Eleanor Rigby." There's also Ringo's lovable if somewhat childlike "Yellow Submarine," plus "Good Day Sunshine" and "Got to Get You into My Life." "Tomorrow Never Knows," Lennon's first psychedelic song, ends the record and helps set the stage for *Sgt. Pepper's Lonely Hearts Club Band* and the Beatles' third and final phase. (See Chapter 15, "The Second British Invasion.")

Gerry and the Pacemakers

Gerry Marsden and the Pacemakers were the second band to break out of Liverpool. "How Do You Do It?," an upbeat, cornball pop song, went to the top of the British charts in 1963 as did the group's second and third singles, "I Like It" and a version of Rodgers and Hammerstein's "You'll Never Walk Alone" from *Carousel*. Gerry and the Pacemakers scored three number-one singles in just eight months, with a fourth barely missing number one. ("I'm the One," a Marsden original, topped at number two.) But, even though these three number ones made Gerry and the Pacemakers the second biggest Liverpool band after the Beatles, today these records have little going for them except nostalgia, and even that's debatable.

But "Don't Let the Sun Catch You Crying" and "Ferry 'Cross the Mersey," both written by Marsden, are two of the best ballads to come out of the early days of the British Invasion. Light, breezy pop, yes, but each was well done and memorable in its own winsome way.

The Best of Gerry and the Pacemakers / Capitol / 1979

There are British and American versions of this album. The American LP is more widely available, but contains eight fewer tracks than its British counterpart. Both records have the hits, but Anglophiles will certainly want to track down the U.K. record since it presents a deeper look at the band and is a good example of the Liverpool Sound.

The Searchers

Also from Liverpool, the Searchers were known for glossy harmonies and hollow, resonating guitars (which influenced the Byrds and the Buffalo Springfield). The Searchers sort of eased into the British Invasion and onto the charts with "Needles and Pins" and "When You Walk in the Room."

The Searchers' first American hit, "Needles and Pins" (written by Americans Jack Nitzsche and Sonny Bono), was the first of several American tunes the group would record in its casual, tender pop style. The Searchers' best material includes versions of "Don't Throw Your Love Away," "Stand by Me," "Da Doo Ron Ron," "Twist and Shout," "What'd I Say," "Sweets for My Sweet," and "Love Potion Number Nine." The latter tune, originally done by the Clovers in 1959, was the Searchers' biggest hit in the States, number three in early 1965.

When You Walk in the Room / Pye / 1980

Undoubtedly the best available Searchers British import anthology, *When You Walk in the Room* contains all the Searchers tracks you'll ever need: "Needles and Pins," "Love Potion Number Nine," the title song, and others. The best thing about the LP, though, is the jangling guitars and the influence they had on the Byrds and other folk rockers.

Dave Clark Five

In terms of popularity, the Dave Clark Five was second only to the Beatles in 1964 and 1965. The group hailed from Tottenham, a working-class suburb of London, and formed when members of the Hotspurs soccer team sought to raise money so that they could compete in matches being held in Holland. The only member who didn't have any musical experience was Dave Clark, but he put together the band, bought a cheap drum kit, and learned the basics, and the Dave Clark Five earned the money they needed by playing a few local dances.

When the band returned, Clark and company decided to stay together. Their increasing popularity encouraged them to record the Contours' "Do You Love Me." Next, Clark and keyboard player Mike Smith penned "Glad All Over," which pushed the Beatles' "I Want to Hold Your Hand" out of the number-one slot on the British charts in 1964.

As a drummer, Clark was basic and efficient. His real talents were in songwriting, arranging, and managing the group. He singlehand-edly negotiated a recording contract that gave the Dave Clark Five twice the royalties per record that the Beatles were getting. Clark ran the DC5 like a business and the group's music sometimes reflected this. Still, the Dave Clark Five did leave behind a number of unforgettable tunes before it fizzled out in 1966. "Glad All Over" and "Bits and Pieces" were banging rockers; "Anyway You Want It" remains a British Invasion classic; and "Because" is a fine, light pop ballad.

Glad All Over / Epic / 1964

Out of print, but available in used record stores, *Glad All Over* is the Dave Clark Five's debut album. It contains the title song, "Do You Love Me," and "Bits and Pieces." Nothing outrageous here or, for that matter, on any of the other Dave Clark Five sixties albums, except period rockers that are still entertaining in a nostalgic sort of way.

Twenty-Five Thumping Great Hits / Polydor / 1978

This is the best Dave Clark Five anthology because it was put together by Clark himself. The LP covers the group's entire history, which means that the last few tracks are clunkers. But side one has all the hits.

The Hollies

Though the Hollies were more popular in Britain than they were in the States, three of their singles—"Bus Stop," "Stop, Stop, Stop," and "Carrie-Anne"—were Top Twenty hits in America.

The group was led by guitarists and chief vocalists Allan Clarke and Graham Nash (later of Crosby, Stills and Nash). Their crystal-clear sound emphasized the group's strong vocal harmonies; songs such as "Carrie-Anne" and "Bus Stop" depicted the band in its best light. Despite initial success in the States, the band stalled after "On a Carousel," and Nash, who was eager to change direction, left the band in 1967. The Hollies had a smash single with "He Ain't Heavy, He's My Brother" in 1970 and then scored their biggest hit ever, "Long Cool Woman (In a Black Dress)," in 1972.

Super Hits / Axis / 1983

This is part of Axis's Super Hits series that includes a number of British Invasion groups. An import, it's widely available in most good record shops; if unavailable, pick up a copy of *Greatest Hits* on Epic Records. The two albums have pretty much the same selections. Twelve tracks in all, including "The Air That I Breathe" (from 1974), "Just One Look," "Look through Any Window," and the hits mentioned above.

The Zombies

The Zombies are known for three superbly crafted, rather sophisticated pop songs: "She's Not There," "Tell Her No," and the richly rewarding "Time of the Season." Led by keyboard player Rod Argent, who wrote most of their songs and these hits, the Zombies were unique in the mid-sixties British rock scene.

Argent was a clever tunesmith; his wafting electric piano and inventive melodies gave "Time of the Season" an airy, seductive feel. Lead singer Colin Blunstone and bassist Chris White, with his throbbing bass riffs, further enhanced the song's drama. These adventurous pop constructions, however, were better appreciated in America than in England. "She's Not There" went to number two in 1964, "Tell Her No" peaked at number six a year later, and "Time of the Season" was number three in 1968. Still other singles and both U.S. albums, *The Zombies* and *Odyssey and Oracle*, flopped. The band broke up, and while its members continued in music, only Rod Argent (with his band, Argent, and solo) recorded anything of substance.

Time of the Zombies / Epic / 1973

Time of the Zombies is a two-record set. Record one contains material from *The Zombies* and another LP called *Early Days*, the latter released in 1969 when demand for the defunct group was still fairly strong in America. The second record contains all the tracks found on *Odyssey and Oracle*. Altogether, *Time of the Zombies* is as comprehensive an anthology as you're apt to find.

The Rolling Stones (Part I)

The Rolling Stones exhibited a better grasp of the inner workings of R&B, played it with a commanding authenticity, and showed a more natural inclination for it than any other British (or white American) group in the early and mid-sixties. All the members of the band—Mick Jagger (vocals), Brian Jones and Keith Richards (guitars), Bill Wyman (bass), and Charlie Watts (drums)—came from solid blues and rhythm & blues backgrounds. All except Bill Wyman had spent time with Alexis Korner and his loosely defined group, Blues Incorporated, where future Stones and a number of other soon-to-be great British musicians served apprenticeships.

Jagger and Richards were boyhood chums who became thoroughly engrossed in American black music. Their obsession with R&B and blues led them to Brian Jones, who shared their interest in the music and had enough formal musical training to enhance his understanding of it. The three of them played with a couple of other drummers and bass players and keyboardist Ian Stewart until the trio enlisted Bill Wyman and convinced Charlie Watts to leave Blues Incorporated for their new band, the Rolling Stones. By 1963 the band was complete and, shortly thereafter, signed a record deal. The Stones didn't stir any interest in the States until 1964. But in 1963 in England, they released their first singles to much acclaim. They also performed frequently enough at venues and on concert slates that would bring them the most attention, so that by the time their debut album was released they were a top British band.

For most of its early years (1963–65), the Stones were primarily an R&B cover band. Most of the tracks on *The Rolling Stones (England's Newest Hitmakers)*, *12 X 5*, *Rolling Stones Now!*, and *Out of Our Heads* were interpretations of tunes originally recorded by Chuck Berry, Solomon Burke, and Willie Dixon, among others. But they were extraordinary interpretations, for the Stones seemed to scrutinize and master each song before recording it. New riffs and new accents could make a song sound as if the Stones had penned it, yet there always remained an obvious, inherent respect for the original version.

Although the Stones had American Top Forty hits with "Time Is on My Side," "The Last Time," "Heart of Stone," "Tell Me," and "It's All Over Now," it wasn't until "(I Can't Get No) Satisfaction" went to number one in July 1965 that the band broke big.

By this time the Stones' image as Britain's bad boys—scruffy, brazen characters, perfect foils for the smiling, wholesome Beatles—was set. The band shrugged off the barbs thrown by America's press and managed to exploit its bad reputation to the hilt. They also lived it. No other rock & roll band, especially in 1965, had the gall to record a song about a sexually frustrated bloke whose girl just so happened to get her period when he needed "it" the most. Bad boys? Absolutely. (See also Chapter 15, "The Second British Invasion.")

The Rolling Stones (England's Newest Hitmakers) / London / 1964

One track after another of solid rhythm & blues make up the Stones' debut album. Buddy Holly's "Not Fade Away" is roughed up, Chuck Berry's "Carol" rocks with a blue-collar British accent that only the Stones could give it, and Willie Dixon's "I Just Want to Make Love to You" is the band's tribute to Chicago blues. Jagger and Richards's "Tell Me" is the hit single and amply displays Mick's flagrantly sexual vocal style. The Stones are young and raw, and that's what makes this record so appealing today.

12 x 5 / London / 1965

There's more chance taking on *12 × 5* than on the debut album. Sometimes, as in the case of the instrumental, "2120 South Michigan Avenue," the risk pays off. Other times, it doesn't. "Under the Boardwalk" is poorly handled; "Suzie Q" doesn't unfold properly. But "Time Is on My Side," Chuck Berry's "Around and Around," "It's All Over Now," and the excellent "Empty Heart" make up for any lost ground.

The Rolling Stones Now! / London / 1965

The Stones project still more straight-ahead rhythm & blues but with even more success here than on the previous two albums. The arrangements are on the mark, and the musicianship of Brian Jones and Keith Richards shapes up the cover songs, making this the best of the Stones' early records. Of course there's a Chuck Berry tune, "You Can't Catch Me," and one by Willie Dixon, "Little Red Rooster" (which is handled magnificently). "Down Home Girl," "Down the Road Apiece," and Jagger and Richards's "Heart of Stone" steal the show.

Out of Our Heads / London / 1965

Even though this record includes the classic "Satisfaction" and "The Last Time," the record stalls somewhat because of the cover songs. "Hitch Hike" is okay, and so is "Mercy, Mercy" (two soul covers), but you can hear in these grooves a restlessness. "Play with Fire" is simple and intriguing, but the real delights (in addition to the two hits mentioned above) are "Spider and the Fly" and "Under Assistant West Coast Promotion Man."

December's Children / London / 1965

This record and *Aftermath* (see Chapter 15, "The Second British Invasion") are transitional albums. Both portray the swing away from the hard R&B stance of the first four LPs and toward an all-original format. Unfortunately, *December's Children* finds the group still adjusting to its new role. "Get Off of My Cloud" and "As Tears Go By" are the LP's best songs.

Big Hits (High Tide and Green Grass) / London / 1966

The Stones' first greatest-hits collection is not necessary if you own all the other LPs listed in this section. The only song here that is not on any of the others is "19th Nervous Breakdown," for some a song good enough to make *Big Hits* worth getting.

The Kinks

The Kinks were one of the few R&B-influenced British Invasion bands that eventually developed its own style. Brothers Ray and Dave Davies were at art school in London when they teamed up with drummer Mick Avory and bass player Pete Quaife. The group's earliest single, a cover of "Long Tall Sally" in 1964, went unnoticed. It was followed by the equally obscure "You Still Want Me." But a few months later, out came "You Really Got Me." Few songs in 1964 possessed the firepower of "You Really Got Me" and its follow-up, "All Day and All of the Night." Because of their fierceness and intensity, these two songs contain some of the earliest traces of British punk and heavy metal. The chainsaw sound Dave Davies got out of his guitar as he power-chorded his way through the tunes was unlike anything anyone had ever heard before in a hit (both went Top Ten).

The Kinks retained their cutting edge, although some of the harshness was eventually toned down. But such songs as "See My Friends," "Who'll Be the Next in Line," "Set Me Free," and "Tired of Waiting for You" were distinctively styled rock & roll tunes. The earliest indication that songwriter Ray Davies would ultimately wind up composing more than just hard rockers came in 1966, when the Kinks recorded "A Well Respected Man," "Dedicated Follower of Fashion," and "Sunny Afternoon." Ray Davies was writing social commentary and satire, and the results were as impressive as his thrashing rock & roll. "A Well Respected Man" closed in on English society's mindless observance of tradition and conservatism, "Dedicated Follower of Fashion" took a poke at the whims of fashion, and "Sunny Afternoon" went after Britain's privileged upper class. All hits, they revealed a side of the Kinks that they would explore more thoroughly in the future.

You Really Got Me / Reprise / 1964

Not all the songs on the Kinks' debut album sound as dangerous or despotic as the title track. Included is the exceptional "Stop Your

Sobbing," which the Pretenders covered in the early eighties. Other notable tunes: "Too Much Monkey Business" and "Got Love If You Want It." This album is out of print.

Kinks Kingdom / Reprise / 1965

The rapid maturity of Ray Davies's songwriting is revealed here with "A Well Respected Man" and "See My Friends." At the same time there's an attempt to stoke the band's rock & roll fire. Such is the case with "Who'll Be the Next in Line." This album is also out of print.

Kinks Greatest Hits / Reprise / 1966

The Kinks' best songs from 1964 through 1966 comprise this, the most popular of all the early Kinks albums. In addition to the hard-rock charttoppers, there's "A Dedicated Follower of Fashion" and "A Well Respected Man," which help explain why the Kinks are one of the best things to come out of the British Invasion.

Manfred Mann

Manfred Mann (named after their keyboardist leader) was another British Invasion band with strong rhythm & blues roots, although it eventually shifted more toward pop. The group had built a sizable following in England during 1963 and 1964. Its debut U.S. single, "Do Wah Diddy Diddy," was written by Jeff Barry and Ellie Greenwich and, when first recorded by the Exciters in 1964, barely made a ripple. But Manfred Mann's version—which accented the stop-and-go rhythm and featured a smart organ riff—went to number one.

A cover version of the Shirelles' "Sha La La" proved almost as successful as "Do Wah Diddy Diddy," but—with the exception of "Pretty Flamingo" in 1966—it wasn't until 1968 that Manfred Mann had another major Stateside hit, a fine interpretation of an unreleased Dylan song, "Mighty Quinn (Quinn the Eskimo)." In the early seventies the group became Manfred Mann's Earth Band and struck big in 1977 with covers of Bruce Springsteen's "Blinded by the Light" and "Spirit in the Night."

The Best of Manfred Mann / EMI / 1978

This British import covers Manfred Mann's best period, the years 1963 through 1966. All the hits are here ("Do Wah Diddy Diddy," "Pretty Flamingo," etc.), and so are two Dylan songs, "If You Gotta Go, Go Now" and "With God on Our Side." Manfred Mann was primarily an interpretative band and thus made no real impact outside the charts. But they were certainly one of the best cover bands.

The Animals

Of all the British Invasion bands that borrowed from American blues and rhythm & blues, the Animals and the Rolling Stones were the most faithful. With Eric Burdon's ratty, slightly raw vocals and his uncommonly strong command of blues and R&B vocal techniques, the Animals landed a number-one record with "The House of the Rising Sun" in 1964. The song, an old New Orleans blues ballad, was an unlikely hit, but the Animals electrified the tune and gave it a new energy, and, incredibly enough, it became an instant classic.

The Animals, like Manfred Mann and the Stones, covered many standard and obscure R&B and blues numbers. Yet Burdon and the group were able to make each song their own. Burdon's surly vocals helped, but Alan Price's short, bluesy organ riffs were the band's trademark. In 1965 the Animals had three more hits: "Don't Let Me Be Misunderstood," "We Gotta Get Out of This Place," and "It's My Life"—all with a firm R&B, blue-collar stroke and some of the grittiest vocals heard anywhere in the mid-sixties.

Numerous ego clashes caused the Animals to break up in 1966. Alan Price pursued a solo career, bass player Chas Chandler discovered and managed Jimi Hendrix, and Eric Burdon moved to California where he formed a new version of the Animals. Abandoning most of his blues and R&B roots, Burdon dove into psychedelia and had a few more hit tunes, namely "San Franciscan Nights," "Sky Pilot," "Monterey," and, in 1970 with War, "Spill the Wine."

The Animals / MGM / 1964

Produced by Mickie Most, two of the best songs on the album, "The House of the Rising Sun" and "Baby Let Me Take You Home" (real title: "Baby Let Me Follow You Down") were taken from Bob Dylan's 1962 debut album on Columbia. *The Animals* introduced the group as one sincere and committed to keeping its blues and rhythm & blues influences intact, even in pursuit of pop-chart success. Out of print.

Animal Tracks / MGM / 1965

Eric Burdon never sounded better than on such tracks as "Don't Let Me Be Misunderstood" and "We Gotta Get Out of This Place." This was the Animals' third album, and for the first time there's an obvious confidence in their music since most American blues artists had raved about what the group was doing. *Animal Tracks* also contained a fine version of Sam Cooke's "Bring It on Home to Me" and a humorous, rambling epic, "The Story of Bo Diddley," which outlined the history of rock & roll. Also out of print, unfortunately.

Animalization / MGM / 1965

This might be the most balanced of all the Animals' early LPs. There's rock & roll with Chuck Berry's "Sweet Little Sixteen," hard-core blues in the form of John Lee Hooker's "Maudie," and a typical Goffin–King song torn down to its basics and brimming with Burdon's steely vocals, "Don't Bring Me Down," undoubtedly one of the best things the Animals ever did. Finally, there's a wonderful ballad, "You're on My Mind," written by Burdon and Price's replacement, Dave Rowberry. All in all, a very satisfying record that is out of print but available on occasion as an import from Britain.

The Best of the Animals / Abkco / 1973

The best of the best-of-the-Animals packages—of which there are many. Fifteen tracks in all, the only inexcusable omission: "Don't Bring Me Down." However, the Animals' superb rendition of John Lee Hooker's "Boom Boom" is included and fits in nicely with the other American blues-based hits. An important LP since most of the early Animals LPs are out of print in this country.

Them

Them ranks as one of the better bands that should have but didn't outlive the British Invasion. This Irish quintet recorded some of the very best R&B-influenced rock of the mid-sixties but never received the notoriety that the Yardbirds, the Animals, and the Rolling Stones did. From the start, Them was mismanaged, misguided, and frequently ripped off. Being from Belfast, the group was alienated from the burgeoning London rock scene and missed out on building an all-important club following there. Still, Them's second and third singles, "Baby Please Don't Go" and "Here Comes the Night," were British hits.

The heart and soul of Them was its chief songwriter and lead singer, Van Morrison. His moody yet bullish voice gave Them a bitter sounding authenticity that easily carried onto vinyl and made the group's debut album a true mid-sixties classic. With Morrison at the helm, Them bore a striking stylistic similarity to the Stones; the two groups gave mid-sixties British rock a certain toughness that was in dark contrast to what the Beatles and other Mersey acts presented. Unfortunately, Them broke up in 1966. The group did manage one tour of America and saw three of its records nudge onto the U.S. charts. "Here Comes the Night" and Morrison's "Mystic Eyes" made it into the Top Forty in 1965. Morrison's other gem, "Gloria," a song that the American Shadows of Knight cut and made a Top Ten hit a year later, peaked at number seventy-one. Much more would be heard from Van Morrison after he emigrated to America and recorded one of his greatest solo LPs, *Astral Weeks*. (See Chapter 11, "San Francisco: New Sounds, New Directions.")

Them / Parrot / 1965

The British version of this album was called *Angry Young Them*. Both contained three of the four best Them tracks: "Here Comes the Night," "Mystic Eyes," and "Gloria" (the missing track: "Baby Please Don't Go"). Also included is Them's version of "Route 66," which the Rolling Stones had covered on their first album. A comparison of the tracks leaves Them coming up short, but not by much.

The Spencer Davis Group

The group might have been called the Spencer Davis Group, but its most important member was young singer/songwriter/musician Steve Winwood. Before he left the group in 1967 to form Traffic, Winwood had left his mark with "Gimme Some Lovin' " and "I'm a Man," two of the very best rockers of the mid-sixties. "Gimme Some Lovin' " was flawless. It began with digging, relentless bass, followed by the patter of drums. Then out of nowhere came a sultry, soaring organ riff (Winwood's) followed by Winwood's best Ray Charles-influenced vocal. The song overflowed with punch and excitement. "I'm a Man" delivered virtually the same results. Before these two recordings, there was "Keep On Running" (sung by Davis), the first of the band's singles to enter the American charts. The Spencer Davis Group was a factor in British rock only from 1965 to 1967. But in those three years it established itself as one of England's more riveting R&B-influenced bands and gave Steve Winwood his start on a road that would take him to the top of the British rock hierarchy.

Gimme Some Lovin' / United Artists / 1967

Along with the title song and "Keep On Running," there's a wealth of rock/R&B/blues material here that makes this LP a classic. "Trampoline" and "Sittin' and Thinkin' " are delightful blues numbers; "Good-Bye Stevie" contains some fine boogie piano from Winwood. But the diamond in the rough is the Motown-influenced "It Hurts Me So," a Winwood original that reveals his singing and writing capabilities almost as nicely as "Gimme Some Lovin' " and "I'm a Man." Available as an import.

The Best of the Spencer Davis Group / Island / 1983

This British import has the best tracks from the group's three sixties albums and offers a thorough look at its considerable contribution to British rock. The Spencer Davis Group was one of those bands that was at home with R&B, blue-eyed soul, and basic rock & roll, but Winwood's restless creativity would lead him in search of more challenging endeavors.

The Who (Part I)

Despite a general lack of attention in America until 1967, the Who was an extremely important band in England from 1964. One of the original Mod bands, the Who redefined rock's arrogance and rebelliousness, especially live. Onstage Pete Townshend's guitar windmills and the manic destruction of his equipment matched up perfectly with Roger Daltrey's bold, brash vocals, bassist John Entwistle's pathetic glare, and Keith Moon's savage beating of his drum kit. It was rock & roll as no one had ever heard or seen it before—without compromise or pretense. It was unabashedly crude and downright belligerent. But it made all the sense in the world.

The story of the Who between 1964 and 1966 is only a small part of the band's long and successful career. But these were the Who's glory days. Before becoming the Who, the band was called the Detours, the Who, the High Numbers, and then the Who again. Like most Mods, the Who members were quite heavily into black American soul and R&B music, though these influences were more noticeable in other early British Invasion groups.

The Who first attempted to break into the charts when it was the High Numbers. "I'm the Face" was released in 1964 and sold disappointingly few copies. But after some very clever promotion tactics put into motion by managers Kit Lambert and Chris Stamp, "I Can't Explain" went to number eight on the British charts in early 1965; in the States it stalled at ninety-three. Next came "Anyway, Anyhow, Anywhere," which also entered the British Top Ten, and then "My Generation," the sixties' first youth anthem, which lodged itself at number two. "My Generation" summed up what the Who was acting out onstage. The song defied the establishment, growing old, and the British code of ethics. Both the melody and the lyrics were supremely menacing; "My Generation" can probably be tabbed Britain's very first punk tune of note.

By this time, the Who possessed a large and faithful following in its home country. Other singles such as "Substitute" and "Happy Jack," British hits in 1966, didn't make it onto the U.S. charts until 1967. The Who's biggest American single of the sixties, "I Can See for Miles," would make it all the way to number nine in 1967, but not until the Who had proven itself at the Monterey Pop Festival that year. (See also Chapter 15, "The Second British Invasion.")

The Who Sing My Generation / MCA / 1966

With the exception of *Tommy* (see Chapter 15), this is the best Who album made in the sixties. Pay no attention to the uneven delivery or to the overall sound quality. Rather, focus on the energy and the uncompromising intensity of "My Generation" and "The Kids Are Alright." Few mid-sixties albums pack as much power as this one.

The Yardbirds

The Yardbirds never enjoyed the grand commercial success many other British Invasion bands did. But with the exception of the Beatles, the Stones, and the Who, no other English band of the time was as influential as the Yardbirds. Aside from the fact that the three greatest British guitarists of the sixties (and seventies as well)—Eric Clapton, Jeff Beck, and Jimmy Page—had been members of the group, the Yardbirds helped pave the way for the blues-rock explosion of the late sixties, opened the doors for heavy metal, and advanced the lead guitar to higher, more expressive levels than ever before.

Clapton was the group's first major guitarist. Under him, the Yardbirds were heavily influenced by American blues, particularly Chicago-style blues. But when the group decided to become a little more pop oriented, Clapton left for John Mayall's Bluesbreakers. The Yardbirds' "For Your Love," a tune written by Graham Gouldman (later of 10cc), was a smash hit, but the group was without a guitar player. Session musician Jimmy Page was offered the role but turned it down. He did, however, highly recommend the guitarist from a group called the Tridents, Jeff Beck.

With Beck on guitar, the Yardbirds kept a basic blues foundation but experimented with new sounds and ideas on "Heart Full of Soul," "Shapes of Things," and "Over Under Sideways Down." When bassist Paul Samwell-Smith quit to produce records, Page finally joined the band. His role, however, was to be bass player until the rhythm guitarist, Chris Dreja, became proficient on bass, at which time Page moved into the second lead guitar slot, behind Beck.

The group had the ultimate one-two guitar punch for a few months. When Beck decided to leave the group for a solo career, Page became the band's sole lead guitarist, and thus began the Yardbirds' third and final stage. Although Page continued the experimentation begun by Beck, the band had lost much of its momentum. After a couple of album flops, the Yardbirds collapsed. Everyone departed save Page, who quickly assembled Robert Plant (vocals), John Paul Jones (bass), and John Bonham (drums): the New Yardbirds. They would become known as Led Zeppelin. (See Chapter 16, "The Origins of Heavy Metal.")

For Your Love / Epic / 1965

This is the Yardbirds' debut LP; much of what's contained on the

HOT HOUSE OF OMAGARASHID
WHAT DO YOU WANT
OVER UNDER SIDEWAYS DOWN
LOST WOMAN
TURN INTO EARTH
JEFF'S BOOGIE
I CAN'T MAKE YOUR WAY
EVER SINCE THE WORLD BEGAN
HE'S ALWAYS THERE
FAREWELL

Courtesy of Epic Records

record isn't the tough blues the band pursued with Clapton at the helm. There are blues strains running in and out of the songs, but there's also a lean toward pop. Sadly, *For Your Love* never fully displays Clapton's blues guitar talents.

Having a Rave-Up with the Yardbirds / Epic / 1965

Clapton played on four tracks, but it's Beck who is most widely heard. "Heart Full of Soul," the follow-up to "For Your Love," is included here, as is "I'm a Man," which demonstrates that, despite Clapton's departure, the band didn't totally abandon the blues. Beck's guitar playing here is magnificent. There's exciting experimentation with Middle Eastern-style leads and dangerous sounding power chords. *Rave-Up* was one of the best albums to come out of England in 1965.

Over Under Sideways Down / Epic / 1966

Once again it's Beck who's in the spotlight. "Lost Woman," the title song, "Jeff's Boogie," and "Hot House of Omagarashid" advance guitar ideas first introduced on *Rave-Up*. Here, however, Beck sounds more sure of himself and the group's direction. He plays without any preconceived notion of what a guitarist should and shouldn't do. With feedback and fuzz-tones interspersed in his leads, this LP lays the groundwork for the guitar-dominated albums in the late sixties.

Yardbird Favorites / Epic / 1977

The definitive anthology of Yardbirds music has yet to be done. In the meantime this record and those listed below will have to do, especially since the band's early LPs mentioned here are available only as imports and are often hard to find. *Favorites* is strong in the blues: "Smokestack Lightning," "New York City Blues," "Good Morning Little Schoolgirls," and "I'm a Man" are included. The other tracks are drawn mostly from *For Your Love* and *Rave-Up*.

Yardbirds Great Hits / Epic / 1977

The Yardbirds' early singles highlight this LP. "For Your Love," "Heart Full of Soul," and "Shapes of Things" are here, and there's some redundancy because both this record and *Favorites* pull tracks from the early LPs. The record would have been stronger had "Over Under Sideways Down," "Tinker, Tailor, Soldier, Sailor," and "Happenings Ten Years Time Ago" been included.

The Yardbirds: A Compleat Collection / Compleat / 1984

Those interested in the Yardbirds under Eric Clapton's reign and when the band was nothing *but* a hard-edged blues outfit will enjoy this two-record set. The included tracks are early ones (1963) and mostly obscure, taken from out-of-print English LPs; sides three and four feature not only Clapton but also American bluesman Sonny Boy Wiliamson jamming with the group.

Other Recommended Albums

History of British Rock Volumes 1-3 / Sire / 1974

These out-of-print anthology albums are difficult to find but well worth the search. There were many one-hit wonders to come out of the British Invasions (see also Chapter 15, "The Second British Invasion") that deserve to be recalled, if only briefly. This three-volume set, along with excellent liner notes, performs the task in fine fashion.

The big groups—such as the Beatles, the Rolling Stones, and the Who—are poorly represented, but those groups demand more extensive investigations anyway, and their early albums are still in print and readily available. But groups like the Troggs, Silkie, Peter and Gordon, and the Swinging Blue Jeans (Vol. 1); Chad and Jeremy, the Tremeloes, and Billy J. Kramer and the Dakotas (Vol. 2); and Badfinger, Unit Four Plus Two, and Matthew's Southern Comfort (Vol. 3) are more adequately represented. Therein lies the real value of *History of British Rock*.

8
THE AMERICAN RESPONSE

The American pop response to the British Invasion was immediate. In many cases it took the form of pure imitation. In 1965, for instance, there was a proliferation of self-contained bands, many of which recorded songs that aped the best qualities of what came from England. Those bands that didn't imitate were, at the very least, inspired and influenced by the English records. No American musician, songwriter, producer, or arranger wasn't affected in some way.

The mid-sixties American pop scene was essentially a hodgepodge of some things borrowed, some things not—all aimed at AM radio and the new generation of record buyers who had surfaced, it seemed, when the Beatles did.

At the time the white pop response was flooding AM radio and the charts with tunes, Motown acts—the Supremes, the Temptations, and the Four Tops—were doing the same. Also beginning to get noticed in a big way were folk rockers Bob Dylan and the Byrds, plus folkies Donovan, and Simon and Garfunkel. With everyone competing for attention, it turned out to be a great era for AM radio. But it was its last hurrah; 1967 would bring FM and the beginning of album-oriented progressive radio.

Some of the sixties' best pop came out of this era. Although much of it was quickly forgotten by 1967, when rock suddenly got heavy, interest in mid-sixties pop was revived in the late seventies.

RECOMMENDED ARTISTS
The Beach Boys (Part II)

Although the Beach Boys minus Brian Wilson continued to tour and sing on the records, the story of the group for the rest of the decade is really the story of Wilson's studio accomplishments. After the surf-music era ended, the strength of the Beach Boys' live shows diminished to the point where they were seen as merely a good-time oldies pop band keeping alive the spirit of surf, sun, and summertime.

Though the Beatles and the British bands dominated the charts in 1964 and 1965, the Beach Boys held their own. They provided one of America's strongest alternatives to the Beatles, thanks to such Brian Wilson gems as "I Get Around" and "Help Me, Rhonda" (both of which made it to number one in 1964 and 1965 respectively), "Fun, Fun, Fun," "Dance, Dance, Dance," "California Girls," and two covers—the Regents' "Barbara Ann" and Bobby Freeman's "Do You Wanna Dance."

Once again, successful singles led to successful albums. In 1964 there were four albums: *Shut Down—Vol. 2*, *All Summer Long*, *Beach Boys Concert*, and *The Beach Boys Christmas Album*. In 1965 there were three: *Beach Boys Today*, *Summer Days (and Summer Nights)*, and *Beach Boys Party*. In 1966 there was only *Pet Sounds*.

Brian Wilson still concerned himself with less pressing issues than, say, Bob Dylan, John Lennon, and Paul McCartney, but his songs continued to grow more sophisticated in terms of production techniques, arrangements, and harmonic and melodic structurings. "Help Me, Rhonda" and "I Get Around" are great American pop songs, and though they had roots in the Beach Boys' surf-music era they were immaculately written and gorgeously recorded.

The Beach Boys and Wilson peaked with *Pet Sounds*, still considered by many the Beach Boys' greatest album. It was definitely Brian Wilson's most ambitious project to date, taking nearly one year to make in an era when LPs were finished in weeks. *Pet Sounds* was the perfect culmination of the Beach Boys' sixties sound. There were no flaws.

The other sixties studio albums the Beach Boys made suffered by comparison. *Smiley Smile* (1967), *Wild Honey* (1967), *Friends* (1968), and *20/20* (1969) all had their finer moments, but all were generally disappointing in light of *Pet Sounds*. *Smile* was eagerly anticipated since Wilson teamed up with L.A. studio whiz Van Dyke Parks to write its material, but it was never released. Various tracks from the album, however, showed up on the records mentioned above, but revealed nothing astonishing.

Smiley Smile had "Good Vibrations," the only song that advanced what was heard on *Pet Sounds*; *Wild Honey* had "Darlin'," one of the truly great Beach Boy songs; *Friends* rates as one of the Beach Boys' worst albums ever, and *20/20* had the infectious little rocker "Do It Again" plus a Carl Wilson treat, "I Can Hear Music."

The general lack of quality on the late-sixties Beach Boys albums is usually attributed to the fact that, while the rest of the group toured, Brian Wilson stayed at home and dropped acid. Wilson never fully recovered from his breakdown, and his desire to top Phil Spector and the Beatles drove him to the breaking point. It would be a long while before Wilson could again use his talents in a constructive way. The Beach Boys paid the price with diminishing record sales.

Shut Down—Volume Two / Capitol / 1964

Shut Down—Volume One wasn't a Beach Boys album; it contained only two Beach Boys tracks. But *Volume Two* was theirs and included "Fun, Fun, Fun," one of the classic hot-rod songs of the sixties, the haunting "Don't Worry, Baby," and a delightful Spectoresque interpretation of Frankie Lymon and the Teenagers' "Why Do Fools Fall in Love." *Shut Down—Volume Two* is also available as part of the *Dance, Dance, Dance/Fun, Fun, Fun* collection released by Capitol in 1971, minus two tracks, "In the Parking Lot" and " 'Cassius' Love vs. 'Sonny' Wilson."

All Summer Long / Capitol / 1964

"I Get Around" was *All Summer Long*'s biggest song. But "The Girl on the Beach," another "Surfer Girl" style ballad, and "Don't Back Down," the last pure surfing song the Beach Boys recorded, are also highlights. Other songs include "Little Honda," "Wendy," and a great cover of "Hushabye," formerly recorded by the Mystics in 1959.

The Beach Boys Today / Capitol / 1965

A classic Beach Boys album that includes such tunes as "Do You Wanna Dance," "When I Grow Up," "Help Me, Rhonda," "Dance, Dance, Dance," and "Please Let Me Wonder." Perhaps more than any other LP, this one reflected Brian Wilson's move away from surf sounds without sacrificing the good-time, sunny feelings. *The Beach Boys Today* is available as the second half of the *Dance, Dance, Dance/Fun, Fun, Fun* compilation minus "Please Let Me Wonder," "In the Back of My Mind," and "Bull Session with the Big Daddy."

Summer Days (and Summer Nights) / Capitol / 1965

Another classic Beach Boys album and widely available as a Capitol reissue but now called *California Girls* because of the record's star title track, which might just be the greatest song Brian Wilson ever wrote. Also on the record is a tribute to Phil Spector, heard in "Then I Kissed Her," and "The Girl from New York City," Brian Wilson's response to the Ad Libs' "The Boy from New York City."

Pet Sounds / Capitol / 1966

Pet Sounds is often considered the Beach Boys' *Sgt. Pepper's Lonely Hearts Club Band.* Despite its brilliance—"Wouldn't It Be Nice," "God Only Knows," "Caroline, No," "Sloop John B.," and the indescribably pretty "Don't Talk (Put Your Head on My Shoulder)"—*Pet Sounds* did not sell as it should have. The Beach Boys' fans had a difficult time digesting the distinctive textures, the magnificence of the arrangements, and lavish backgrounds. Had *Pet Sounds* been released after *Sgt. Pepper* instead of before it, perhaps people would have been better prepared for what they heard.

The Monkees

For a band created by TV executives hoping to exploit the Beatles' impact on pop culture, the Monkees were at least partially responsible for a batch of pretty decent pop tunes in the mid-sixties. In the beginning the Monkees neither wrote nor played on the songs they recorded. They did little except follow the directions of TV producers Bob Rafelson and Bert Schneider and the musical direction of music publisher/producer Don Kirshner, and act silly any time anyone pointed a camera at them.

Davy Jones, Michael Nesmith, Peter Tork, and Mickey Dolenz were the Monkees. Tork was a folksinger of sorts and Nesmith did have some music in his background, but as a whole the boys were chosen because of their zaniness and cute looks. It was exploitation at its fullest, but it worked. A TV comedy series called "The Monkees" became a top-rated program and helped a number of their records become huge hits. In a three-year period (1966–68) the Monkees had three number-one singles ("Last Train to Clarksville," "I'm a Believer," "Daydream Believer"), a number two ("A Little Bit Me, a Little Bit You"), and two number threes ("Pleasant Valley Sunday," "Valleri"). The group's impact on pop music and pop culture was considerable. Many of the elements of Beatlemania were acted out one more time during the height of Monkeemania: Monkee dolls, trading cards, lunch boxes, and other merchandise abounded.

Most of the hits were written by Don Kirshner's writing team of Tommy Boyce and Bobby Hart, and by Neil Diamond. They were beautifully effective pop songs—catchy, cleverly penned in the best Brill Building tradition, and cute. Davy Jones sang most of the leads with the rest of the group as back ups. Until the LP *Headquarters*, top L.A. session players provided the instrumentation. Although the concept behind the Monkees was strictly commercial ("serious" listeners ridiculed the band mercilessly), the records were good pop fun.

The Monkees Greatest Hits / Arista / 1969

The typical greatest-hits package—all the smash singles plus "(Theme from) The Monkees" and one or two tracks from the original albums. Mid-sixties pop freaks might want to check out the original Monkees albums, some of which have been rereleased. But for the average listener, *The Monkees Greatest Hits* or any of the other best-of collections on the market (there are many of them) should suffice.

Paul Revere and the Raiders

If you ignored the corny Revolutionary War costumes, you'd perceive that Paul Revere and the Raiders were responsible for some truly excellent pop-rock songs. Tunes like "Hungry," "Just Like Me," and "Kicks," one of the first antidrug songs, were all produced with a tidy pop sensibility, yes. But underneath was an undeniable rock spirit that penetrated the teeny bopper goo that the group instigated with their outfits and goofy antics on Dick Clark's afternoon TV program, "Where the Action Is."

Originally called the Downbeats, the group was part of the Pacific Northwest rock scene that produced the Ventures and the Kingsmen. (See Chapter 2, "Twangy Guitars: The Instrumental Groups.") Despite a couple of local hits, it wasn't until the band moved to California, teamed up with producer Terry Melcher, and was selected to appear regularly on "Where the Action Is" that it got its big break. Paul Revere (his real name) played keyboards and had his name out front, but it was Mark Lindsay, the cute lead singer and saxophone player, who got most of the media attention and camera close-ups.

The years 1965 and 1966 were good to the Raiders, but by 1967 the group was viewed as an unhip product of the pop establishment. The Raiders fell out of the limelight but launched one last assault on the charts in 1971. "Indian Reservation (The Lament of the Cherokee Reservation Indian)" became the group's one and only number-one hit.

Midnight Ride / CBS / 1966

Midnight Ride contains "Kicks" and "Hungry," both written by Barry Mann and Cynthia Weil. The songs possess strong hooks in the chorus and thick bottoms. Mark Lindsay sang both songs with a rock vigor that is as effective today as it was twenty years ago. Two other rock tracks worthy of note: "Steppin' Out" and "Louie, Go Home." Available as a rerelease.

Paul Revere and the Raiders' Greatest Hits / CBS / 1967

The first of CBS's two best-of collections (the other was released in 1973 and called *The All-Time Greatest Hits of Paul Revere and the Raiders*). There are a couple of deletions here, most notably, "Steppin' Out." Check out the Raiders' version of "Louie Louie" as well as "Good Thing," penned by Terry Melcher and Mark Lindsay.

The Association

The Association wrote and recorded easy-flowing, mainstream pop songs that were ideally suited for AM radio. The Association's first major single was "Along Comes Mary," a controversial song because of its alleged reference to marijuana, which turned out to be the group's most potent hit single.

More representative of their style were the two number-one singles, "Cherish" (1966) and "Windy" (1967). In 1967 came "Never My Love," which peaked at number two. All three songs were willowy love songs, carefully constructed and recorded. Though the Association sold millions of records and during a three-year stretch (1966–68) five of their songs were Top Ten smashes, their stylistic impact was minimal.

The Association's Greatest Hits / Warner Bros. / 1968

Like most sixties pop bands, the Association definitely was not album oriented, and so this greatest-hits package is their only LP worth considering. It contains all the hits mentioned above plus "Everything That Touches You," "Time for Livin'," and "Requiem for the Masses." A great album for recalling AM's mid-sixties pop glory days.

The Grass Roots

The Grass Roots were a little-known group out of Los Angeles before they got involved with songwriter P. F. Sloan and his cohort, producer/songwriter Steve Barri. The Grass Roots' first single was a Sloan–Barri composition, "Where Were You When I Needed You" (1966). It was a moderate hit, but the group's third single, "Let's Live for Today," and then later "Midnight Confessions" (their best song) broke into the Top Ten. Steve Barri produced most of the Grass Roots' material, including their biggest-selling album, *Golden Grass*. He emphasized the group's rich, full vocals and a mature, intelligent pop delivery.

The Grass Roots continued to record into the seventies. The group's best period, though, was from 1966 to 1968. "Sooner or Later" their last Top Ten hit, came in 1971.

Golden Grass / Dunhill / 1968

A twelve-song collection of the Grass Roots' best songs through 1968, *Golden Grass* includes "Where Were You When I Needed You,"

"Let's Live for Today," and "Midnight Confessions." Some of the tracks are a bit ordinary, but nothing here is unlistenable.

The Sir Douglas Quintet

Another mid-sixties product of the American backlash was the Sir Douglas Quintet. The band's producer, Huey Meaux, seemed to go by the philosophy, "if you can't beat 'em, join 'em" because he made Doug Sahm's San Antonio–based group (Sahm was Sir Douglas) sound, look, and act British. The group's debut on the pop charts was the rollicking, thinly disguised Tex-Mex rocker "She's about a Mover." Sahm's "hey heys" supplied the British connection, but Augie Meyers's Farfisa organ riffs kept the sound inherently local.

Later, when Sahm got involved in the San Francisco music scene, he had another hit with "Mendocino." But Sahm's prime importance is that he helped introduce the sound of Tex-Mex into pop-rock. Sahm continues to carry the music's banner and records great if not commercial records.

The Best of Sir Douglas Quintet / Takoma / 1980

This record, which has "Mendocino" and "She's about a Mover," also includes as a bonus a cross-section of Sahm's best material from the sixties and the seventies. A great history lesson in the development of Tex-Mex.

Sam the Sham and the Pharaohs

Doug Sahm and the Sir Douglas Quintet weren't the only ones scoring with Tex-Mex rock & roll in the mid-sixties. Domingo Samudio, better known as Sam the Sham, led the Pharaohs up into the top of the charts a couple of times: with the timeless rocker "Wooly Bully" and "Lil' Red Riding Hood," Sam's clever play on seduction.

Sam the Sham and the Pharaohs donned Arab turbans and tunics to capitalize on the visual gimmickry popularized by Paul Revere and the Raiders and the Young Rascals. Arabs playing Tex-Mex? The image was a tough one to swallow, but it didn't much affect the band's ability to rock. With Sam's sexy vocals and cheesy organ riffs, and Butch Gibson's simple yet surprisingly effective saxophone runs,

Sam the Sham and the Pharaohs proved that some of the greatest sixties party music came from Tex-Mex bands.

Wooly Bully / Polydor / 1984

A dandy compilation from France that includes Sam the Sham's best moments. Of course, "Wooly Bully" stands out among the others, but take note of the colorful versions of "Memphis Beat," "Big City Lights," and Sam's own "JuJu Hand." Dance tunes one and all.

? (Question Mark) and the Mysterians

No overview of mid-sixties Tex-Mex would be complete without mention of ? [Question Mark] and the Mysterians. Their 1966 number-one single, "96 Tears," is as much a sixties classic as Sam the Sham's "Wooly Bully" and the Sir Douglas Quintet's "She's about a Mover." More Farfisa organ, more party music.

96 Tears / London / 1978

Unlike *Wooly Bully*, which contains mostly cover material (though nicely done), ? and the Mysterians wrote most of their own songs. "96 Tears" is the tune that naturally draws the most attention, but "I Need Somebody" and "Nd Side" are nearly as strong, especially in the vocals department. Available as a Japanese import.

The (Young) Rascals

The Rascals, called the Young Rascals at first, were the best American white R&B/rock band of the sixties. Felix Cavaliere (organ, vocals), Dino Danelli (drums), Eddie Brigati (vocals), and Gene Cornish (guitar) wore stage costumes—Little Lord Fauntleroy outfits complete with knickers and Edwardian shirts. But the get-ups were as unnecessary as they were pathetic. The Rascals would make it on their music alone.

The Young Rascals originated in the New York–New Jersey area after Cavaliere, Brigati, and Cornish left Joey Dee and the Starliters (see Chapter 3, "Early Sixties Pop") and hooked up with drummer Dino Danelli.

The Young Rascals released "I Ain't Gonna Eat Out My Heart Anymore," which set the stage for a slew of hit songs. Most of them incorporated a strict R&B delivery that consisted of intense, soulful vocals and Cavaliere's swirling organ (the band had no bass or lead guitar).

The Rascals' first big hit was a number-one cover of the Olympics' "Good Lovin' " in 1966. Eight Rascals songs that year and in 1967 and 1968 made it to the Top Twenty. "Groovin' " and "People Got to Be Free" also were number-one records.

The Rascals could do it all. They mastered the popular R&B songs of the day: "Midnight Hour" and "Mustang Sally." They knew how to sing about love: "How Can I Be Sure." They knew how to rock: "Good Lovin'," "Come On Up." They could send out a social message: "People Got to Be Free." And they perfected the intelligent pop ballad: "Groovin'," which turned out to be one of the greatest (AM radio) songs of the decade. But by 1968, despite an earnest desire to embrace psychedelia, the group faltered. Cavaliere and Brigati strayed from their R&B roots and found it exceedingly difficult to write or perform psychedelic-style songs without a lead guitarist. This stifled the band musically, caused internal problems (as did ego conflicts and opposing social philosophies), and led to the Rascals' breakup.

The Young Rascals / Atlantic / 1966

Only one song, "Do You Feel It," was a Rascals original on their debut album. Yet the interpretations of "Mustang Sally" and "In the Midnight Hour" plus excellent renditions of the more obscure "Slow Down" and "Baby, Let's Wait" reveal just how good an R&B band the Rascals was. Also included: "I Ain't Gonna Eat Out My Heart Anymore" and "Good Lovin'."

Groovin' / Atlantic / 1967

This rates as the Rascals' best album. Side one has "A Girl Like You" and "How Can I Be Sure"; side two has "Groovin' " and "You Better Run," all Top Twenty hits. Cavaliere and Brigati emerge here as top-notch composers and vocalists, and instrumentally, the band is as tight and ambitious as ever. Only one track out of eleven was not written by the band.

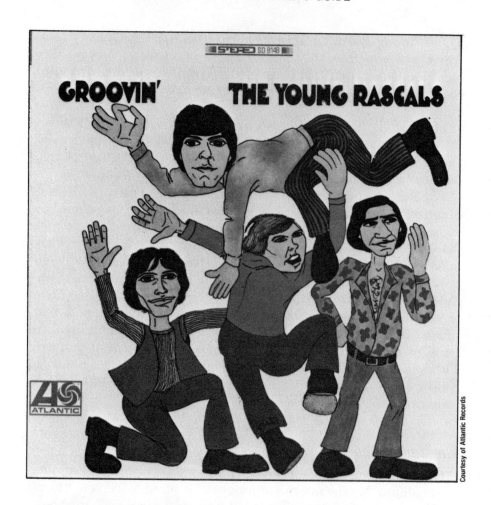

Courtesy of Atlantic Records

Timepeace / Atlantic / 1968

Timepeace is an excellent anthology of the band, from its rawest R&B beginnings ("Mustang Sally"), through its pop-rock stage ("Groovin' "), to its one last taste of gold, "A Beautiful Morning."

Mitch Ryder and the Detroit Wheels

Mitch Ryder and the Detroit Wheels knew how to play R&B-tinged rock only one way—fast and furious. Few bands in the mid-sixties could match Ryder and his Wheels' uninhibited, rapid-fire energy. With Ryder sounding like he was one note shy of going hoarse, Johnny "Bee" Badanjek's machine-gun drumming, and Jim McCarty's frenetic lead guitar riffs, the band seemed bent on self-destruction or, at the very least, exhaustion.

Originally called the Rivieras, Ryder and the Detroit Wheels left Detroit for New York and signed on with producer Bob Crewe. Crewe encouraged the Wheels to let it rip on such songs as "Jenny Take a Ride!" and "Devil with a Blue Dress On/Good Golly Miss Molly." Both hits made the Top Ten. "Jenny Take a Ride!" was actually a medley of Little Richard's "Jenny Jenny" and Chuck Willis's "C. C. Rider." After "Little Latin Lupe Lu" failed to break into the Top Ten (it got to number seventeen), Crewe went back to the original formula. "Devil with a Blue Dress On/Good Golly Miss Molly" went to number four.

The last Top Ten hit for Ryder and the Wheels was "Sock It to Me—Baby," a straightforward sex song that raised its share of eyebrows. This was followed by one last medley, "Too Many Fish in the Sea/Three Little Fishes."

Like the Rascals, Mitch Ryder never really adapted to the swing away from R&B-influenced rock in the late sixties. By the decade's end Ryder and the Wheels had gone their separate ways.

Wheels of Steel / Dow / 1983

This British import is a ten-inch LP that contains eight superb tracks. Included here: "Jenny Take a Ride!," "Sock It to Me—Baby," "Little Latin Lupe Lu," "You Get Your Kicks" (all off the Wheels' LP, *Breakout*), "Devil with a Blue Dress On/Good Golly Miss Molly," "Too Many Fishes in the Sea/Three Little Fishes," and "Shake a Tail Feather" (from the LP *Jenny Take a Ride*). One added advantage of *Wheels of Steel* is its remarkable clarity, which is superior to any of the other greatest-hits Wheels packages.

Greatest Hits / Virgo / 1972

This has three more tracks than *Wheels of Steel* ("I Like It Like That," "Turn on Your Love Light," "I Got You"), but otherwise it's the same record. Go with *Wheels of Steel* for its sound.

Tommy James and the Shondells

Despite the confectionary nature of most of Tommy James's hits, he made a fairly serious attempt to make pop a bit more meaningful.

"Hanky Panky" was his first chart single; it went to number one in 1966 even though the song had originally been released four years earlier and flopped. A disc jockey in Pittsburgh rediscovered the tune, began playing it, and Tommy James was on his way to stardom.

"Hanky Panky" was pure pop and much fun. Yet the follow-ups, especially "I Think We're Alone Now" and "Crimson and Clover," which captured the essence of teen sexual desire, and "Crystal Blue Persuasion," which concerned drugs, were actually pretty heavy pop songs. James's voice was made to sing pop, and virtually all his songs were produced with AM airplay in mind.

Twenty-Six Great Hits / Adam VIII / 1976

This is one of the most complete anthologies of Tommy James and the Shondells on the market. It's a no-frills package, to be sure (no liner notes), but contains everything important recorded by James in the sixties. Aside from the sixties hits are James's early-seventies solo singles "Draggin' the Line" and "Celebration." A two-record set.

The Turtles

Traditionally the Turtles have been labeled a sixties folk-rock outfit, partially because their first big hit was an interpretation of Bob Dylan's "It Ain't Me Babe" (1965). Before that the Turtles had been a surf band called the Crossfires; after 1966 they were a tremendously witty pop group responsible for some of the most elaborate pop gems of the sixties.

Led by Howard Kaylan and Mark Volman, the Turtles scored a number of chart hits. From 1965 through 1968 seven singles crashed into the Top Twenty. "Happy Together," arguably one of the two or three greatest pop constructions of the era with its intricate arrangement and great harmonies, reached number one in 1967. Other bright, bouncy pop songs included "She's My Girl," "She'd Rather Be with Me," "You Know What I Mean," and "Elenore." The earlier folk-rock period produced, in addition to "It Ain't Me Babe," two P. F. Sloan songs, "Let Me Be" and "You Baby."

Underneath all this pop success, however, was Kaylan and Volman's lampoonery, which could barely be contained. It was difficult for them to take *anything* seriously, including themselves. They couldn't remain pop stars despite their success; they saw through it. What they ultimately became was one of rock's great satire bands. Few listeners caught the tongue-in-cheek genius of "Elenore." But there was a good reason for not catching it: The song was also a great pop tune in the "Happy Together" tradition, full of lovely vocals and a gorgeous melody that still sounds good.

The satiric "Elenore" was just the beginning. One of the great unsung albums of the late sixties was the Turtles' *Battle of the Bands*, on which the group spoofed rock & roll by recording each track as if it were done by a different band. Some of the fictitious groups included were the Atomic Enchilada, Fats Mallard and the Bluegrass Fireball, the U.S. Teens Featuring Raoul, and the Fabulous Dawgs. There was even a self-parody by the Cross Fires. The album, a commercial flop, is still brilliant.

When the Turtles broke up, Howard Kaylan and Mark Volman signed on with Frank Zappa and the Mothers of Invention. Later, as Flo and Eddie, the duo expanded their penchant for being loony while continuing to vocalize with amazing results.

It Ain't Me Babe / Rhino / 1982

A rerelease of the Turtles' only folk rock album. Three Dylan tunes (the title track, "Love Minus Zero," Like a Rolling Stone") and two P. F. Sloan numbers ("Eve of Destruction" and "Let Me Be") make *It Ain't Me Babe* a good, not great, album.

Happy Together / Rhino / 1983

A rerelease of the Turtles' most memorable pop album. All the best songs on here are also on *Happy Together Again* (see below), but this LP is much easier to find.

The Battle of the Bands / White Whale / 1968

The Battle of the Bands includes the funniest stuff the Turtles ever recorded. The only hit found here is "Elenore," but "Chicken Little Was Right," "Oh Daddy!," and "Surfer Dan" are simply delightful.

Happy Together Again / Sire / 1974

If all anthologies were as well done and thorough as those released by Sire Records, the great bands of rock would all be well documented by now. This two-record set consists of twenty-nine tracks ranging from "Santa and the Sidewalk Surfer," cut in 1963 as an "early satiric commentary of the surf scene," to "Teardrops," a 1970 single. In between are all the hits plus some great previously unreleased songs like "Can I Go On" and "Gas Money." The LP also comes complete with informative liner notes by Ken Barnes and comments on every song from Volman and Kaylan. Undoubtedly one of the greatest rock anthologies ever released.

The Bobby Fuller Four

Only in the last couple of years has rock rediscovered the Bobby Fuller Four. It took a raw, invigorating version of Fuller's "I Fought the Law" by the Clash to instigate a new round of interest in him and his music. Although the song was Fuller's only hit, the rest of his repertoire is filled with excellent pop rockers.

Fuller's biggest influences, by far, were Buddy Holly and the Beatles. Like Holly, Fuller based his sound on richly textured guitar riffs supported with just enough bottom to make the songs rock. This has led some critics to tag—unfairly—Fuller as a Holly imitator. But Fuller's songs were thicker sounding; musically, more things were going on in his records. Also, the production of Fuller's songs was influenced by the Beatles' and the Byrds' albums.

"Let Her Dance," a bright, uptempo gem of a tune, was the group's debut single; it did well but not as well as its follow-up, "I Fought the Law." The latter tune, which was written by Sonny Curtis, Buddy Holly's lead guitarist, broke into the Top Ten in 1966. It looked as if Fuller was on his way to becoming a big star when he died. His death was ruled a suicide, but there is evidence to suggest foul play.

So many other things were happening in the mid-sixties that Fuller's death didn't cause a great stir at the time. But looking back and listening to his best material, it's easy to envision how much rock would have benefited had Fuller lived.

The Bobby Fuller Memorial Album / President / 1966

This British import shines a light on Fuller's better recordings,

including, of course, "I Fought the Law" and "Let Her Dance." But the ten other tracks hold up nearly as well. All the songs on side two, save for "I Fought the Law," were written and recorded just prior to Fuller's death.

Best of the Bobby Fuller Four / Rhino / 1981

Rhino Records has done as much as anyone to keep Bobby Fuller's music alive. This fourteen-track collection brims with bright up-tempo rockers that fall somewhere between American pop and British Invasion rock. Almost all of them were written by Fuller and most are excellent.

The Bobby Fuller Tapes, Vol. 1 / Rhino / 1983

Albums such as these are usually suited for collectors and avid fans only, since much of what's included probably wasn't supposed to be released in the first place. Although the material doesn't rate as highly as the tracks found on the LPs mentioned above, it's worthwhile. All the songs were recorded between 1960 and 1964, before "I Fought the Law" was a hit. There are more Holly-inspired songs here plus some surf tunes and Texas-style rockabilly.

The Beau Brummels

The Beau Brummels are best remembered for two very good (and very Beatles-influenced) 1965 hit singles: "Laugh, Laugh" and "Just a Little." Lead singer Sal Valentino's voice, sincere and very British-sounding, was very well suited for guitar player Ron Elliott's originals. Produced by Sylvester Stewart (Sly Stone of Sly and the Family Stone), these two singles helped the Beau Brummels become one of the first successful American bands after the British Invasion.

Historically speaking, the Beau Brummels are also significant for being the first San Francisco–based rock group to gain real national attention.

Introducing the Beau Brummels / Rhino / 1982

A Rhino rerelease of the original Autumn Records LP, this contains "Laugh, Laugh," "Just a Little," and eight other Elliott tracks that further illustrate the group's capabilities and strong Beatles influence. Judging from the overall quality here, it's a shame the Beau Brummels didn't successfully move into the next phase of rock that began in its own backyard.

The Velvet Underground

Of all the American groups that began in the wake of the British Invasion, no group aroused so little commercial attention yet ultimately had so much influence on rock's future as the Velvet Underground did. The group formed in New York City in 1965 under the leadership of Lou Reed and John Cale. Almost at once the Velvet Underground broke from the pack and established its own course and its own intentions, namely defining rock as art.

Lou Reed's voice was the Velvet Underground's trademark. It was soft, even sensuous and comforting, but deceptively so. Underneath was a streetwise poet who knew firsthand the joys and anguish of heroin, the hustle, and distorted visions that existed inside the belly of Manhattan. Reed's lyrics dealt with desperation and delusion, but he expressed a stern conviction to find some sort of meaning from it all. Backed by a band that played wildly original and disconnected melodies, he often found what he was looking for.

The Velvet Underground broke up in 1969. Years ahead of its time, the band never found an audience outside New York City. But before the split, the group set the stage for such seventies rock genres as art rock and punk and such artists as David Bowie, Roxy Music, and the Talking Heads.

The Velvet Underground & Nico / Polygram / 1967

The Velvets' debut album was their best. With the support of scenemakers such as Andy Warhol (he supplied the LP's cover art), Reed and company sought to divorce rock from any pretense and pap. They succeeded marvelously with "Femme Fatale," "Heroin," and "The Black Angel's Death Song." Nico is a featured vocalist, but her input doesn't come close to Reed's. Although avant-garde by any definition, the music on this album possessed as much light for the coming generation of rockers as almost any other made in 1967.

White Light/White Heat / Polygram / 1967

Due to resurging popularity of the Velvet Underground, Polygram has re-released this LP, originally issued by Verve Records in 1967. Its tracks are mostly rampaging excursions into the uncertain world of guitar frenzy and distortion and strange side trips that depict the Velvet's supreme anti-pop devilishness. Nothing is sacred on *White Light/White Heat*; nothing is spared. A song like "Sister Ray," for instance, is often overwhelming in its nervy art-rock thrusts into mid-sixties pop rock sensibilities. A fascinating record always worth its time on the turntable, *White Light/White Heat* is, and forever will be, a genuine aural experience.

The Velvet Underground / Polygram / 1969

Another Polygram re-release. Compared to what's heard on *White Light/White Heat*, these songs are rather subdued and less fierce.

There's much more acoustic music here, allowing glimpses of the band and its sense of poetic imagery. Pay special attention to "What Goes On," one of the better examples of Lou Reed's songwriting skills.

OTHER RECOMMENDED ALBUMS

Nuggets Volumes 1–4 / Rhino / 1984

If there is one record company truly dedicated to the preservation of sixties rock, it's Rhino Records. Along with its long list of excellent sixties reissues and anthologies, the label's *Nuggets* series is indispensable. The four volumes released thus far do a superb job of filling the gaps in the sixties rock story.

Volume 1, *The Hits*, is the best of the four volumes. Virtually every track is a song worth discovering or rediscovering. Volume 1 contains the finest selections from a good many of the numerous bands in the mid-sixties that recorded interesting and exciting music but not enough to fill a full album. This record's highlights are the Leaves' "Hey Joe," "Dirty Water" by the Standells, the Blues Magoos' "We Ain't Got Nothin' Yet," the Seeds' "Pushin' Too Hard," and "Open My Eyes" by the Nazz.

Volume 2, *Punk*, is not as essential or absorbing as *The Hits*, but punk fans will undoubtedly love the Vagrants' "Respect" and the Chocolate Watchband's "Are You Gonna Be There (At the Love-In)?" And everyone will enjoy "Gloria" by the Shadows of Knight.

Volumes 3 and 4 consist of sixties pop-rock selections. Volume 3 is better than Volume 4 simply because the songs and the groups ("Lies"/the Knickerbockers; "Turn Down Day" and "Red Rubber Ball"/Cyrkle; "Time Won't Let Me"/the Outsiders; and "Let Her Dance"/Bobby Fuller Four) were more popular and had more of an impact on the pop charts than those included on Volume 4.

9
MOTOWN

If any one person can be singled out as having the greatest impact on black music in the sixties it is Berry Gordy, Jr. Gordy built the Tamla/Motown/Gordy records empire and developed the Motown Sound, one of the grandest, most commercially accessible, and, at the same time, artistic sounds of the decade.

The Motown Sound incorporated the basic elements of soul, gospel, and rhythm & blues mixed with a unique and remarkable pop sensibility. It was a sound built atop a powerful rhythm section led by hard, snappy drums and thick, inventive bass lines. From there the usually simple yet wonderfully catchy melodies would grow with guitars and keyboards, strings and horns, percussion in the form of handclaps and tambourines, and, finally, vocals that were polished beyond belief—all enhanced by an undeniable Motown beat.

It was a patterned sound, and many Motown hits came from the same mold (the Four Tops' "I Can't Help Myself" and "It's the Same Old Song"; Martha and the Vandellas' "Heat Wave" and "Quicksand," for example). But the style was more durable than any other in the sixties. In 1965 and 1966 alone, Motown placed at least thirty-three hits in the Top Twenty.

Gordy's Motown operation was a family operation. For the most part, Gordy used the same session players on all the tracks cut in Detroit during Motown's heyday. Robert White and Joe Messina were the guitarists, Earl Van Dyke played keyboards, Uriel "Pistol" Jones and Benny Benjamin were the drummers, James Jamerson was the bass player, James Giddons played vibes, and Eddie Brown, percussion. (Motown tunes were also cut in New York and Los Angeles and other musicians were used there.)

The songwriters and producer/arrangers included Smokey Robinson, Eddie Holland, Brian Holland, and Lamont Dozier, Norman Whitfield, Mickey Stevenson, Harvey Fuqua, Nicholas Ashford, and Valerie Simpson. No other record company could boast such a stable of talent. Berry Gordy fed this talent into his well-oiled organization, applying the Motor City's assembly-line production philosophy to making records.

Gordy knew a hit record when he heard one. A former record store owner, auto assembly-line worker, and songwriter for such artists as Jackie Wilson, Gordy began Tamla Records in 1959 in a small office on West Grand Boulevard in Detroit. He called the place Hitsville, U.S.A. Marv Johnson, Tamla's first successful artist, recorded a number of fairly decent singles in 1959 and 1960. Gordy's first big hit was Barrett Strong's "Money (That's What I Want)," which went to number two on the R&B charts. But it wasn't until the Miracles signed on with Gordy that the Motown Sound began to take form. Their "Shop Around" went to number two—but on the *pop* charts. From then on, Gordy refined Motown's sound and expanded its roster until it became the largest black-owned record company in America.

Motown's success was Gordy's success and he ruled the corporation, never compromising his authority or his standards. Gordy released only the best product possible. Songs were frequently remixed, rerecorded, and rewritten. Gordy developed local artists whom he controlled. No Motown artist recorded before he or she was primed and prepared to give his or her best performance. Because of this, Gordy encouraged in-house competition among songwriters, producers, arrangers, musicians, and performers.

But most important, Gordy relentlessly stuck to a proven formula for making records. He instructed his songwriters and producers to exploit a particularly successful feel through several records until fading chart strength dictated otherwise.

Motown was a solid and successful organization until 1968, when cracks in the empire began to appear. That year Holland-Dozier-Holland, the ace songwriting and production team, left to form their own company. In addition, Gordy was becoming bored with merely making records. He got involved in film on the West Coast and in 1971 moved Motown to Los Angeles. Motown carried on throughout the seventies and into the eighties. The hits were fewer and harder to come by, but acts like Stevie Wonder, Marvin Gaye, Diana Ross, and the Jackson 5 helped Motown remain a potent force.

RECOMMENDED ARTISTS

Smokey Robinson and the Miracles

Motown would never have known the success it did without Smokey Robinson. Not only were the Miracles one of the label's best-selling acts through the mid-sixties, but Robinson was also one of the label's best songwriters and producers.

The Miracles consisted of Robinson, Ronnie White, Pete Moore, Bobby Rogers, and Claudette Rogers, who later married Smokey. The group signed with Gordy in 1959. With a lilting falsetto that always sounded true, Robinson sang lead. He was rarely aggressive or overly anxious; he simply did what he had to do in order to make a song work. Most of the time it meant a delivery comprised of a soft, sensitive touch that blended beautifully with the other Miracles.

In addition to producing the Miracles, he also produced Mary Wells, the Temptations, the Supremes, the Marvelettes, Martha and the Vandellas, and others.

Despite Robinson and the Miracles' success—fourteen Top Twenty hits—they didn't have a number-one single until 1970, two years before Robinson and the group would amicably part company. The Hit, "The Tears of a Clown" has a bright melody, meticulously phrased lyrics, and instrumentation that fits like a glove and is one of the best examples of Robinson and the Miracle's virtuosity.

Robinson was an incredibly versatile songwriter. He could pen a deep, emotional ballad ("You Really Got a Hold on Me") or an uptempo dance tune ("Going to a Go-Go"). He also wrote countless songs for other Motown artists: "My Guy" for Mary Wells, "The Way You Do the Things You Do" for the Temptations, and "Ain't That Peculiar" for Marvin Gaye. Smokey Robinson might be considered

Courtesy of Motown Records

the most *complete* artist the decade produced. He left his mark on so many recordings that it's often difficult not to regard Robinson's sound *as* the Motown Sound.

Hi . . . We're the Miracles / Motown / 1961

The Miracles' debut album has been rereleased by Motown and is easily available. Wrongly overlooked because Robinson's later material was so strong, this record is much more of a group effort and contains some excellent singing. Includes the hit "Shop Around" and a fine rendition of "Money" plus "After All," sung by Claudette Rogers Robinson.

Going to a Go-Go / Motown / 1965

With three classic Miracles' songs on it—"The Tracks of My Tears," "Going to a Go-Go," and "Ooo Baby Baby"—this is the Miracles' best studio album. Robinson never wrote or sounded better. Also here: "Choosey Beggar," one of Robinson's great unheralded songs, and "My Baby Changes Like the Weather," which has a delightful fifties feel. Highly recommended.

Anthology / Motown / 1974

This three-record set, complete with photo booklet, is the Miracles' definitive retrospective release. The collection begins with "Got a Job" (1958) and ends with "I Can't Stand to See You Cry" (1972). The great songs in between are simply too numerous to list here. If there is only one Smokey Robinson and the Miracles album in your collection, it should be this one.

Mary Wells

Mary Wells was the first Motown artist Smokey Robinson produced and wrote for, and she became the label's biggest female star in the early sixties. Her good looks and sensuous voice made her sound a lot older than she was; virtually all of her hits were recorded before she was twenty-one years old. "Two Lovers," "The One Who Really Loves You," "You Beat Me to the Punch," and her biggest hit, "My Guy" (number one in 1964), all bore Robinson's stamp.

Mary Wells was a fine though not spectacular singer. Her departure from Motown in 1965 essentially ended her career. Her only Top Forty single after leaving Motown was "Use Your Head" on Twentieth-Century Records. Mary Wells's failure was the first bit of evidence to suggest just how highly the Motown organization figured in its artists' success. Her fall was the first of several (which included Florence Ballard's, among others) to demonstrate that the Motown machine was more important than the talent of any one performer in its domain.

Greatest Hits / Motown / 1964

This basic collection of Wells's Motown hits is sufficient for any listener who merely wants to sample her best songs. Robinson had something to do with eight of the twelve tracks on the record. Included here: "My Guy," "Two Lovers," and the profoundly catchy "The One Who Really Loves You."

Marvin Gaye

Marvin Gaye was originally brought into the Motown fold as a session drummer. But before long he was making records of his own. From his very first single, "Stubborn Kind of Fellow," released in 1962, to his departure from Motown twenty years later, Gaye was one of the label's most adaptable artists.

Gaye's early recordings were steeped in rich, satisfying rhythm & blues. Such songs as "Stubborn Kind of Fellow," "Hitch Hike," and "Can I Get a Witness" contained soulful vocals and superb instrumentation. Yet occasional production flaws prevented a few of them from reaching their maximum commercial potential. On both "Stubborn Kind of Fellow" and "Hitch Hike," for instance, the flute carries the midsection solo spot. A saxophone or a piano would have given the songs a harder, even more convincing edge.

As Gaye matured as a songwriter and recording artist, he smoothed and sweetened his singing style. As one writer put it, "The most remarkable thing about Marvin's vocal abilities was, however, the way he could combine the tough and tender sides of his style into one song."

Gaye cut many duets with female labelmates, among them a couple of hit records with Mary Wells in 1964. Then in 1967 he cut "It Takes Two" with Kim Weston. But the best was yet to come. In 1967 he and Tammi Terrell recorded "Ain't No Mountain High Enough," the first of seven hit singles for the duo. After "Ain't No Mountain High Enough" came "Your Precious Love," "If I Could Build My Whole World around You," "Ain't Nothing Like the Real Thing," and "You're All I Need to Get By," all first-class recordings from start to finish.

The years 1966 through most of 1968 were fairly lean; none of Gaye's solo efforts managed to break into the Top Twenty. But then came Gaye's version of a Gladys Knight and the Pips hit, "I Heard It through the Grapevine," and Gaye had a number-one hit all his own. In Gaye's rendition, the song was a complete triumph in soul sophistication and production, and Gaye sang it as he had sung his early R&B records. He crossed the tune's subtle funkiness and his

own perfect sensitivity and made the Norman Whitfield composition the biggest hit of 1968.

After "Grapevine" came "Too Busy Thinking about My Baby" and "That's the Way Love Is," both Top Ten songs. Things were rolling along in high gear until Terrell died of a brain tumor in 1970. Gaye, shocked and saddened by her death, didn't regain his form until a year later with the landmark *What's Going On.*

From that point on, Marvin Gaye took more control of his work. "Mercy Mercy Me (The Ecology)," "Inner City Blues," "Trouble Man," and "Let's Get It On" were early-seventies hits. But the rest of the seventies were personally troubling and not nearly as fruitful. In 1982 Gaye returned with the Grammy-award winning "Sexual Healing." He died in 1984 after his father shot him during a family argument.

That Stubborn Kinda Fellow / Motown / 1963

Even a superficial listen to this record indicates just how influential an artist Gaye was. Such white rock singers as Mick Jagger and Rod Stewart owe much to Gaye. There's also a bold confidence apparent on "Hitch Hike," "Pride and Joy," and "Get My Hands on Some Lovin' " that is rarely found on debut records. It was obvious from the contents of this LP that Gaye would eventually become a major force in soul music.

United / Motown / 1967

On *United* Gaye and Tammi Terrell sound like they were born to sing together. The vocal trade-offs on "Ain't No Mountain High Enough" and the way Terrell draws the soul out of Gaye on "You Got What It Takes" are simply awesome. Only "Somethin' Stupid" fails to impress.

Anthology / Motown / 1974

Like all the other Motown *Anthology* albums, this three-record set is an excellent compilation. It's the most thorough compilation of Gaye's vast body of work, up to 1972. For a complete collection of Gaye records, be sure to include copies of *What's Going On* and *Let's Get It On*, his two principal seventies albums.

Stevie Wonder

During the early sixties Stevie Wonder was affectionately known as Little Stevie Wonder. He was ten years old when Ronnie White brought him to meet Berry Gordy. Gordy saw the young blind boy named Steveland Morris as a younger Ray Charles. At Gordy's insistence, Stevie Morris became Little Stevie Wonder.

In 1963 Wonder's third single, "Fingertips—Part Two," and the album from which it came, *Little Stevie Wonder, the 12 Year Old Genius* (recorded live at the Apollo), hit number one.

Wonder was eager to make records. However, only "Uptight (Everything's Alright)," an upbeat rocker, was a big hit in the two and a half years after "Fingertips." Wonder's sound was still in its formative stage; there was much experimenting to see just exactly how and what he should record. Wonder sang Dylan's "Blowin' in the Wind," and it broke into the Top Ten, as did "A Place in the Sun." By then, Wonder's voice had begun to deepen, and he didn't sound so little anymore.

Wonder's own approach to singing and recording began to take shape with "I Was Made to Love Her" in 1967. Wonder then recorded ballads like "My Cherie Amour" and "Yester-Me, Yester-You, Yester-day" and continued to refine his vocals with challenging tunes such as "For Once in My Life."

In the seventies Wonder fulfilled the promise of his youth after assuming full artistic control of his work and writing such outstanding albums as *Signed, Sealed & Delivered, Talking Book, Music of My Mind, Innervisions,* and *Songs in the Key of Life.*

Stevie Wonder, the 12 Year Old Genius / Motown / 1963

This record best captures Wonder's little-boy qualities that, when propped up with a hot rhythm section, make him a joy to listen to. "Fingertips, Parts One and Two" are included here, as is Wonder's homage to Ray Charles in the form of "Hallelujah, I Love Her So" and "Don't You Know."

I Was Made to Love Her / Motown / 1967

A problem with Wonder's mid-sixties LPs is that too many were stuffed with ordinary filler material. Both *I Was Made to Love Her* and *For Once in My Life* are worthwhile albums if you don't mind Wonder singing other people's hits. On *I Was Made to Love Her*, there's "My Girl," "Please, Please, Please," "Respect," and a couple of others, all nicely done but better by the original artists. Still the title tune is exceptional and a definite highlight of Wonder's sixties recording career.

Greatest Hits / Motown / 1968

Better than *I Was Made to Love Her* is this album, since, for the most part, Wonder was a singles artist. "Uptight," "I Was Made to Love Her," "Fingertips," and "Blowin' in the Wind," along with eight other hits, make this an adequate representation of Wonder's best moments.

The Temptations

The Temptations were Motown's biggest and best male vocal group. Their songs sold millions of records and repeatedly hit the Top Ten. They were stylish, dynamic, and versatile: Any of the group's five members could sing lead, and onstage their choreography was second to none. Though the Tempts' golden years were from 1964 to 1968, the group carried on into the seventies, despite personnel changes and shifts in sound and direction. In 1971 "Just My Imagination (Running Away with Me)" was a number-one record; the following year "Papa Was a Rollin' Stone" made it to number one, too.

The group, which signed to Motown in 1960, consisted of Otis Williams, Eddie Kendricks, Eldridge Bryant, Melvin Franklin, and Paul Williams. The first couple of tunes the Temptations recorded—written and produced by Gordy—had no real impact on the charts. Enter Smokey Robinson. Under his wing the Tempts (with David Ruffin replacing Bryant) had their first hit single, his "The Way You Do the Things You Do" in 1964. Eddie Kendricks sang the lead. "I'll Be in Trouble" and "Girl (Why You Wanna Make Me Blue)" were the follow-ups that, although fine tunes, didn't break into the Top Twenty. Later that year Robinson gave them "My Girl," on which Ruffin sang the lead. The song shot to number one, and the album that followed it, *The Temptations Sing Smokey*, is one of the best the group ever recorded.

Much of the Temptations' early success can easily be traced to Robinson. He not only produced and wrote much of their material (including "Since I Lost My Baby," "It's Growing," "My Baby," and "Get Ready") but developed their sound. It was a full-bodied, lively sound, for the most part, and with a seamless web of vocal harmonies that were consistently rich. But by 1966 the demands of working with so many Motown acts caused Robinson to bow out of the picture. Enter Norman Whitfield.

Whitfield was no stranger to the Temptations; he had written (with Eddie Holland) "Girl (Why You Wanna Make Me Blue)" and had produced a few of the group's B sides. From the start he sought to add a more ambitious edge to their records. The songs Whitfield cowrote with Eddie Holland—"Ain't Too Proud to Beg," "Beauty Is Only Skin Deep," "(I Know) I'm Losing You," "It's You That I Need"—resulted in a commercial response bigger than the Tempts had experienced under Smokey's direction.

It was with Whitfield that the Temptations became the first Motown act to embrace what became known as psychedelic soul. Influenced and vastly impressed with what Sly and the Family Stone had done with black music, Whitfield set a course for the Tempts that would tap the same hard-rock sound, making the group's records heavier than ever before. There was an increased use of guitars, sound effects added whenever appropriate, and lyrics that dealt with controversial social issues.

It was an ideal time for the change, too. David Ruffin had left the group for a solo career, and Dennis Edwards of the Contours took his

place. Lead vocals now were shared fairly equally among the group's members, and songs such as "Cloud Nine," "Run Away Child, Running Wild," and "Don't Let the Joneses Get You Down" were all hits in 1968 and 1969. In 1970 came "Psychedelic Shack" and "Ball of Confusion (That's What the World Is Today)."

Even though his records were hits, some Motown purists dismiss Whitfield's accomplishments with the Temptations because he led them away from the more comfortable R&B/pop groove. Whitfield was an adventurous producer who believed radical change was necessary for Motown to keep up with the pace of pop music in the late sixties and early seventies. However, during the Tempts' psychedelic soul era, Whitfield and the Tempts also recorded more traditional sounding Motown songs—"You're My Everything" (1967), "I

Wish It Would Rain" (1968), and "Just My Imagination" (1971). In short, Whitfield gave the Tempts a sound that helped them remain a top group long after their contemporaries had faded from the scene without abandoning completely the group's original groove. For that, he is to be commended.

The Temptations Sing Smokey / Motown / 1965

For those who prefer the Tempts' Smokey Robinson period, this LP is an absolute must. It includes the Temptations' hits "The Way You Do the Things You Do" and "My Girl" as well as a terrific version of the Miracles' "You've Really Got a Hold on Me." The sweet, timeless quality of this LP makes it as rewarding to listen to today as it was in 1965. Rereleased by Motown and available in most record stores.

Cloud Nine / Gordy / 1969

This is a good representation of the Temptations' work with Norman Whitfield. The LP was recorded when Whitfield was still formulating the Temptations' "new" sound. None of Whitfield's psychedelic soul albums, however, rival the albums Robinson made with the group. Because Whitfield had less of a grasp of what comprised a solid LP than Robinson did, there is more filler material on his records.

Anthology / Motown / 1973

The Temptations' *Anthology* album might be a cut above the other Motown anthologies because writer Vince Aletti's liner notes tell the history of the songs contained on the three-record set so well. The thirty-seven tracks in this deluxe package cover both Robinson's and Whitfield's work with the group.

Martha and the Vandellas

Martha and the Vandellas were Motown's only true female soul group. Unlike the Supremes, who heavily crossed over into pop, or the Marvelettes, who emulated the girl-group sound, Martha Reeves and her Vandellas belted out soul tunes in classic soul fashion.

Reeves was a secretary at Motown before getting a chance to record. With Gordy's guidance, Martha and the Vandellas were formed in 1962, and Holland, Dozier, and Holland came up with songs for them to record. The group's debut single, "Come and Get These Memories," got as far as number thirty in 1963 and established the group's strong, vigorous style. Of all the songs Martha and the Vandellas cut for Motown, none so clearly and convincingly reflected their talent as "Heat Wave" and "Dancing in the Street," unquestionably two of the most memorable records ever to come out of Motown.

"Heat Wave" demonstrated just how far Martha Reeves would go to get her point across. The song's aggressive, energetic rhythm came on full force from the very first note—the same instant Reeves took total charge of it. Her vocal performance was perfect in every sense.

"Dancing in the Street" was every bit as exciting as "Heat Wave" but possessed more tenacity and a slightly sexier groove. Reeves took the Marvin Gaye–William Stevenson tune and overwhelmed it with nearly-flawless soul vocalizing. The song became an instant masterpiece and has been interpreted countless times. Most of the other hits of Martha and the Vandellas were written by Holland-Dozier-Holland. "Quicksand" (the carbon copy of "Heat Wave"), "Nowhere to Run," "Jimmy Mack," and "I'm Ready for Love" were all Top Ten smashes.

Reeves and her Vandellas were certainly excellent singers and did much to make their records successful. But the Hollands and Dozier supplied the songs, and when the songwriters left Motown, Martha and the Vandellas' hits stopped. By the end of 1967 they were considered has-beens, eclipsed at Motown by the Supremes' success. Soul was heading in a new direction, and all Martha Reeves and the Vandellas could do was watch it pass.

Anthology / Motown / 1974

Unlike most of the other classic Motown *Anthology* record sets, this one consists of only two records. Sides one, two, and three are outstanding; they include all the early hits plus "I'll Have to Let Him Go," recorded in 1962, and an assortment of tunes written by Richard Morris and Sylvia May. Side four is the group's best from 1969 to 1972.

The Supremes

The Supremes epitomized the Motown method for success. From the beginning the group was molded and polished under Gordy's personal supervision, not just in terms of music, but in such things as etiquette and dress. Diana Ross, Florence Ballard, and Mary Wilson captivated Gordy, for he knew that if he made the right decisions, they could turn into the big group he'd been looking for.

The Supremes were that—and more. With Ross singing lead, the Supremes tallied twelve number-one singles, a record topped by only Elvis Presley and the Beatles. The Supremes made millions for Gordy and Motown and were the most successful crossover act the label ever had. By brandishing a sound and a style that was based in pop rather than true soul or R&B, the Supremes reached heights never thought possible for a female vocal group, let alone a black female vocal group.

Gordy showed unusual patience with the Supremes. The group's early records were flat and uninspired; producer Smokey Robinson had difficulty determining their sound. When it became apparent that the Supremes were going nowhere, Gordy assigned Eddie and Brian Holland and Lamont Dozier to the task. It was the perfect combination. Beginning with the number-one "Where Did Our Love Go" in 1964, the team racked up four more straight number ones: "Baby Love," "Come See about Me," "Stop! In the Name of Love," and "Back in My Arms Again."

The standard Motown formula was employed to keep the Supremes' string of hits going. Many of the songs bore a remarkable similarity in melodic construction. Most important, Holland, Dozier, and Holland meticulously wrote each song to fit Ross's nasal vocals. The songs' dynamics were arranged so that Ross could make the most of her voice at just the right moment.

No American recording act could equal the Supremes' gargantuan success from 1964 through 1967. When Holland, Dozier, and Holland left and Florence Ballard was replaced by Cindy Birdsong, a new era began. The group came to be known as Diana Ross and the Supremes. Because Gordy was preparing Ross for a solo career, the success of the Supremes became secondary. In 1969 Diana Ross left the group and embarked on a successful solo career.

The Supremes Sing Holland-Dozier-Holland / Motown / 1967

Those who must have at least one Supremes studio album should pick up this one. Holland, Dozier, and Holland weren't the only songwriting team to work with the Supremes, but they were far and away the best. Though not as good, another worthwhile album to look into is the one that preceded this, *Supremes A Go-Go* (Motown 1966).

Anthology / Motown / 1974

Because the Supremes were a singles group, only a couple of their albums work well enough to consider here. *Anthology* is the best Supremes release. The three-record set, complete with a booklet of notes and photographs, covers the group's entire history up to and including 1969's best efforts. Included are all of the hits and then some.

The Four Tops

Like the Temptations, the Tops exuded an aura of polish and professionalism that was impossible to miss either on record or in person. Live, the Tops were almost as good as the Tempts when it came to showmanship. Yet the Four Tops and the Temptations each had a distinctive style. Levi Stubbs, the Tops' lead singer, was a dominating presence on nearly all the group's sixties records. His voice was forceful, magnetic, even intimidating. Songs like "I Can't Help Myself," "Reach Out I'll Be There," and especially "Bernadette" were built around Stubbs. Neither Ruffin nor Kendricks of the Temptations possessed such power.

The Four Tops—Stubbs, Renaldo Benson, Lawrence Payton, and Duke Fakir—had been together since 1953. Yet it was only during a few years in the mid-sixties that the Four Tops made their mark on pop. With the exception of their first big hit, "Baby I Need Your Loving," an impeccable ballad strung out on emotional pleas and hopes, just about all of the Tops' monster records were uptempo, blood-pumping soul songs that put to good use Stubbs's vocals and Holland-Dozier-Holland's songwriting and precision production. "I Can't Help Myself" (1965) was the Four Tops' first number-one single. A couple of months later "It's the Same Old Song" peaked at number five. "Something about You" and "Shake Me, Wake Me (When It's Over)" barely snuck into the Top Twenty, but "Reach Out

I'll Be There" went to number one. The Four Tops registered two more Top Ten tunes—"Standing in the Shadows of Love" and "Bernadette"—before Holland-Dozier-Holland departed. Unlike every other Motown group, the *original* Four Tops are still touring and recording. Seventies hits include "Keeper of the Castle," "Ain't No Woman (Like the One I've Got)," and "When She Was My Girl."

Reach Out / Motown / 1967

This album contains such vintage soul stirrers as "Reach Out I'll Be There," "Standing in the Shadows of Love," and "Bernadette," plus fascinating interpretations of "If I Were a Carpenter" and "Walk Away Renee." Unfortunately, there are also garbage versions of "Last Train to Clarksville" and "I'm a Believer," tunes the Four Tops had no business recording. Skip over the shoddy stuff and get to the real meat of this record. Even on the filler tunes, Stubbs's vocals are commanding and strong.

Anthology / Motown / 1974

Motown did an adequate job with the Four Tops' three-record compilation. Sides one, two, and three contain the bulk of the Four Tops' classic recordings. Four, five, and six make you wish that Holland, Dozier, and Holland had never left Motown.

Jr. Walker and the All Stars

Jr. Walker recorded for Motown, but his records didn't ape the Motown sound. They had a distinctively funky edge and made the fewest concessions to pop. He was primarily an instrumentalist who became a vocalist with some reluctance.

Walker formed the All Stars in Detroit in 1961. His first hit for Motown, the hot, sassy "Shotgun," carried his trademark: a slick tenor saxophone that never strayed too far and always managed to sound gutsy without becoming crude. "Shotgun" was one of the best dance records of 1965 and the first of a number of saxophone-dominated follow-ups.

Walker sang on most of his songs, many of which he wrote himself or took from Johnny Bristol, a Motown songwriter/producer. But Walker's range was a bit limited, and often his saxophone playing would pull his voice out of jams with crisp, trim solos. Perhaps his most effective vocal output, aside from that heard on "Shotgun," was on "What Does It Take (To Win Your Love)?" Released in 1969, it was his biggest-selling single.

Anthology / Motown / 1974

The original LP *Shotgun* is a great Jr. Walker album, for it features him and the All Stars in their funkiest, most soulful light. But it's out of print and rarely seen in used-record bins. Fortunately, Motown saw fit to include Walker and the All Stars in the label's Anthology series. This two-record set is the most thorough overview of Walker's career ever released. The best material is found on side one: "Shotgun," "Do the Boomerang," "(I'm a) Road Runner," and "Money." Once again, notice how the Motown formula is worked into each song and how Walker always adds a new twist.

All the Great Hits / Motown / 1972

This LP is a nice compact collection of Walker's best tracks. It includes only ten songs, all of which appear on *Anthology*. For those not interested in a full dose of Walker, *All the Great Hits* covers the basics. One glaring omission is "(I'm a) Road Runner."

OTHER RECOMMENDED ALBUMS

The Motown Story / Motown / 1970

It's all here in this five-record boxed set that includes not only the greatest chartbusters ever to come out of Motown but mini-interviews with the artists and a narrator to pull everything together. Just about all the important Motown artists are represented with at least one song. For anyone who's more than a casual fan, this package is a must.

The Motown Story: The First Twenty-Five Years / Motown / 1983

Essentially, this is an updated and expanded version of *The Motown Story*. This edition covers the seventies in addition to the sixties and includes selections by the Commodores, Rick James, and the Jackson 5.

10
FOLK ROCK

Throughout the early sixties a vibrant folk scene in America attracted listeners disillusioned with pop music and all its offshoots, unable to fully relate to jazz or R&B, and vastly interested in music with "meaning." Folk scenes thrived in college towns and cities like New York, Boston, and San Francisco.

The two common threads inherent in all folk tunes were simple melodies with chord structures easy enough for anyone to play and lyrics that claimed more than "I love you baby, yes I do." Many folk artists didn't get the chance to record. If they did, it was usually on one of the small folk labels located in New York, although more popular folk groups like Peter, Paul and Mary and the Brothers Four not only made records with larger record companies but made records that made it onto the pop charts.

By 1964 folk's biggest star was Bob Dylan. His incisive, bittersweet songs and scruffy, country-boy-in-the-big-city image epitomized what a folkie was supposed to be all about. Intelligent, witty, funny, Dylan was folk's most important artist since the glory days of Woody Guthrie. His lyrics were not only listened to but read as poetry. His songs of social protest were incredibly effective and did much to set folksingers singing about the bomb, civil rights, and war.

These were the folk roots of folk rock. As for the rock part, one has to look no further than the British Invasion. As much as Dylan is credited with initiating the big jump from acoustic to electric guitars and giving folk a backbeat, it was the Beatles who enlightened him and the others who quickly followed his path (the Byrds, the Lovin' Spoonful, and others). For Dylan, rock had finally become meaningful enough to embrace once again. What the Beatles wrote and sang about and what the Rolling Stones were playing, were relevant. Even the most ardent folkies listened.

The single most important early folk-rock record might have been Dylan's "Like a Rolling Stone," but the first came from England. In 1964 the Animals had a number-one hit with "The House of the Rising Sun," a traditional folk tune set to electric guitars, bass, organ, and a subtle backbeat. The song had appeared on Dylan's eponymously titled debut album in an acoustic version. The Animals' version—whether they knew it or not—was folk rock.

Folk rock in its purest form (if there ever was such a thing) existed around 1965 and 1966. After that, performers—including the Byrds and Dylan—moved into other areas such as country rock. Despite its relatively brief heyday, folk rock was influential. Musically, the blend of folk and rock created a brand-new sound, as evidenced by the sensitive guitars of the Byrds and taken further along by the Buffalo Springfield. Folk rock also gave rock a whole new audience, as most folkies gradually came to accept both music forms. Finally, from folk rock came country rock as well as the whole singer/songwriter genre in the seventies. Joni Mitchell, James Taylor, Carly Simon, Cat Stevens, Jackson Browne, and many others owe something to folk rock.

Note: From folk rock came a number of artists who fell into the general category but in reality were more folk than rock. Artists such as Joan Baez, Judy Collins, Tim Hardin, Buffy Sainte-Marie, Eric Andersen, Dave Van Ronk, Tom Paxton, Phil Ochs, and Arlo Guthrie played mostly folk music or folk pop that attracted a folk-rock audience. All of these artists are worth checking into, but due to space considerations, can't be discussed here.

Bob Dylan

Along with Elvis Presley and the Beatles, Bob Dylan was one of rock's most important artists. In the sixties he was the music's most respected sage, its inner spirit, and, very often, its guiding light. An ordinary guitar player with a voice that could just as easily offend as it could bring joy, Dylan was, however, a supreme songwriter and rock's most accomplished poet.

Almost singlehandedly, Dylan revamped the art of rock and pop songwriting and elevated it to new and exciting heights. For the first time in the music's history, the lyrics carried as much weight as the melody and, in some cases, even more. In addition, no topic or theme was off limits. Dylan wrote prolifically about racism, political oppression, injustice, and war. Within a year of his emergence on the rock scene, he had a dedicated legion of songwriters imitating every stroke of his pen.

Dylan was indeed a giant. What he wrote and sang had an astounding impact on the growth and future course of rock, not to mention his effect on the baby-boom generation. He brought a respect to the musical form that it never lost. And because of him, such hybrid rock forms as folk rock and, later, country rock were born.

Originally, Dylan's main interest was with rock & roll, but it was as a folksinger that he first achieved prominence. Born Robert Allen Zimmerman, he left his Hibbing, Minnesota, home in late 1960 to visit Woody Guthrie, who lay dying in a New Jersey hospital. Dylan had become intensely interested in meeting Guthrie ever since he read the great American folksinger's autobiography, *Bound for Glory*.

Dylan's earliest album, *Bob Dylan*, released on Columbia Records in 1962, didn't reveal any significant writing talent since all but two songs on the record were penned by other songwriters. But Dylan had soaked up enough of Guthrie's inspiration and genuine folky flavor to give the record an irresistible visceral charm.

Dylan's next LP, *The Freewheelin' Bob Dylan*, was different. It contained nothing but originals and almost instantly unveiled Dylan as a major new artist in folk music. Dylan had shifted gears, something he would do numerous times in his career; he cut down the country nasal twang that ran through most of the tracks on his debut album and fostered a more urban, serious, and mature vocal delivery. More important, however, was the type of songs that he recorded for *Freewheelin'* and its follow-up, *The Times They Are A-Changin'*. The songs bristled with a topical fervor that made them impossible to ignore. Dylan was something of a musical social commentator as he wrote song after song about the most heated social issues of the day.

Whether Dylan seized upon such song topics as civil rights and injustice because he was sincerely concerned or merely as a means to advance his career is not altogether known. But for whatever reason, Dylan mastered the concept of folk protest music.

Dylan was a folksinger's folksinger in the early sixties, and most of his songs were presented in traditional folk music fashion—with acoustic guitar, harmonica, maybe the addition of a stand-up bass for certain tunes. But as rock & roll grew by leaps and bounds in 1964 and 1965 with the advent of the Beatles and other British groups, Dylan found himself fighting the urge to experiment with electric instruments.

In the summer of 1965 he could hold back no longer. At the Newport Folk Festival that year—on the same stage where he had won so many supporters and admirers at the 1963 fest—Dylan walked out in front of his audience with an electric guitar. Backed by the Paul Butterfield Blues Band, he broke into "Maggie's Farm" and made history. Although the boos and shouts of "traitor!" echoed off the stage, Dylan broke with tradition and pushed into a brand new area of music. Folk rock had been born.

It was the perfect combination for Dylan. The lyrical depth and coffeehouse warmth of folk and the physical energy of rock gave Dylan the best medium for the songs he was writing at the time. As a result, his three greatest albums—*Highway 61 Revisited, Bringing It All Back Home,* and *Blonde on Blonde*—are from this period.

It was also in 1965 that Dylan began his association with the Hawks, the group that eventually became known simply as the Band. The time Dylan spent with the Band might have been his zenith as a recording and performing artist, for the folk-rock accomplished onstage and in the studio was some of the most richly textured rock music made in the sixties. Dylan was brimming with new ideas and new attitudes concerning pop music, and, with the Hawks supporting him, Dylan was untouchable as a force in American rock.

It's hard to imagine how far Dylan would have gone with the Band or what new path he would have chosen if he had not had a near-fatal motorcycle accident just outside Woodstock, New York, in the summer of 1966. The mishap forced Dylan to retreat from public life and convalesce for over a year. Holed away in Woodstock, he and the Band recorded numerous tracks, many of which would surface first on bootleg albums and later as the much praised *Basement Tapes* in 1975.

But Dylan didn't record a follow-up to *Blonde on Blonde*, his last studio LP prior to his accident, until he decided to go to Nashville, of all places, to make *John Wesley Harding*. Released in 1968 the LP depicted a recuperated Dylan who once again had opted for a new direction. Rock's most intriguing artist had already gone from rock to folk to folk rock and now to country, and each time he shifted the direction of popular music in the process as well.

A subdued, delusive record in the way the songs appeared so basic, lyrically speaking, and yet so complex in terms of allegories and outlaw imagery, *John Wesley Harding* was a landmark record. It helped open the doors to country rock and surely set off the country music fad that swept through rock in the late sixties and early seventies.

From *John Wesley Harding*, Dylan stepped further into country by cutting *Nashville Skyline*, a pure, unfiltered country LP that included a duet with Johnny Cash. It was Dylan's last sixties album and the last one before being beset by a spell of mediocrity that nearly cost him the respect earned as a result of his earlier accomplishments. Listening to, say, *Bringing It All Back Home* and then to *Self-Portrait*, the abominable follow-up to *Nashville Skyline* in 1970, it was, and still is, almost impossible to accept that the same man made both records.

In the seventies and early eighties, Dylan's attempt to regain the power and prestige he possessed in the sixties has been virtually all uphill. Dylan's flirtations with religion, both Christianity and Judaism, and the manner by which he incorporated it into his music hurt his output tremendously. Also to blame was his inability to stir up any new trends or commitments to old ones. Finally, the coming of age of a new generation of rockers who had not known Dylan's incredible sixties legacy firsthand demanded he prove his worth all over again. When he couldn't, more than one fan and critic wrote him off. But just as Dylan seemed truly ready for retirement, he would release a record (*Blood on the Tracks, Infidels*) that would reignite interest in him and his music all over again.

The Freewheelin' Bob Dylan / Columbia / 1962

Freewheelin' contains some of the best protest songs written in the twentieth century. Tunes like "Masters of War," "A Hard Rain's A-Gonna Fall," "I Shall Be Free," "Talking World War III Blues," and the classic "Blowin' in the Wind" popularized the protest lyric and opened up a social awareness in rock never known before. Dylan's voice sounds less whiny than it did on his debut LP, *Bob Dylan* (Columbia / 1961), and both his vocal and guitar delivery are more relaxed and confident. Unlike his first album, which contained only a sampling of original compositions, *Freewheelin'* is all Dylan.

The Times They Are A-Changin' / Columbia / 1964

The Times They Are A-Changin' continues the run of early-sixties Dylan protest songs. Aside from the title song, all of the other protest songs deal with still unresolved social and moral issues and retain an amazing amount of freshness. "The Ballad of Hollis Brown" is simple and stark and one of the most haunting tunes Dylan has ever written. "The Lonesome Death of Hattie Carroll" and "When the Ship Comes In" are both magnificent reflections of Dylan's lyrical genius. Effectively produced by Tom Wilson, *The Times They Are A-Changin'* stands beside *Freewheelin'* as early folk/protest masterpieces.

Another Side of Bob Dylan / Columbia / 1964

Another Side of Bob Dylan is just that. Whereas *Freewheelin'* and *The Times They Are A-Changin'* are steeped in protest and discontent, *Another Side* finds Dylan contemplative and personal. "Ballad in Plain D," a beautifully introspective tune, is too often overlooked when early Dylan classics are recalled. The same holds true for "Spanish Harlem Incident." The more noted songs on the LP—"All I Really Want to Do," "It Ain't Me Babe," "My Back Pages," and "Chimes of Freedom"—were popularized by other artists. Sonny and Cher struck gold with "All I Really Want to Do," the Turtles hit with "It Ain't Me Babe," and the Byrds recorded "All I Really Want to Do" plus "My Back Pages" and "Chimes of Freedom."

Bringing It All Back Home / Columbia / 1965

One of the greatest albums of the sixties, *Bringing It All Back Home* is a landmark record for a number of reasons. The LP unveiled Dylan's electric side for the first time on vinyl. It also

solidified his immense lyrical talents and proved that Dylan's poetic talents could easily stretch beyond the protest lyric. *Bringing It All Back Home* included the timeless "Mr. Tambourine Man," which the Byrds quickly interpreted in a number-one hit version. The album also contained "It's Alright, Ma (I'm Only Bleeding)," "It's All Over Now, Baby Blue," and the wonderfully clever and insane "Bob Dylan's 115th Dream." A must album for anyone even remotely moved by Dylan, folk rock, the sixties, or all of the above.

Highway 61 Revisited / Columbia / 1965

Highway 61 Revisited is essentially an elaboration of the electric style introduced on *Bringing It All Back Home*. "Like a Rolling

Stone," Dylan's first hit single, heads the list of powerful songs here, most of which are hard-edged rockers. *Highway 61* proved that this "new" sound—the merger of acoustic folk with electric rock and blues—wasn't something Dylan would soon abandon.

Blonde on Blonde / Columbia / 1966

Recorded in Nashville and released as a double LP (unheard-of at the time), *Blonde on Blonde* is still widely acclaimed as Dylan's best. Hits like "Rainy Day Women #12 & 35," "I Want You," and "Just like a Woman" graced the set. But tunes such as "Visions of Johanna," "Absolutely Sweet Marie," and "Memphis Blues Again" are the more memorable of the bunch. *Blonde on Blonde* saw Dylan once again express his emotions in love songs not always easy to comprehend. The complex imagery and romantic visions that run back and forth in many of *Blonde on Blonde*'s songs occasionally shroud Dylan's true intentions but also represent some of his most challenging and mature lyrical work to date. Musically, *Blonde on Blonde* is a joy—with solid playing courtesy of session aces like Charlie McCoy, Kenny Buttrey, and Al Kooper. Perhaps a touch overrated by critics, but a great Dylan album nevertheless.

The Basement Tapes / Columbia / 1975

Although *The Basement Tapes* was released in the mid-seventies, the tracks that comprise this double-record set were previously unreleased demos spruced up and remixed from the days of Dylan's recuperation from the motorcycle accident. The twenty-four tunes contain Dylan and the Band (Dylan sang lead on two-thirds of them; members of the Band, the other third) and artfully reveal how well the two got on together. There's a priceless informality to the songs as Dylan's voice weaves effortlessly around the licks and rhythms, creating a magnificent statement of mid-sixties American rock & roll. *The Basement Tapes* proved what many people thought—that Dylan and the Band made the best one-two combination in pop music.

John Wesley Harding / Columbia / 1968

Dylan liked the results of working in Nashville and recorded *John Wesley Harding* there. The first album Dylan had done since his motorcycle accident, it revealed yet another change of direction. The prominent country flavor of the LP outshone the rock and folk elements. "I Dreamed I Saw St. Augustine," "Dear Landlord," and "I'll Be Your Baby Tonight" flowed effortlessly. Dylan's lyrics were also headed in a different direction: *John Wesley Harding* contains biblical references and symbolism, although the record isn't overtly religious. Included on the album is "All Along the Watchtower," which Jimi Hendrix turned into one of the most forceful rock songs of the late sixties.

Nashville Skyline / Columbia / 1969

Nashville Skyline is an important record for two reasons: It culminated Dylan's incredible sixties output in daring fashion, and it had vast implications for a new, developing genre of pop music, country rock. *Nashville Skyline* went far beyond *John Wesley Harding* in embracing country music. It was a rather adventurous record because the music and the lyrics were so blatantly simple and light. A few standouts are: "Girl from the North Country," sung with Johnny Cash; "Nashville Skyline Rag," a delightful instrumental; and the hit ballad "Lay Lady Lay." There was, however, one more noticeable difference heard on *Nashville Skyline*: Dylan's voice had changed. Gone was the early-sixties scruffiness and the mid-sixties nasality. In their place was a kind of a spruced-up, tinny drone. One critic wrote that Dylan's new voice reminded him of a piece of aluminum.

Bob Dylan's Greatest Hits / Columbia / 1967

Released during Dylan's convalescence from the motorcycle accident, *Greatest Hits* contains only the thinnest of samplings of Dylan's early-sixties accomplishments. There are ten tracks on the LP; all of them are excellent, but there are far too many that were left off the record for it to be of any real value. Recommended for Dylan neophytes only.

Bob Dylan's Greatest Hits Vol. II / Columbia / 1971

A much more comprehensive collection than its predecessor, *Greatest Hits Vol. II* is a two-record set and much more representative of Dylan's greatest work. In addition to the best tracks from *Bringing It All Back Home*, *The Times They Are A-Changin'*, and *Nashville*

Skyline is a nice collection of previously unreleased tracks ("You Ain't Goin' Nowhere," "I Shall Be Released"). A worthwhile LP even for those who own all of Dylan's sixties albums since it brings together his best under one cover.

The Byrds

The Byrds were the first successful folk-rock group. Their neat, melodic blend of folk and rock coupled with the magnetic attraction of Jim (a.k.a. Roger) McGuinn's twelve-string Rickenbacker guitar sound and the group's impeccable vocal harmonies did much to popularize the hybrid music form.

Guitar player/singers McGuinn, Gene Clark, and David Crosby came from folk backgrounds; bass player Chris Hillman had played bluegrass, and Michael Clark had never played the drums until he joined the Byrds. They had all been impressed by Dylan, but it was the Beatles who moved them away from pure folk and toward folk rock.

The Byrds recorded Dylan's "Mr. Tambourine Man" partially because of the Animals' success with "House of the Rising Sun" (which Dylan had not written). Producer Terry Melcher not only convinced the group that "Mr. Tambourine Man" was the one to record but pulled together the jangling guitar sound that became the Byrds' trademark. Number one in 1965, the song had a clean, fresh sound. Gene Clark had written most of the Byrds' early originals, but after "Mr. Tambourine Man," the group recorded more Dylan material. *Mr. Tambourine Man* included Dylan's "All I Really Want to Do," "Spanish Harlem Incident," and "Chimes of Freedom," all done with the same type of arrangement as "Mr. Tambourine Man." "All I Really Want to Do" was the follow-up single, but Sonny and Cher cut their version of it and beat the Byrds in the race up the charts.

The Byrds' version of "Turn! Turn! Turn!," a Pete Seeger folk classic based on a Bible verse, also went to number one. The album by the same name followed in early 1966 and it contained two more Dylan tunes, "The Times They Are a-Changin' " and "Lay Down Your Weary Tune." The Dylan–Byrds connection, however, eventually wore thin. By their third album, *Fifth Dimension*, the Byrds were writing more material and expanding their folk-rock sound. Much of this was due to the departure of Gene Clark, for it forced McGuinn and Crosby to begin composing. The results were startling. "Eight Miles High" predated psychedelia and acid rock with its soaring lead guitar and supposedly pro-drug lyrics. (Clark did contribute to the writing of the song.) With one tune the Byrds transcended the mellow sway of folk rock and pressed ahead in an exciting new direction.

On the next album, *Younger than Yesterday*, Hillman contributed more songs than any other member. "So You Want to Be a Rock 'n' Roll Star," penned by Hillman and McGuinn as a response to the manufacturing of groups like the Monkees, was the record's best track.

The Byrds, it seemed, could do no wrong. But there were problems. Crosby and McGuinn began to disagree about the group and their material. In addition, Crosby had been considering joining the Buffalo Springfield, with whom he played at the Monterey Pop Festival. Hillman and McGuinn then kicked out Crosby, and Gene Clark rejoined the Byrds. He had left the group initially because of his fear of flying; he then said he had conquered his problem, but soon left again. To make matters even worse, in the midst of recording their next album, drummer Michael Clarke quit the group and moved to Hawaii to work in a hotel.

The Notorious Byrd Brothers, completed with sessionmen, was a transitional album that linked the Byrds' folk and psychedelic strains with the country roots Hillman would exploit on *Sweetheart of the Rodeo*. The Byrds' final studio album of the sixties was *Dr. Byrds and Mr. Hyde*. The LP didn't quite restore the Byrds' reputation, though it did contain some truly fine tracks. "This Wheel's on Fire," "Drug Store Truck Driving Man," and "Bad Night at the Whiskey" were highlights. But the LP's cover revealed why the record sounded fragmentary and unsettled: cowboys and spacemen. McGuinn wanted the Byrds to become a spacy, jazz-influenced electronic outfit even though the other members of the group wanted to play country.

The Byrds moved into the seventies not knowing exactly what direction they would follow. *The Ballad of Easy Rider* was a hit album in 1970, as was *Untitled*, a two-record live/studio set. But these records were followed by *Byrdmaniax* and *Farther Along*, two LPs best forgotten, and some greatest-hits packages.

Following the deaths of guitarist Clarence White, who was killed by a drunken driver, and Gram Parsons, who died of heart failure, the group's tenure as one of the most influential American rock bands came to an end.

Mr. Tambourine Man / Columbia / 1965

Mr. Tambourine Man was folk rock's first great album by a group or artist other than Dylan. The songs kind of lilt rather than chug along, and there's a sweet country warmth to the vocals and guitars. The record had a tremendous impact on future folk rockers; it set the guidelines for the whole genre. Only Dylan's *Highway 61 Revisited* and *Bringing It All Back Home* packed as much significance around 1965.

Turn! Turn! Turn! / Columbia / 1966

A continuation of what was heard on *Mr. Tambourine Man*, complete with the same glowing results. On songs such as "Lay Down Your Weary Tune" and "He Was a Friend of Mine," producer Terry Melcher and the Byrds polish up the guitar-heavy deliveries of the song without killing off the folky spirit.

Fifth Dimension / Columbia / 1966

Fifth Dimension is a striking departure from the previous two albums. The songs' themes are more adventurous, and the Byrds take risks melodically, and set their own code of hipness with the psychedelic songs "Eight Miles High," "Mr. Spaceman," and "Captain Soul." The folk roots begin to become less of a factor in the Byrds' song makeup although the folk-rock guitar sound is still evident.

Younger than Yesterday / Columbia / 1967

What the Byrds set out to do on *Fifth Dimension*—expand their scope and sound and rid themselves of what was left of their folkie image—is completed here. "So You Want to Be a Rock 'n' Roll Star" is a veritable masterpiece.

Sweetheart of the Rodeo / Columbia / 1968

Sweetheart of the Rodeo was as important an album as *Mr. Tambourine Man*, but for a different reason. Whereas *Mr. Tambourine Man* ushered in folk rock, *Sweetheart of the Rodeo* paved the way for the advent of country rock. Gently presented in classic Byrds fashion, the record brought a clarity and a fresh new approach to rock & roll. A Dylan tune, "You Ain't Goin' Nowhere," plus "Pretty Boy Floyd," "I Am a Pilgrim," and "Blue Canadian Rockies" make this record excellent.

Simon and Garfunkel

One of the most commercially successful acts to come out of folk rock was Simon and Garfunkel. Paul Simon and Art Garfunkel, childhood buddies, had been playing together and occasionally recording for a number of years when their single "Sounds of Silence" unexpectedly shot to number one in 1965. A delicate yet penetrating account of isolation, the song epitomized the burgeoning popularity of folk rock. Simon and Garfunkel's voices blended beautifully and, set against an acoustic guitar backdrop which was often elaborated with bits of electric guitar, bass, and drums, the instrumentation accented lyrics that some called rock poetry.

Simon was the duo's songwriter. A former English literature and law school student, he was a sophisticated composer whose meticulously crafted images and notions of life, love, and alienation came across sounding cerebral without being pretentious. Almost at once Simon was cheered as one of rock's great new songwriters, a claim which tunes such as "Sounds of Silence," "I Am a Rock," "Homeward Bound," "Dangling Conversation," and the LPs *Bookends* and *Bridge Over Troubled Water* bore out remarkably well.

Toward the end of the sixties, however, Simon and Garfunkel began to drift apart. Garfunkel got involved in acting, due in part to the relatively minor role he played in the duo (he merely sang, while Simon sang, wrote, produced, and arranged the songs and played guitar), while Simon continued with his deep interest in music. In 1971 the two went their separate ways.

Paul Simon recorded a number of excellent solo albums in the seventies that are certainly worth investigating, most notably *Paul Simon, There Goes Rhymin' Simon*, and *Still Crazy After All These Years*. None of Art Garfunkel's recording efforts in the seventies matched Simon's.

Throughout the seventies and early eighties Simon and Garfunkel occasionally performed and recorded together. The highlight of their reunions came in 1981 when the two gave a free concert in New York's Central Park. *The Concert in Central Park*, a delightful two-record set, resulted from the performance and is a must for Simon and Garfunkel aficionados.

Sounds of Silence / Columbia / 1966

Wednesday Morning 3 A.M. was the duo's initial release and contained the original version of "Sounds of Silence," but the song was spiced up in the folk-rock vein for this album, and it is the version that became the number-one single. Also included: "I Am a Rock," one of the follow-up singles to "Sounds of Silence," "Richard Cory," a song based on the Edward Arlington Robinson poem by the same name; and "April Come She Will."

Parsley, Sage, Rosemary and Thyme / Columbia /1966

The soft-rock sensibility heard on *Sounds of Silence* is even more obvious here. The LP had two hit singles—"Homeward Bound" and "The Dangling Conversation"—in addition to social commentaries like "A Simple Desultory Philippic (Or How I Was Robert McNamara'd into Submission)" and the experimental "7 O'clock News/Silent Night."

Bookends / Columbia / 1968

The first of two classic Simon and Garfunkel LPs, *Bookends* is, as critic Dave Marsh wrote in *The New Rolling Stone Record Guide,* a "kind of snapshot album of American life in the late sixties." Simon's songs are meaningful and far-reaching, and the production wonderfully eloquent. "Mrs. Robinson" is noteworthy because it was the theme song from the movie *The Graduate,* but "Save the Life of My Child," "Old Friends," and "America" are just as memorable.

Bridge Over Troubled Water / Columbia / 1970

It was two years from *Bookends* to the release of the duo's other classic LP, *Bridge Over Troubled Water,* but the time and effort Paul Simon put into writing its songs and perfecting the arrangements were well spent. *Bridge Over Troubled Water* was a landmark album for three reasons. First, it was a commercial blockbuster, ranking with Carole King's *Tapestry* (1971) as the era's biggest-selling records. Second, the title song was Paul Simon's greatest artistic triumph. (Other notable tracks: "The Boxer," "El Condor Pasa," "Keep the Customer Satisfied," "Cecilia.") Finally, the LP celebrated the success—and parting—of the duo in splendid fashion.

Donovan

Donovan Leitch was England's answer to Bob Dylan in 1965. Strongly influenced by American folk music, Donovan imitated the common-man poetic vision of Woody Guthrie and Dylan and blended it with his own Celtic folk heritage. During the folk-rock boom he recorded two fine albums, *Fairy Tale* and *Catch the Wind*, which solidified his appeal as England's best folk balladeer of the mid-sixties.

But compared with Dylan's stark, strained voice, Donovan was a nightingale whose untainted, innocent vocals and soft, warm melodies lacked impact and grit. Nevertheless Donovan's catchy songs and sunny deliveries made him a fairly popular figure in both England and America. Songs like "Universal Soldier," "Colours," and "Catch the Wind" were particular favorites.

As folk rock began to wane, however, Donovan abandoned his scruffy, Dylan-ized image and dove headfirst into flower power. In no time he embodied all the trappings and hues of a psychedelicized love child—which, not surprisingly, suited his vocals and songs quite naturally. Donovan scored big with hits such as "Sunshine Superman," "Mellow Yellow," "Hurdy Gurdy Man," and "Atlantis."

Donovan's music suffered, however, as his fascination with flowery bliss and mysticism grew tedious. By decade's end, he had faded into obscurity.

Fairy Tale / Hickory / 1965
Catch the Wind / Hickory / 1965
Golden Hour of Donovan / Pye / 1965

These records are out of print but occasionally available as British imports. All three contain Donovan's best songs—simple, uncluttered folk and folk-protest tunes in the tradition of Dylan and Guthrie, *Fairy Tale's* "To Try for the Sun," "Sunny Goodge Street," "Jersey Thursday," and Buffy Ste.-Marie's "Universal Soldier" are standouts. The same can be said for *Catch the Wind's* title song, plus "The Alamo" and "Ramblin' Boy." *Golden Hour* is an excellent round-up of Donovan's best folk efforts; it includes the cream of *Fairy Tale* and *Catch the Wind* and some other gems like "The War Drags On" and "Hey Gyp (Dig the Slowness)."

Wear Your Love Like Heaven / Epic / 1967

Perhaps the most representative sample of Donovan's flower-power recordings, *Wear Your Love Like Heaven* was also part of a deluxe two-album set that included *A Gift from a Flower to a Garden*. The songs and themes are obviously dated, even wimpy, by today's standards. But tunes like "Mad John's Escape," "Someone Singing," and "Little Boy in Corduroy" help illustrate how fluffy some aspects of rock got in the late sixties.

Donovan's Greatest Hits / Epic / 1969

A standard "best of" LP that sums up Donovan's sixties achievements without getting excessive. Included are all the big pop-chart hits that are best remembered today—"Sunshine Superman," "Mellow Yellow," etc.

The Buffalo Springfield

The Buffalo Springfield was a pivotal group in American rock, for not only did it seed such major groups as Crosby, Stills and Nash; Crosby, Stills, Nash and Young; Poco; and Loggins and Messina, but the Springfield tied together the essential elements of folk rock and helped introduce the concept of country rock.

The lineup was superb: Richie Furay on rhythm guitar and vocals; enigmatic Canadian folkie Neil Young on first lead guitar and some vocals; Steven Stills, a folkie with a rock & roll heart, playing second lead guitar and sharing the lead vocals with Furay; Dewey Martin, formerly of the Dillards, playing drums; and first Bruce Palmer, then Jim Messina, playing bass. Stills and Furay were the mainstays of the Buffalo Springfield. Their voices, clean and sweet, and their jangling guitars seemed to drive the Springfield's songs, while Young's soaring leads gave the band a unique emphatic intensity.

That the Buffalo Springfield lasted only two years (1966–1968) surprised no one. Stills and Young were competitors and clashed constantly. By the time the group's third and final album was released, its members had parted company and the Buffalo Springfield was over. Soon afterward, Stills teamed up with David Crosby and Graham Nash to form one of America's first supergroups, Crosby, Stills and Nash; Richie Furay and Jim Messina founded

STEREO SD33-226

Buffalo Springfield Again

Courtesy of Atco Records

Poco, one of the first great country-rock outfits; Neil Young embarked on a solo career with help from the band Crazy Horse; and Dewey Martin futilely attempted to keep the Buffalo Springfield name alive with different members.

Buffalo Springfield / Atco / 1966

The group's debut album includes its 1967 Top Ten hit, "For What It's Worth," plus Stills's "Sit Down, I Think I Love You" and Young's "Nowadays Clancy Can't Even Sing." The band's folk roots are more evident here than on the next two albums, but so is a genuine rock quality that routinely overwhelmed the less forceful folk strains.

Buffalo Springfield Again / Atco / 1967

Stills and Young put their personal rivalry to good use on *Buffalo Springfield Again*, the band's finest album. The musicianship is remarkably robust, and the solo work enlightening. Young's "Mr. Soul" and Stills's "Rock 'n' Roll Woman" are the jewels.

Last Time Around / Atco / 1968

On *Last Time Around* the magic first heard on *Buffalo Springfield Again* was fragmented into twelve separate songs, each with its own life force and direction. Richie Furay's "Kind Woman" is a wonderful country track that he later made popular with Poco. "I Am a Child," Young's haunting tune, is equally memorable. Yet the enthusiasm of *Again* is noticeably absent. On *Last Time Around* it was more a case of each musician in the band delivering and then walking out.

Buffalo Springfield / Atco / 1973

This two-record anthology does an admirable job of defining the group's musical wealth and importance. The twenty-three tracks include a previously unreleased nine-minute version of "Bluebird." Almost half the songs are Stills's, eight are Young's, and three are Furay's. Together they represent the very best of a band that was way ahead of its time.

The Lovin' Spoonful

The Lovin' Spoonful emerged from the New York City folk scene in the mid-sixties. John Sebastian and Zal Yanovsky were originally with a folk group called the Mugwumps that included Denny Doherty and Cass Elliot, later of the Mamas and the Papas. Sebastian, who wrote most of the group's best songs, was also responsible for the Spoonful's eclectic sound which combined rock and pop with liberal scatterings of jug-band music, folk, and country. It was a richly textured, tasteful sound, and in the mid-sixties inspired the East Coast folk-rock boom. The group recorded happy-go-lucky, easy-flowing songs sweetened by an innocent, likable charm. The Spoonful's very best song, "Do You Believe in Magic," epitomized its rather unique approach. Sebastian was an interesting, if not pure,

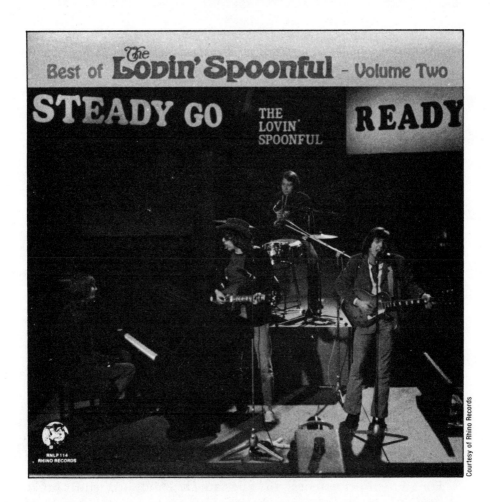

vocalist, and when he sang the lyrics came through right on target. "Daydream" was a lazy, even goofy, song but a big hit, as were "You Didn't Have to Be So Nice," "Rain on the Roof," and "Did You Ever Have to Make Up Your Mind." The Spoonful's most potent tune was "Summer in the City," a forceful, aggressive number that was more rock than folk rock. The band lasted until 1968. John Sebastian then pursued a solo career.

The Best of the Lovin' Spoonful / Buddah / 1976

Even though all the group's sixties albums are out of print, the Lovin' Spoonful's best music is well preserved on this LP. It contains the group's big hits, while *The Best of the Lovin' Spoonful, Volume*

Two, consists of obscure but worthwhile album tracks from those deleted albums. The Buddah record is a no-frills package of twelve cuts ("Do You Believe in Magic," "Daydream," "Summer in the City," etc.) and a few dumb lines about how legendary the Spoonful is.

The Best of the Lovin' Spoonful, Volume Two / Rhino / 1984

Anything of import that was not included on the Buddah LP is here. Fourteen selections in all (including two Sebastian gems, "Younger Girl" and "Darling Be Home Soon"), *Volume Two* is the perfect complement to the above LP and comes with liner comments by John Sebastian.

The Fugs

The Fugs were a bunch of beatniks from New York City's East Village who tried to come to terms with the sixties in the most offensive and obscene manner possible. Most of their songs were pornographic, left-of-center satires aimed at any and all oppression, complete with sound effects and all-around weirdness. Songs like "Dirty Old Man," "Coca-Cola Douche," and "Kill for Peace" were downright rude. Yet "Boobs a Lot," "Slum Goddess," and "I Feel like Homemade Shit" were hilarious. The Fugs were hardcore protest folk rockers. Nothing was sacred. As one writer put it, "the Fugs pissed on everything."

For all their perverseness, the Fugs attacked and successfully broke down many barriers, forging the trail for groups like the Mothers of Invention and Captain Beefheart and His Magic Band. The two principal Fugs, Ed Sanders and Tuli Kupferberg, were poets and wrote most of the material. Despite songs sung off-key with out-of-tune instruments aching in the background, the lyrics—often twisted and demented—were indeed sharply phrased and poetically sound. Songs like "Nothing," "Frenzy," and "Virgin Forest" bear this out well.

The Fugs faded out as the more musically ambitious Frank Zappa and his Mothers of Invention got a grip on satire and fully incorporated it into rock in the last years of the decade. From that point on, rock's best satire would hail from the West Coast.

The Fugs' First Album / ESP / 1965

This was a pretty heavy album for 1965. There's a lot of hilarity and biting satire: "Slum Goddess," "Supergirl," and "I Couldn't Get High." But the most popular tune of the record was Steve Weber's "Boobs a Lot." Although the Holy Modal Rounders' version attracted more attention, the Fugs' interpretation was rawer and funnier. You won't find yourself playing this more than a couple of times a year, but when you do it works wonders for your sense of humor.

The Fugs / ESP / 1966

Ed Sanders, Tuli Kupferberg, and company thoroughly savage a good many of society's big hangups. "Dirty Old Man," about a pervert, is a bit too much. But "Kill for Peace" is a great mockery of war and is all too relevant.

The Youngbloods

The Youngbloods used folk rock as a base but regularly experimented with strains of jazz, country, R&B, and San Francisco-inspired rock. (After moving from Boston, the group settled near San Francisco.) The group consisted of Jesse Colin Young, bass and vocals; Jerry Corbitt, guitar and vocals; Joe Bauer, drums; and Banana Levinger, guitar and keyboards. Their sound was airy and mellifluous. Young's voice was just too silky smooth and soft to be anything else, even when the group tried to sound like a hardened R&B band.

The Youngbloods recorded two notable albums and one anthem-like single before they folded. Both *The Youngbloods* and *Elephant Mountain* were critical successes, but sold disappointingly. "Get Together," a tune written by Dino Valenti of Quicksilver Messenger Service, first appeared on *The Youngbloods* in 1967. In 1969 it was rediscovered and became a theme song for the counterculture.

Best of the Youngbloods / RCA / 1970

Although the Youngbloods' LPs are available to some extent, none is really either that good or that necessary. Just about all of what the

Youngbloods cut that was worthwhile is here, even if this record sounds a bit too sixties-ish and the songs sort of float around.

Fairport Convention

Fairport Convention provided England with much of that country's best folk rock. But, despite its popularity at home, the band barely achieved cult status here. *Fairport Convention*, the group's self-titled American debut, was released in 1969, by which time the folk-rock boom was giving way to country rock. Also Fairport based its repertoire on traditional British folk music, which many Americans found hard to understand and enjoy. Nevertheless, Fairport Convention's layers of subtle instrumentation plus the folkish melodies that Richard Thompson and Sandy Denny included in their originals made Fairport's first couple of albums fresh and fascinating. Lead singer Denny was a good, not great, vocalist. A soothing motherly charm was her best quality. Thompson and, for a short time, Ian Matthews also sang lead. But with old members departing and new ones always trying to fit in, the band never really jelled. By 1969, two years after its founding, two of the band's most important members—Matthews and Denny—and bassist Ashley Hutchings and drummer Martin Lamble had gone.

Unhalfbricking / Island / 1969

Three of the eight songs on this British import are Dylan songs: "Percy's Song," sung by Ian Matthews; "Million Dollar Bash" and "If You Gotta Go, Go Now," the latter sung in French. All three are fresh interpretations that hold up remarkably well. "Cajun Woman," a Thompson tune, and Denny's beautiful "Who Knows Where the Time Goes" (popularized in the United States by Judy Collins) make this LP one of Fairport's most engaging records.

The Band

It's difficult to categorize the Band. It fits into no single genre, for no group in rock had ever recorded music similar to the Band's before *Music from Big Pink* and no one has done so since.

The Band's story is somewhat of a contradiction. Their music was intensely original and purely American, yet only Levon Helm was an American; the other four members (Robbie Robertson, Rick

Danko, Richard Manuel, and Garth Hudson) were Canadian. The Band's roots were in folk, traditional rock & roll, rockabilly, country, blues, and rhythm & blues, and its songs echoed these influences marvelously. Its members had played together since 1959, yet they got their first recording contract nearly ten years later, partially because they were Bob Dylan's backup group.

Before being hired as Dylan's supporting musicians, they were the Hawks and backed up Arkansas rocker Ronnie Hawkins. Hawkins and the Hawks toured incessantly. Finally Helm and the others split from Hawkins. Known mostly as Levon and the Hawks, the group played dives and beer joints until they were discovered by Dylan. With the exception of Helm, the group backed Dylan on his 1965–66 world tour during which he made the jump from playing solo acoustic folk to playing electric folk rock with a band. Some fans approved; some did not. Helm was unwilling to take the booing and the abuse, so he quit.

After the tour, the Band moved to upstate New York, invited Helm to rejoin them, and set out to record on their own.

Robertson and Manuel wrote most of the material on their brilliant debut, *Music from Big Pink*. Dylan, however, cowrote two songs and contributed his tender ballad "I Shall Be Released." The music was earthy and wonderfully rich. The album was eagerly received by the blossoming rock press but failed to sell well. The Band toured the States, played Woodstock, and released *The Band* in 1969. Like the first record, *The Band* emphasized tradition, the simple life, and family, and offered beautiful pastoral glimpses of down-home America. A rugged individualism permeated both records, but on *The Band* the group hit all the right chords and sang all the right words. It was a masterpiece, pure and simple, and remains one of the greatest rock & roll albums.

The Band continued touring and recording until 1976, when its members called it quits in San Francisco with a farewell concert from which the documentary film *The Last Waltz* was made. Guest appearances by Dylan, Muddy Waters, Eric Clapton, Neil Young, and Van Morrison, among others, made *The Last Waltz* and the Band's last concert a huge success. In between *The Band* and *The Last Waltz* soundtrack were the seventies LPs *Stage Fright, Cahoots, Moondog Matinee, Northern Lights—Southern Cross,* and *Islands,* each first-rate and worth checking into.

Since *The Last Waltz* the Band has re-formed but without Robbie Robertson.

Courtesy of Capitol Records

Music from Big Pink / Capitol / 1968

Two things separate this LP from all that came before it. One is the instrumentation: All the members except Robertson jumped from instrument to instrument (such was their musical skill), giving the impression that there are at least a dozen players. Helm, for instance, played drums one way; Manuel played them another. That made the bottom sound and beat of the tracks different and unique each time.

The other element is the Band's unbelievable tightness. There's not a botched line or a shallow spot anywhere. The top tracks include the mesmerizing "The Weight," a one-of-a-kind organ rocker, "Chest Fever," and the poignant "I Shall Be Released."

The Band / Capitol / 1969

The Band is as great an album as *Sgt. Pepper* or *Beggar's Banquet*. The songs are crisper and more insightful than those on the debut. There's a timeless quality here that few, if any, other sixties rock & roll albums possess. "The Night They Drove Old Dixie Down" exudes American history and rural Southern tradition. "Rag Mama Rag" is a study in instrumentation; many things are going on, and yet it all comes together. "Up on Cripple Creek" is backwoodsy and light, but "King Harvest" is serious and poetic. All in all, an American landscape set to music.

11
SAN FRANCISCO
New Sounds, New Directions

Contrary to popular belief, there was no single San Francisco Sound in the mid- and late sixties. *Sounds*, yes. But what went on in the Bay Area was, musically speaking, far too mercurial ever to be lumped under one general description. Case in point: The music of the Grateful Dead, one of San Francisco's earliest and most popular bands, was a far cry from the music of the Jefferson Airplane, one of its most successful. What the Airplane played was miles from what Country Joe and the Fish were playing over in Berkeley. And no one was playing anything like what came from It's a Beautiful Day or Santana.

The common denominator was the city itself, a place that traditionally endorsed a free-spirit mentality and tolerated the artsy, the absurd, the freaky. With a history of permissiveness that stretched back to the Gold Rush, San Francisco was ripe for what happened there, musically and culturally, from 1965 to 1969.

In addition to calling San Francisco home, these bands also shared a desire to do things differently, to go beyond the traditional boundaries of pop music and rock & roll. Most of the groups disregarded the idea of Top Forty hit singles and ridiculed rock music as big business. There was also a commitment to the community, and many San Francisco groups routinely played free concerts and benefits, building up strong local followings along the way.

The term "acid rock" was tagged onto a number of San Francisco bands, and rightfully so. There's no question that the widespread use of LSD and other hallucinogenic drugs had a profound effect on the music. Musicians had always flirted with drugs, but never quite like this. Playing while being zonked on acid or speed led to long, shapeless soloing and unbearably long jam sessions. Ten-, twenty-, even thirty-minute solos were not uncommon, nor were all-night jams. Actually such indulgences were standard for many San Francisco groups, and they had a lasting effect on rock in general.

There was also a psychedelic code that stated music was something you *experienced* rather than merely listened or danced to. This code was the result of the famous "acid tests" held in the days when LSD was legal. With the aid of acid and psychedelic light shows, a person could penetrate the inner dimensions of the music and become part of it. At least that was the theory.

The Grateful Dead used its folk, jug-band, and bluegrass roots to good use. Steve Miller, despite his solid blues background, often sounded British. Janis Joplin and Big Brother and the Holding Company started and ended with the blues. Creedence Clearwater Revival took from rockabilly, Chuck Berry, and Elvis Presley to create a new salt-of-the-earth rock sound. Santana used Latin and jazz elements; It's a Beautiful Day's David LaFlamme played classical violin.

San Francisco was a melting pot of contemporary music, and just after the Monterey Pop Festival in June 1967, which showcased all of the Bay Area's major bands, many of them had recording contracts. In one way, the festival was the beginning of the end. Money and travel outside California entered into the picture. The innocence departed and the unusually close relationship most bands shared with their followers collapsed.

RECOMMENDED ARTISTS

The Grateful Dead

The Grateful Dead was the first San Francisco band to play acid rock. Supported primarily by author Ken Kesey (*One Flew over the*

Cuckoo's Nest) and Owsley, the Bay Area's original LSD entrepreneur, the Grateful Dead supplied the music for most of the acid tests sponsored by Kesey's Merry Pranksters. Essentially these were community turn-ons before the drug became illegal.

The Dead evolved from the Warlocks in 1966. Jerry Garcia and Bob Weir were the guitarists, Phil Lesh played bass, Pigpen McKernan was the organ player, and Bill Kreutzmann was the drummer. Together they brought into the group bluegrass, jug-band, country, and blues influences, and from the start, they were San Francisco favorites. A sense of community spirit embodied the band, and there was an honest commitment to advance the hippie lifestyle. The Dead played countless free concerts and had a strong local following.

The Dead's early years as a band were spent trying to get a handle on its music amid all the activity going on in the Haight-Ashbury section of San Francisco, especially in the summer of 1967, the Summer of Love. The band was casual when it came to the music it would play and how it would play it. As musicians go, Garcia was never an exceptional guitarist, but he was more proficient than his detractors claimed. His main trouble was he simply didn't know when to quit playing (and still doesn't). The others were more than adequate. Excessive drug taking, however, warped their sense of how their songs should sound on vinyl. The Dead remain, first and foremost, a performing band. It's onstage that its marathon meanderings make sense.

Even though the Dead played the Monterey Pop Festival, Woodstock and other rock fests, it remained pretty much a San Francisco band until 1970, when it recorded its two best studio LPs: *American Beauty* and *Workingman's Dead*. Songs like "Uncle John's Band" and "Casey Jones" off *Workingman* and "Truckin'," "Sugar Magnolia," and "Friend of the Devil" were crisp country rockers. *The Grateful Dead, Anthem of the Sun*, and *Aoxomoxoa* were strictly for fans.

The Grateful Dead has been subjected to abuse and criticism, yet it has endured as an American rock & roll institution. Through the seventies and eighties the Dead relied almost exclusively on its fervent following, the Dead Heads, for support. With the Dead Heads' unflinching dedication, the band never needed to push beyond the status quo—and never has. Of all the bands to survive the sixties, the Dead has progressed the least.

The Grateful Dead / Warner Bros. / 1967

There's not much in the way of flashy musicianship or focused songs on the Dead's debut LP. But it has a wonderful timepiece quality about it. "The Golden Road (to Unlimited Devotion)," "Cream Puff War," and "Morning Dew" have a colorful Haight-Ashbury feel to them, and Pigpen's organ riffs give the tunes flair. Basically, *The Grateful Dead* is rough on all fronts, but it's worth listening to once or twice a year, if only to stir up old memories.

Skeletons from the Closet / Warner Bros / 1974

The usual best-of collection, this contains a couple of things each from *The Grateful Dead* and *Aoxomoxoa*, but the best tracks are from *American Beauty* and *Workingman's Dead*. It's a good record for those not serious enough to actually *own* any of the Dead's studio or live LPs.

Quicksilver Messenger Service

In its original form, Quicksilver Messenger Service was more conscious of and more successful with extended jams and long, roving guitar solos than most other San Francisco bands. Guitarist John Cipollina provided much of the solo action while Gary Duncan backed him up on rhythm and the occasional second lead. Quicksilver's initial impetus was to think solo instead of vocal, or so it seemed. It wasn't such a bad idea since no one in the group could sing better than Cipollina played.

The original group—Duncan and Cipollina, David Freiberg on bass and vocals, and Greg Elmore on drums—released two laudable albums before shifting gears under singer Dino Valenti's domain. The self-titled debut, released in 1968, contained folksinger Hamilton Camp's "Pride of Man," redressed in a rock vein, and Duncan and Freiberg's "The Fool," a popular concert tune. *Happy Trails*, considered by many to be Quicksilver's most memorable album, was mostly a live record and highlighted Cipollina. *Shady Grove*, also released in 1969, was less a Quicksilver LP and more a display of British keyboards ace Nicky Hopkins's ability to dominate both a record and a band. His tenure with Quicksilver, however, was short-lived, and his exit led the way for ex-folkie Valenti, who had been released from prison after serving time on a drug rap, to assume control of the band. Valenti had written two vintage sixties songs, "Hey Joe" and "Get Together," and his echoey, whiny vocals later on gave Quicksilver a brand-new sound. Such early-seventies albums as *What about Me, Just for Love,* and *Comin' Thru* are lyrically and socially a bit more aware, thanks to Valenti. By 1973 Quicksilver folded due to personnel changes and an inability to shake off its outdated image.

Quicksilver Messenger Service / Capitol / 1968

John Cipollina was among the top San Francisco guitarists, and his work is featured here. This debut LP contains "Pride of Man," one of the strongest studio tracks that the pre-Valenti Quicksilver recorded.

Happy Trails / Capitol / 1969

Once again it's Cipollina in the limelight. The soloing, however, doesn't sound pretentious, indulgent, or boring, as some records from the period do. Some of the LP was recorded live at the Fillmores East and West. "Who Do You Love" and "Mona" stand out, but sound nothing like the originals in their bluesiest form. Though *Happy Trails* sounds a bit dated, it's a representative sample of what rock concerts were like in the sixties.

Anthology / Capitol / 1973

Anthology provides a decent enough overview of the history of Quicksilver under Cipollina and then Valenti. Record one contains tracks from *Quicksilver Messenger Service, Happy Trails,* and *Shady Grove.* Record two takes from the best of Valenti's seventies albums. All of Quicksilver's records that were out of print have been rereleased. Those not interested in them will do fine with *Anthology.*

Janis Joplin

To say that Janis Joplin was the greatest white female blues singer ever would raise little argument. Her accomplishments were legendary. Yet Joplin's career as a working blues/blues-rock artist lasted only four years. She began singing with the San Francisco group Big Brother and the Holding Company in 1966; in October 1970 she was dead of a drug overdose.

After returning to San Francisco from her native Texas, Joplin joined Big Brother, the Avalon Ballroom's house band. From that point on, she sang the blues (as no other white woman did before her); lived the blues (despite her success and stardom, she was unhappy); and died the blues (drugs, alcohol, and cheap sex seemed to dominate her life). Joplin lived hard but sang harder. Her idol and main influence was Bessie Smith. Her ragged, gravelly voice, which would have been irritating were it not for Joplin's emotion and intense realism, was abused by dope and booze. She'd drink Southern Comfort so that she could go beyond the limits of her natural vocal range and then push her voice until it cracked, grew hoarse, and undoubtedly hurt. But the pain didn't seem to matter. What did matter was the moment. The blues was a feeling more than anything else for Joplin, and she sought to embrace it, enhance it, and deliver it to her listeners with every note she sang.

Joplin's big break came at the Monterey Pop Festival. Along with Jimi Hendrix and the Who, Joplin stole the show, and she and Big Brother immediately signed a recording contract with Columbia Records. Their debut, *Cheap Thrills*, a live album recorded at the Fillmore West, became a best-seller in 1968. Eventually internal feuding and a barrage of criticism aimed at the group's lack of musical ability prompted Joplin to go solo. In 1969 she recorded *I Got Dem Ol' Kozmic Blues Again, Mama*, with the Kozmik Blues Band. Loved by some and hated by others, the album contains two classic tracks, "Try" and "To Love Somebody." It was no secret that Joplin was better onstage than in the studio; this at least partially explains why she toured so much and recorded only two studio LPs.

Pearl, her second and final studio album, was recorded in 1970 and released posthumously. It features a new band, Full-Tilt Boogie, and includes Joplin's most remembered song, "Me and Bobby McGee," plus "Cry Baby," "Half Moon," and "Mercedes Benz," a tune she wrote herself. *Pearl* was an excellent record; Joplin seemed in control of her life, and her vocals were more demanding and compelling than ever before. Sadly, she didn't live to enjoy its success or widespread critical acclaim.

Cheap Thrills / Columbia / 1968

This is Joplin's (and Big Brother's) best sixties album. It includes the brilliant "Piece of my Heart" and "Summertime," as well as "Ball and Chain," "I Need a Man to Love," and "Combination of

Courtesy of Columbia Records

the Two." Big Brother's crude performance works beautifully with Joplin's raw sensuality.

Pearl / Columbia / 1971

Even though this album was recorded in the seventies (and thus doesn't fit the format of this book), Joplin was a sixties artist and her blues evolved out of the decade's fascination with the blues. Since *Pearl* is such a great record and much better than *I Got Dem Ol' Kozmic Blues Again, Mama*, it's included here. It's a hard and wonderfully invigorating album, and it contains Joplin's most stirring studio tracks.

The Sons of Champlin

The Sons of Champlin (or simply the Sons, as they were often called) were a particular favorite with San Francisco and Marin County locals. Unfortunately, the band (like It's a Beautiful Day) had no connection whatsoever to acid rock and never benefited from the hype. Formed in 1965 by Bill Champlin, the Sons, along with the Charles Lloyd Quartet, were two of San Francisco's first jazz-rock outfits. But where Lloyd favored "serious" jazz, Champlin rubbed bits and pieces of rock (especially in the rhythm section) with the occasional R&B element to create improvisational jazz riffs and unorthodox melodies. Champlin called on his reed and brass players to do much of the soloing while he handled the vocals and keyboards.

The Sons finally got a recording contract with Capitol Records and in 1969 released a two-record set called *Loosen Up Naturally*. They made a couple more albums, *The Sons* and *Follow Your Heart*, both interesting, but few listeners outside of San Francisco seemed to appreciate them.

Loosen Up Naturally / Capitol / 1969

This is a tough album to locate; it's been out of print for some time. The best place to look for it would be, of course, in the Bay Area, but it does turn up now and again in used record stores and flea markets elsewhere. The playing here is imaginative and tight, and the jazz-rock instrumentation is better here than on any other Sons record. Interesting tracks include "Black and Blue Rainbow" and "1982-A." Worth tracking down.

The Jefferson Airplane

The Jefferson Airplane embodied the sound of acid rock perhaps better than any other San Francisco band. It was a sound dominated by Jorma Kaukonen's brash, biting lead guitar, Jack Casady's throbbing bass, and Grace Slick's charged vocals.

The Airplane was originally formed by folksinger Marty Balin who envisioned a band similar in design to that of the Lovin' Spoonful or the Byrds. Guitarists Paul Kantner and Jorma Kaukonen and Signe Anderson, the original female vocalist, were all

folkies. Bassist Jack Casady joined, and guitar player Skip Spence was coaxed to try his hand at drums.

The Airplane played at the San Francisco club that Balin was managing, the Matrix, and quickly acquired a large following. The group's debut album, *The Jefferson Airplane Takes Off*, a modest success in 1966, was a fairly gentle folk-rock record with Balin out front. Things changed dramatically when Spence left to play guitar with a band he was forming called Moby Grape and Anderson became pregnant. Spencer Dryden, an experienced drummer, replaced Spence. Anderson's replacement, the former lead singer of the Great Society, Grace Slick, brought with her two songs from the Great Society, "Somebody to Love" and "White Rabbit." These songs became hit singles, provided the foundation for the group's next LP, *Surrealistic Pillow*, and exposed the nation to acid rock. *Surrealistic Pillow* only hinted at the Airplane's folk-rock origins with Balin and Kantner's "Today" and Balin's "Comin' Back to Me." "Somebody to Love," "White Rabbit," "3/5 of a Mile in Ten Seconds," and "Plastic Fantastic Lover" announced the group's next direction.

Slick's aggressive posture in the band and Balin's attempt to regain control led to a growing rivalry that could be heard when the two shared the lead vocals. As the Airplane became a full-fledged hard-rock outfit, Balin's role diminished considerably. *After Bathing at Baxter's* and *Crown of Creation* included more songs by Slick and by Kantner. Eventually, the Balin–Slick feud led to the Jefferson Airplane's breakup.

Before the end, the group released two exceptional albums: *Bless Its Pointed Little Head*, one of the best live LPs from a San Francisco band (right up there with *Happy Trails* from Quicksilver), and *Volunteers*, arguably the group's greatest studio record. These albums captured the Airplane's most striking elements in excellent fashion. The loud, thrashing guitar work was free and improvised yet refined. Slick and Balin each provided some stunning vocals, and the songs they and Kantner wrote were insistent and rousing. The Airplane's moment of glory might have occurred at Woodstock when the band put it all together for the whole world to see and hear.

The Airplane barely made it into the seventies. Balin left the group in 1971; Kaukonen and Casady formed Hot Tuna. Kantner and Slick had a baby, and Kantner recorded *Blows against the Empire*, the first release from the first band to be called the Jefferson Starship. In its most recent incarnation, the Starship is a mainstream rock act that since summer 1984 has continued without Kantner.

Surrealistic Pillow / RCA / 1967

The first commercially successful acid-rock album. As previously mentioned, it contains two classic tracks: "Somebody to Love," a driving, relentless rocker that featured Grace Slick, and the drug-inspired "White Rabbit," which bears sundry little clues about acid and mind expansion. An extremely influential record in 1967.

Bless Its Pointed Little Head / RCA / 1969

Recorded live at the Fillmore East in New York City and the

Fillmore West in San Francisco, *Bless Its Pointed Little Head* depicts the Airplane as one of the finest performing acid-rock bands. There's an intensity that runs through all ten tracks and a powerful, firm precision which is magnified by Kaukonen's and Kantner's guitar work. Slick and Balin rarely sounded better live, and as a whole the band is tight and beautifully efficient on all fronts. Few live albums from this era hold their own today; this one does.

Volunteers / RCA / 1969

With *Bless Its Pointed Little Head* and *Volunteers* out in the same year, 1969 was the zenith of the Jefferson Airplane's recording career. Like other groups that initially began singing about hippies and love, by decade's end the Airplane (as well as the Beatles and Rolling Stones) was writing about revolution. The hopeful, conciliatory "We Can Be Together" balances the strident anger of the title track. "Good Shepherd," "The Farm," and a nice version of "Wooden Ships," made popular by Crosby, Stills and Nash, are included.

Moby Grape

If only Moby Grape could have survived the ton of hype Columbia Records dropped on it in 1967 and the foolish production that marred its second LP, the group might have gone on to greater heights than any other San Francisco band. As it turned out, Moby Grape lasted one year.

Skip Spence and guitarists Peter Lewis and Jerry Miller, bass player Bob Mosley, and drummer Don Stevenson formed the group after Spence left the Jefferson Airplane in 1966. *Moby Grape* was a fine debut record, comprised of well-crafted, country-flavored rockers laced with elements of pop, blues, and a free-spirit attitude. Each of the group's members save Stevenson sang, and the musicianship was impressive.

Columbia recognized the quality of *Moby Grape* and—unbelievably—released more than half the album's songs as singles—all at once. Needless to say, the band suffered miserably for the blunder. It tried to undo the damage with double-record LP *Wow* in 1968. Unfortunately, *Wow* hardly equalled *Moby Grape*; record one consisted of studio tracks, and record two was a long, inconclusive jam with guests Al Kooper and Mike Bloomfield. The album flopped and the group folded.

Moby Grape / Columbia / 1967

Moby Grape would have been much better off had it *not* been part of the San Francisco music scene in 1967. The majority of the songs here, such as "Omaha" and "Hey Grandma," have a San Francisco feel but easily transcend hippie rock and are strong pop tunes. Notice the instrumental proficiency and the balanced contributions. If any one album deserved to be heard in 1967, it was this one.

Country Joe and the Fish

While the Jefferson Airplane was turning on San Francisco crowds with its brand of acid rock, Country Joe and the Fish were doing their thing across the Bay in Berkeley. Ex-folkie/protest singer Joe McDonald and his band, the Fish, openly advocated the use of LSD through mind-bending songs and guerrilla theatrics. McDonald and the Fish were also the Bay Area's most politically aggressive band. McDonald's sharp-witted satire was particularly incisive when it came to the draft, the Vietnam War, and Richard Nixon. The group's lyrics were infinitely more important than its musical accomplishments, which were minimal. But with McDonald performing the role of protest singer and acid dropper, the tunes he wrote and recorded with the Fish were some of the most barbed and sarcastic of the age.

McDonald and the Fish peaked at Woodstock when a half million kids shouted along with McDonald his famous "F-U-C-K" cheer before going into his and his group's most identifiable number, "I-Feel-Like-I'm-Fixin'-to-Die-Rag." Joe and the Fish faded from the scene in 1970.

I Feel Like I'm Fixin' to Die / Vanguard / 1967

I Feel Like I'm Fixin' to Die contains "I-Feel-Like-I'm-Fixin'-to-Die-Rag," McDonald's sarcastic antiwar song that became an anthem for draft resisters, peaceniks, and the New Left. "Janis," a haunting ballad McDonald wrote for Janis Joplin, reveals his quieter side. Another Country Joe and the Fish LP worth checking into is the debut, *Electric Music for the Mind and Body*, which contains another political rocker, "Superbird." Hard to come by.

The Steve Miller Band

Another Texan who found San Francisco to his liking was Steve Miller. Like Joplin, he was into the blues. He moved from Chicago, where he had a blues band with Barry Goldberg (later of the Electric Flag), to San Francisco in 1966. He put together a new band with guitarist and close friend Boz Scaggs. After a performance at the Monterey Pop Festival, Miller's band signed with Capitol Records.

The Steve Miller Band had more success with merging the blues and psychedelia than most. A loose, adventurous spirit permeated his early records. His first album, *Children of the Future*, was recorded in England with producer Glyn Johns, who engineered the Beatles' *Sgt. Pepper* sessions. Johns also produced *Sailor*, *Brave New World*, and *Your Saving Grace*. Each garnered critical approval, but none produced a Top Forty single. More progressive FM radio stations picked up on Miller's music and enabled him to develop a loyal underground following.

The early seventies were bad years for Miller; a broken neck and hepatitis sapped his energy. *Anthology*, a compilation of the first four LPs, was released in 1972 and introduced Miller to a new audience and laid the groundwork for *The Joker* and its number-one title single in 1973–74. *Fly Like an Eagle* followed, and from it, "Rock'n Me" also went to number one. But these catchy pop albums and singles were vastly different from what Miller recorded in the sixties.

Children of the Future / Capitol / 1968

There's more blues here than on any of Miller's other records. Two blues standards, "Fanny Mae" and "Key to the Highway," grace side two. The more interesting material is found on side one and includes "Children of the Future," with its rainbow of moods and mystic meanderings, "Pushed Me to It," clocking in at thirty-six seconds, and "You've Got the Power," at fifty-five seconds. This is the only Miller record Boz Scaggs played on.

Sailor / Capitol / 1968

An ethereal tone is set with "Song for Our Ancestors," followed by "Dear Mary." Because Miller had replaced the traditional blues with more inventive melodies and psychedelic imagery, there's a bit more depth here than on *Children of the Future*. Also included is the 1968 flop which was a 1974 hit, "Livin' in the U.S.A."

Brave New World / Capitol / 1969

Brave New World rocks a bit harder than its predecessors. "Can't You Hear Your Daddy's Heartbeat," "Got Love 'Cause You Need It," and "Space Cowboy" (Miller's popular sequel to "Livin' in the U.S.A.") move faster. Despite a couple of shallow spots, there are more than enough positive, even glowing, elements to make the record important.

Creedence Clearwater Revival

While most of the other San Francisco area bands were caught up in the "psychedelic scene," Creedence Clearwater Revival recorded an eponymously titled debut album of basic, unadulterated rock & roll in 1968. What Creedence played was so traditional in its scope and sound that it really had no business being affiliated with the Bay Area in the late sixties even though all its members were from El Cerrito, just outside of Berkeley.

While other bands emphasized albums instead of singles, open-ended jams instead of tidy studio productions, and big, bountiful guitar solos rather than perfect samples, Creedence's members opted for the standard approach to music and record making. They also dressed and acted like country boys rather than hippies. Creedence consisted of brothers John and Tom Fogerty on guitars, Stu Cook on bass, and Doug Clifford on drums. John Fogerty sang lead and wrote all the songs. The band revolved around him, and when he left in 1972 Creedence limped along, then folded.

In a short time, John Fogerty and Creedence Clearwater Revival made an important contribution to rock & roll. Like Robbie Robertson of the Band, Fogerty painted portraits of America with his lyrics. Coupled with the music he wrote—a first-class blend of Memphis-style rockabilly, traditional rock, and rhythm & blues—Fogerty's songs presented an America almost forgotten in the sixties. He found a certain romantic vision in the land, its people, and its culture. He was particularly fond of writing about the South, that is, New Orleans, Memphis, bayou country, and rivers and riverboats.

Strangely, Creedence was a phenomenally successful Top Forty singles band. Its sound was earthy, economical, and not the least bit flowery or heavy. Because the songs were so well crafted and so much a part of us, Creedence Clearwater Revival's hit singles sold millions of records between 1969 and 1971. "Proud Mary," "Bad Moon Rising," "Down on the Corner," "Travelin' Band," "Up around the Bend," "Lookin' Out My Back Door," and "Have You Ever Seen the Rain" were all in the Top Five, and four other singles made it to the Top Ten. As for albums, Creedence released one in 1968 (*Creedence Clearwater Revival*), three in 1969 (*Bayou Country, Green River, Willy and the Poor Boys*), two in 1970 (*Cosmo's Factory, Pendulum*), and one in 1972 (*Mardi Gras*). In a way, Creedence was the *perfect* American rock & roll band: Its music was respected and critically acclaimed as well as popular and widely accessible, and it sold in the millions. After nine years away from recording and performing, John Fogerty released a widely hailed solo album, *Centerfield*, in 1985.

Bayou Country / Fantasy / 1969

"Proud Mary," Creedence's biggest and best-known song, highlights this very Southern sounding record. "Born on the Bayou" slithers and slips through the grooves like a big ol' swamp snake, "Keep on Chooglin' " boogies, and a raucous version of "Good Golly Miss Molly" moves like an angry boar. This album is a slice of Americana passed through the soul of rock & roll.

Green River / Fantasy / 1969

Green River is quite possibly Creedence's best album. With the title song and "Commotion," both hard-edged rockers; "Bad Moon Rising," a darker view of America; and "Lodi," the greatest song written *about* rock & roll bands, all on the same vinyl, it's hard to imagine anything better (although *Willy and the Poor Boys* comes mighty close). Fogerty's voice is gritty and authentic while brother Tom, Cook, and Clifford show every bit of the ten years of experience they'd had playing with one another.

Willy and the Poor Boys / Fantasy / 1969

Willy and the Poor Boys has both an urban and country feel to it, with "Down on the Corner" and "Poorboy Shuffle" on one hand and "Cotton Fields" and "Midnight Special" on the other. "Fortunate Son" presents a sharp-eyed view of how things really work, and "It Came Out of the Sky" is a straight-ahead rocker. Few American rock & roll bands had as good a year as Creedence did in 1969.

Cosmo's Factory / Fantasy / 1970

The last great Creedence studio album, *Cosmo's Factory* includes "Travelin' Band," "Lookin' Out My Back Door," and "Up around the Bend," all Top Ten chart entries in 1970. Also included: "I Heard It through the Grapevine" and the brilliant "Who'll Stop the Rain." An absolute must album for any Creedence fan as well as those interested in plain old great rock & roll.

Chronicle / Fantasy / 1976

A number of Creedence best-ofs and a couple of live LPs were released in the seventies and early eighties, but this two-record set is the best. Since all four of the sixties studio LPs are still in print (the three mentioned above, plus the band's debut), and the three listed here are exceptional, regard *Chronicle* as a greatest-hits compilation, not as an acceptable substitute for the studio LPs.

Van Morrison

After Van Morrison left Northern Ireland and Them (see Chapter 7, "The First British Invasion"), he eventually settled in the San Francisco area. Although he did much of his important work in the seventies (*Moondance, His Band and the Street Choir, Tupelo Honey,* and *St. Dominic's Preview*) Morrison had a hit single in 1967 with "Brown Eyed Girl," and—more importantly—released his solo debut, *Astral Weeks.*

Even though *Astral Weeks* did not sell very well, the burgeoning rock press hailed it as a masterpiece and critics fell over themselves praising its melodic richness and poetic sophistication. Mass appeal, however, was just around the corner. In 1970 *Moondance* produced a Top Forty single, "Come Running," followed a few months later by the Top Ten hit "Domino" from *His Band and the Street Choir.*

From that point, Morrison became one of the most influential artists of the seventies.

Astral Weeks / Warner Bros. / 1968

It's difficult to pinpoint what makes *Astral Weeks* such a powerful, absorbing album. The lyrics are almost too introspective and their meanings are frequently shrouded in Celtic mythology. But what is obvious—and stunning—is the depth of Morrison's feelings and his intensity. Musically, *Astral Weeks* incorporates nearly every idiom in Morrison's reach, especially Irish folk themes and light, airy jazz. *Astral Weeks* possesses a special warmth that is not soon forgotten, and that alone makes it a classic.

It's a Beautiful Day

David LaFlamme's group, It's a Beautiful Day, had little use for acid rock's guitar screeching. Instead LaFlamme put together an ensemble that played mellow, classically flavored music that empha- sized his violin playing. (LaFlamme, a classically trained musician, first achieved local notoriety with Dan Hicks and the Hot Licks, a country-swing group.) It's a Beautiful Day was the antithesis of the more volatile and aggressive bands such as the Jefferson Airplane and Moby Grape.

The group made two very good albums before succumbing to mediocrity in the early seventies. *It's a Beautiful Day* became an FM favorite because of the song "White Bird." *Marrying Maiden* con- tained more jazz and rock riffs. The group also recorded a well received live album at Carnegie Hall in 1972.

It's a Beautiful Day / Columbia / 1969

In addition to "White Bird," "Hot Summer Day" and "Bombay Calling" are excellent tracks and capture the essence of It's a Beautiful Day's floating instrumentation and light, mellow vocals. LaFlamme handles all the lead vocals, backed by singer/percussion- ist Pattie Santos. Linda LaFlamme, David's wife, plays keyboards.

Marrying Maiden / Columbia / 1970

Marrying Maiden is an interesting concoction of country, jazz, and

rock elements brought together by David LaFlamme's violin. He reveals some of his Hot Licks roots on "Hoedown," but the more enduring instrumental is "Don and Dewey," one of the truly exceptional violin-dominated tracks in rock.

Santana

Santana had been playing its Latin-influenced blues and rock in San Francisco for nearly two years before making its triumphant appearance at Woodstock in 1969. Santana came to the festival as complete unknowns outside the Bay Area but left as one of the year's most exciting new bands. Lead guitarist Carlos Santana's incredible speed and dexterity fueled the group. The deep, polyrhythmic percussion of Jose Chepito Areas and Mike Carrabello added to the band's wild, exotic energy.

Carlos Santana moved from Mexico to San Francisco just as the Bay Area music scene was beginning to come alive. His Santana Blues Band eventually became simply Santana as it turned away from standard blues and toward Latin rock. The uptempos of Santana's originals were ideally suited for playing live; thus the big splash at Woodstock.

That band recorded only *Santana*, its debut, in 1969. But, through the seventies, Carlos Santana and a constantly changing lineup recorded first-class albums that expanded the definition of Latin rock and should be investigated.

Santana / Columbia / 1969

A few weeks after Woodstock, Columbia rushed out the group's debut to capitalize on its new found notoriety. The vibrant, fast-paced songs introduced at the festival were reproduced in the studio with only a minimal loss of energy. "Evil Ways" became the best-selling single of the best-selling album, but nearly every tune on it bristles with intensity and Carlos Santana's guitar virtuosity.

12
BLUES ROCK

Blues and rock have always had a special relationship with each other. Without the blues, there would be no rock & roll. The standard melodic structure of the blues has been borrowed countless times by rock artists. At the same time the blues, especially in the sixties, benefited tremendously from rock's close connection with it. Both in Britain and the United States, rock fans increasingly discovered the wealth of music that came from blues artists such as B. B. King, Muddy Waters, Willie Dixon, and others.

In the post–World War II years, many black Southern rural musicians migrated to Northern cities, where they recorded on small independent labels such as Chicago's Chess Records. This exposed white musicians to the blues more than ever before. It was inevitable that some of them would find the music's earthy richness and authenticity rewarding enough to imitate.

By the mid-sixties there were strong blues scenes not only in Chicago and New York but in Texas, Boston, Memphis (there had always been one in Memphis, of course), and even in some college towns such as Ann Arbor, Michigan. Over in England, London had a particularly vibrant blues scene, though it was based around white admirers of black blues musicians rather than around the original musicians. Chicago, though, was the blues capital. Most of the great urban blues players lived and played there, and when English blues fans sent to the States for records, they sent their orders to the blues labels of Chicago.

The black-white connection in blues resembled a musical fraternity of sorts. Many of the black musicians were much older than the white kids who looked up to them. Except in Chicago, young blacks found the blues too much a reminder of the Jim Crow days; with the rise of a new black awareness, the blues was considered ancient history. Even though the music that young blacks listened to—Motown, Memphis and New York soul, jazz—was derived from the blues, they generally wanted no part of it in its purest form.

But white musicians, among them Paul Butterfield and Mike Bloomfield in Chicago, were eager to take whatever information black blues players would give them. The blues seemed to attract the better white musicians, ones who would become students of the music.

Although Butterfield and Bloomfield formed the Paul Butterfield Blues Band and Al Kooper got the Blues Project rolling in New York, there weren't too many others who actively worked to bring American blues together.

In England, the opposite was true. London was the place to be if you were a blues and R&B player or aspired to become one. The revered musicians there were white blues fans Alexis Korner, Cyril Davies, John Mayall, and Chris Barber, a promoter (among other things) who booked American blues greats to play London venues. Because London's blues scene was so tight, England was in a better position to launch the blues-rock trend of the mid- and late sixties. John Mayall's Bluesbreakers, Cream, Fleetwood Mac, Savoy Brown, and Ten Years After, among others, rose to the top at home and in the United States, while dozens of lesser known but equally committed blues-rock groups—Alexis Korner's Blues Incorporated, Chicken Shack, the Graham Bond Organisation, and Cyril Davies's All Stars, to name a few—were almost unknown here.

Note: Many black blues players who were part of the blues-rock movement aren't included here because of space limitations and the fact that they played more blues than rock. Nonetheless, B. B. King,

Albert King, Freddie King, Junior Wells, Buddy Guy, Luther Allison, Jimmy Dawkins, Muddy Waters, John Lee Hooker, Howlin' Wolf, and many others deserve credit for their immense contributions and should be investigated.

RECOMMENDED ARTISTS

John Mayall

One can't talk about British blues rock without first paying homage to John Mayall. Mayall and his Bluesbreakers were among the first to kick off the sixties blues-rock movement in England. A blues fanatic since his early teens, Mayall had a deep and genuine commitment to the music. He often saw himself as England's blues progenitor; his purpose in life was to carry on and expand upon the blues tradition first set forth by such great American bluesmen as Albert King, Freddie King, Robert Johnson, and Elmore James.

Just about all of England's great blues-rock players passed through the ranks of Mayall's Bluesbreakers, a group first formed in 1963. Its most famous member was Eric Clapton, who joined Mayall after his split with the Yardbirds. But guitarists Mick Taylor (the Rolling Stones), Peter Green (Fleetwood Mac), Jon Mark (the Mark-Almond Band), and Harvey Mandel (Canned Heat) also played with the group, as did bass players Jack Bruce (Cream), John McVie (Fleetwood Mac), and Andy Fraser (Free) and drummers Mick Fleetwood (Fleetwood Mac), Aynsley Dunbar (Mothers of Invention, Journey), Keef Hartley (Keef Hartley Band), and Jon Hiseman (Colosseum). The founders of Fleetwood Mac, Cream, and the Mark-Almond Band met while Bluesbreakers.

As a musician and vocalist, however, Mayall was never as good as those who played with him. He was a fine harp player, but his guitar work and keyboard skills were ordinary, and his voice lacked range and grit. Mayall was, of course, aware of this. But he always encouraged his band members to go as far as they could, and when members outgrew the outfit, they moved on to bigger things with Mayall's blessing. Mayall delved into jazz rock and jazz-blues rock, especially in the late sixties and the seventies, but his LPs never equalled his work with the Bluesbreakers.

Blues Breakers John Mayall with Eric Clapton / London /1966

This is Mayall's and the group's finest moment. Clapton is simply superb, especially on the instrumental tracks "Steppin' Out" and "Hideaway." No other English blues guitarist played with such emotion and total command. Mayall's harmonica riffs provide a balance of sorts, so Clapton doesn't steal the entire show, but in the end it's those riveting guitar solos that are most fondly recalled. A most important album for understanding the roots of the British blues-rock scene.

A Hard Road / London / 1967

What you hear on this record are really the blues sounds that would come from Fleetwood Mac shortly thereafter. Peter Green, one of the original members of Fleetwood Mac, is the lead guitarist; notice the stylistic differences between him and Clapton. Also on the record is Fleetwood Mac bass player John McVie.

Crusade / London / 1968

With Green gone, Mayall picked up the young Mick Taylor to play lead guitar, and the band's sound was affected. Mayall also employed horns here, so there's a different feel, although Mayall made sure that things didn't stray too far from the blues.

The Paul Butterfield Band

The Paul Butterfield Blues Band became part of rock history when it backed up Bob Dylan at the Newport Folk Festival in 1965, the first time Dylan appeared in public playing an electric guitar. Dylan was scorned by many purists for switching from acoustic to electric folk and folk rock. The Butterfield Blues Band only benefited from the exposure.

Band leader/singer/harmonica player Paul Butterfield sang the blues as well as any white kid could. Only longtime Chicago blues players on the South Side of town drew meaner harp licks. As a white blues pioneer who helped ignite the mid-sixties American blues-rock scene, Paul Butterfield's only rival was his guitarist and close friend Mike Bloomfield. The Paul Butterfield Blues Band boasted what was perhaps the best white blues guitar team in the sixties, Bloomfield and Elvin Bishop; a black rhythm section of Sam Lay on drums and Jerome Arnold on bass, both fresh from their stint with Howlin' Wolf; Mark Naftalin on keyboards; and, of course, Butterfield. Not only did the band cut two classic LPs in the middle of the decade— its self-titled debut in 1965 and *East-West* in 1966—but it paved the way for the acceptance of groups like the Blues Project, the Electric Flag, and Canned Heat by rock audiences.

Although the Butterfield Blues Band played the blues, and later blues rock and R&B, with a deep reverence for their black blues mentors, the group rarely imitated its idols. The band cleaned up the blues it recorded; Bloomfield's and Bishop's guitar work had finesse

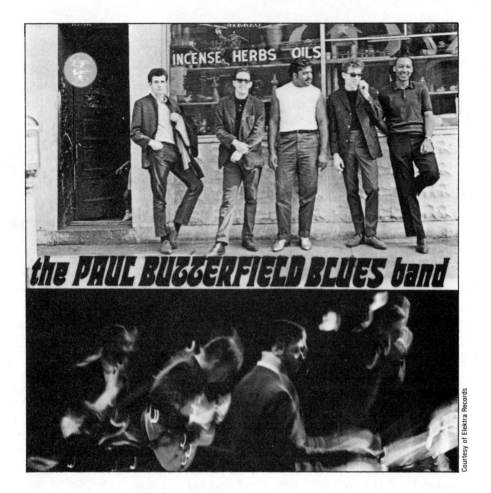

Courtesy of Elektra Records

and polish; and so their albums lacked the roughness inherent in black blues records. Nevertheless, the band was respected by black blues elders. By 1967 Bloomfield had left to form the Electric Flag. Without Bloomfield around, Butterfield went for a bigger sound that included a horn section and was inspired more by R&B. After a couple of albums that sold disappointingly, Butterfield disbanded the group in the early seventies.

The Paul Butterfield Blues Band / Elektra / 1965

Even though this album is more concerned with pure traditional blues than Butterfield's conception of the music, it lays the foundation for his later expansion and enlargement of the blues. Nick

Gravenites's "Born in Chicago" is handled beautifully, as is "I Got My Mojo Working," "Shake Your Money Maker," and a Bloomfield original, "Screamin'." Both Bloomfield and Bishop shine here.

East-West / Elektra / 1966

It's too bad this album is out of print because, along with *The Paul Butterfield Blues Band*, *East-West* is a crucial American blues-rock LP. With guitar riffs that glisten against a steadfast and solid rhythm section, Bloomfield and Bishop distinguish themselves as the best American white blues guitarists of the era (the proof is on "East-West"). Not to be outdone, Butterfield exhibits bolder, more personal vocals than before.

The Blues Project

After the Paul Butterfield Blues Band, the Blues Project was the second most important early blues-rock outfit in the United States. With Danny Kalb and Steve Katz on guitars, Al Kooper on keyboards, Roy Blumenfeld on drums, Andy Kulberg on bass and flute, and Tommy Flanders handling the lead vocals, the Blues Project's lineup was formidable.

The band formed in New York City in 1965 and played blues and folk blues standards in Greenwich Village. Some of these performances are captured on *The Blues Project Live at the Cafe Au Go Go*, one of the better live blues-rock albums of the sixties. Recorded in 1966, the LP includes excellent renditions of such traditional blues as "Spoonful," "Who Do You Love," "Back Door Man," and "Goin' Down Louisiana."

After Flanders left the Blues Project to go solo, Kooper, Kalb, and Katz shared lead vocals. They strongly emphasized mixing traditional blues with folk rock, gentle folk ballads, and R&B, much as they had with Flanders, though with a bluesier approach. By the time the Blues Project released *Projections*, the group had matured enough to handle a bit of experimentation. The colorful "Flute Thing," an instrumental written by Kooper, was an instant classic and remains the group's most memorable tune.

Despite critical praise and a loyal following in New York City, the Blues Project never amounted to much elsewhere. Before the decade was out, Kooper and Katz were gone, only to resurface in Blood, Sweat and Tears, while Kulberg and Blumenfeld formed Seatrain.

Blues Project Live at the Cafe Au Go Go / Verve / 1966

Recorded live in November 1965, this album depicts the earliest incarnation of the Blues Project. Flanders, an ex-folksinger, had a clear voice, and his work on "Catch the Wind," "Violets of Dawn," and "I Want to Be Your Driver" is uplifting. Kalb's and Katz's guitars don't quite equal Bloomfield's and Bishop's, but their efforts certainly come close.

Best of the Blues Project / Verve / 1973

Projections, the Blues Project's most notable studio album, is out of print (although it was reissued in Japan a few years ago). This collection has most of the essentials from that album, however, including "Flute Thing."

Cream

Cream was the most successful blues-rock band to come out of England in the sixties. Its influence was such that only the Beatles and the Rolling Stones had more impact on the continued development and expansion of rock in the latter part of the decade. Guitarist Eric Clapton, bass player Jack Bruce, and drummer Ginger Baker were together only two years, from 1966 to 1968. But their achievements in that time were momentous.

Cream gave birth to the power trio. Despite the minimal instrumentation, the group's music was incredibly sophisticated and full. Much of this was due to the frequent overdubbing of Clapton's guitar and producer Felix Pappalardi's recording techniques.

More than any other band in the sixties, Cream demonstrated just how far blues rock could go. The group transcended the boundaries respected by John Mayall's Bluesbreakers and Paul Butterfield's Blues Band and used the blues as a base from which to pursue hard rock.

Cream also introduced to rock the high art of soloing. Many of Clapton's guitar solos were patterned after the work of black blues guitarists B. B. King, Elmore James, and others. But by playing his leads faster, louder, and with much more energy, he created his own style and became rock's most revered musician. Baker introduced the expanded drum solo. His drum style was extremely busy and aggressive, and he used the double bass drum better than anyone else.

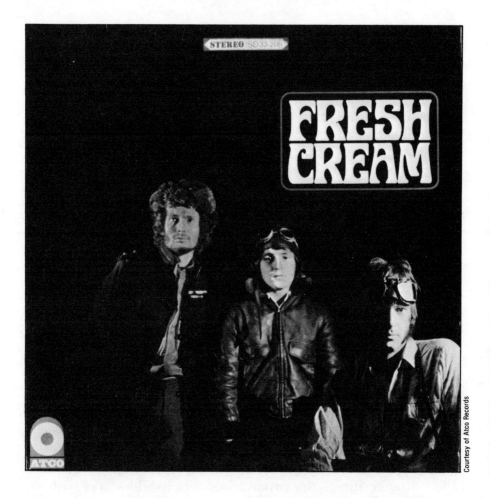

Finally, Bruce's bass playing was probably the most revolutionary of the sixties and early seventies. Frequently, his bass sounded like the second lead guitar in the band. Along with Led Zeppelin, Cream popularized the sweeping, guitar-heavy blues rock that inspired early heavy metal and hordes of imitators in the early seventies on both sides of the Atlantic. (See also Chapter 16, "The Origins of Heavy Metal.")

Cream was not technically the first supergroup. Only Clapton, ex-Yardbird and Bluesbreaker, was an acknowledged star before Cream. Baker and Bruce were highly respected players but little known to the record-buying public in America. Both Bruce and Baker had played in Alexis Korner's Blues Incorporated in the early sixties. From there Bruce became a member of the Graham Bond Organisation, John

Mayall's Bluesbreakers, and Manfred Mann. Baker also had played with the Bond Organisation and in a later version of Blues Incorporated. Cream came together after Clapton jammed with Bruce and Baker.

The band had three best-selling albums, two hit singles ("Sunshine of Your Love" and "White Room"), and could sell out arenas, something not as common in the late sixties as today. But ego problems and drug abuse took their toll. In November 1968 Cream gave its last concert. *Goodbye* was released posthumously.

Fresh Cream / Atco / 1967

Six months after the formation of Cream, *Fresh Cream* was hailed as a major rock album. Clapton's guitar talent would be more obvious on future Cream LPs, but Bruce's cosmic blues vocalizing and his fascinating bass playing are the album's strengths, along with Bruce's ability to take his blues-based songs ("I Feel Free" and "N.S.U.") far beyond the usual blues boundaries. *Fresh Cream* also contains the studio version of "Toad," one of the all-time great drum songs. On that tune and every other one on the record, Baker's drum playing is stunning.

Disraeli Gears / Atco / 1967

The trio's first hit single, "Sunshine of Your Love," is included here. Felix Pappalardi was in charge of production and he emphasized psychedelic colorings over traditional blues elements. On tracks like "Strange Brew" the psychedelic-blues hybrid works with delightful results. The musicianship is again impeccable. Bruce, with lyricist Peter Brown, wrote most of the material.

Wheels of Fire / RSO / 1968

Record one of this double album was recorded in the studio and record two was recorded live. Bruce's "Politician" and an interpretation of Booker T. Jones's "Born under a Bad Sign" accentuate the group's blues-rock roots. But the hit song here is "White Room," another Bruce–Brown composition.

The live record consists of "Crossroads," "Spoonful," "Traintime," and "Toad." Clapton's work on "Crossroads" might very well be the best of any he did with Cream.

Goodbye / RSO / 1969

The success of *Wheels of Fire* prompted the group to use the same studio/live format on this single-record release. The live versions of "I'm So Glad" and "Politician" are excellent and demonstrate Cream's awesome power live. But the real gem is "Badge," which Clapton cowrote with George Harrison. If "Crossroads" features Clapton's best blues guitar, "Badge" features his best rock guitar. His hauntingly poetic lead is not soon forgotten.

Fleetwood Mac

The Fleetwood Mac of the sixties was a far cry from the Fleetwood Mac of the late seventies and eighties. In 1967, when drummer Mick Fleetwood and guitarist Peter Green left John Mayall's Bluesbreakers to form their own band (Bluesbreaker bassist John McVie followed shortly thereafter), they teamed up with guitarist Jeremy Spencer and recorded some of the more interesting blues to come out of England.

At first the group was called Peter Green's Fleetwood Mac. Green and Spencer wrote most of the band's originals and shared lead guitar and lead vocals. Just about all of what they recorded was strongly influenced by Chicago blues. Green's guitar work was very much the product of his intense study of B. B. King. Spencer, on the other hand, lived and breathed Elmore James, and his dashing bottleneck riffs provided a sharp stylistic contrast to Green's playing. Both *Fleetwood Mac* and *English Rose* reveal an intense commitment to blues authenticity and sold considerably well in England.

In 1968 guitarist Danny Kirwan joined, and Fleetwood Mac used the blues as a springboard to record more colorful, perhaps more commercial material. The group expanded its stylistic vocabulary and the results were songs like the haunting instrumental "Albatross," a number-one hit in England in 1968. (Fleetwood Mac was virtually unknown in the states at this time.)

By the end of the sixties, first Green and then Spencer left the group for religious reasons. Kirwan was fired in 1972. Not only was the band besieged with personnel changes but there was an obvious uncertainty about its direction. Despite the confusion, such seventies LPs as *Bare Trees* and *Future Games*, moody, mellow rockers though they were, are excellent. In 1974 Fleetwood Mac added guitarist Lindsey Buckingham and vocalist Stevie Nicks and moved into its hugely successful pop-rock period.

The Original Fleetwood Mac / Sire / 1977

Since the first two Fleetwood Mac LPs, *Fleetwood Mac* and *English Rose*, are out of print, this album is all that's widely available from the band's earliest days. Though the songs are pretty conventional, the playing is inspired. "Drifting," "First Train Home," and "Can't Afford to Do It" give a good account of Fleetwood Mac's strict blues direction before the arrival of Kirwan.

Then Play On / Reprise / 1969

The most intriguing aspect of this album is the way Kirwan turned Fleetwood Mac into a probing, spacey blues-rock outfit. The songs are lush without being excessive, the melodies are less defined than before, and there is much experimentation going on among Kirwan, Green, and Spencer while Fleetwood and McVie supply a very inconspicuous rhythmic backing. The most memorable track is Green's "Oh Well."

Savoy Brown

Blues guitar player Kim Simmonds played much the same role that John Mayall did in the British blues-rock scene but with less spectacular results. The dozens of musicians who passed through his Savoy Brown didn't achieve the same success or fame that Eric Clapton, Mick Fleetwood, or Mick Taylor did after leaving Mayall, although Dave Peverett (guitar), Tony Stevens (bass) and Roger Earl (drums) did go on to form Foghat in the early seventies.

Simmonds was a steady, tried and true blues guitarist who had more fans in the States than in England. He based his guitar style on what Clapton was playing—basic, tough, working-man licks with strong ties to traditional blues.

Savoy Brown was a tireless band; it spent much time on the road, but was never really rewarded for its efforts with great record sales. Still, the group was a cog in the English blues-making machinery in the mid- and late sixties, and so deserves mention here.

The Best of Savoy Brown / London / 1977

Just about all of Savoy Brown's early records are out of print. None is so exceptional that it's worth hunting down, so this compilation will suffice. There are eight tracks here; two of them, "Hell Bound Train" and "Louisiana Blues," are over nine minutes long and showcase Simmonds quite nicely. "Train to Nowhere" and "I'm Tired" display the earthy vocals of singer Chris Youlden.

Canned Heat

Canned Heat was an L.A.-based blues band led by two blues freaks, Bob "the Bear" Hite and Alan Wilson. The group's first two hit singles, "Going Up the Country" and "On the Road Again," helped boost their popularity on the rock-festival circuit. They played the Monterey Pop Festival, Woodstock, the Isle of Wight festival in Britain, and others. Most of the group's tunes were long-winded boogie sessions punctuated by Wilson's guitar and harp and either his light, ticklish voice or Bob Hite's lumberjack growl.

Canned Heat, however, broke no new ground, and none of its albums, save the best-of LP listed below, are solid enough to recommend here. Musically, with the exception of Wilson, the group displayed little virtuosity. Yet popularity enabled the group to turn on rock listeners who might not have ever given the blues a second thought.

Canned Heat's last hit single, a remake of Wilbert Harrison's "Let's Work Together," carried the group into the seventies. But shortly thereafter the group faded into obscurity. Wilson overdosed on barbiturates in 1970; Hite died of a heart attack in 1981.

Canned Heat Cookbook / Liberty / 1970

Canned Heat was always better live than in the studio. *Cookbook* contains the band's best recorded efforts: "Going Up the Country," "On the Road Again," "Bullfrog Blues," and "Same All Over." "Fried Hockey Boogie," a pathetic boogie tune, shouldn't be here; ignore it.

Johnny Winter

Of all the American blues-rock guitarists, Johnny Winter got the biggest billing. Producer Steve Paul took Winter from the Texas bars to New York City, where Winter signed an unusually generous recording contract with Columbia Records. Much hype surrounded the signing, but Winter lived up to expectations.

Winter's hair-raising guitar solos were steeped in the Texas blues tradition; most of his licks were wildly frenetic. When matched with his earthy, visceral blues vocals, the results were striking. The media picked up on Winter's guitar talents and his appearance. Johnny, like his keyboardist brother Edgar, was an albino and, dressed in jet black, he appeared ghostlike.

Winter's self-titled Columbia debut contained thick-edged, heavy blues. But *Second Winter*, his second LP of 1969, contained equal parts rock and blues and reached a much larger audience. Winter was an incessant performer and probably played more rock festivals in 1968 and 1969 than any other rock musician.

In the seventies Winter moved more toward hard rock but never totally abandoned his blues roots. He formed Johnny Winter And, with Rick Derringer as second guitarist. By 1977, however, Winter was back playing the blues. *Nothin' but the Blues* and *White Hot and Blue* were the best LPs of his blues renaissance.

Johnny Winter / Columbia / 1969

This hastily recorded album demonstrates Winter's blues crafts-manship, which far overshadowed any shallow spots in the song selection and production. Tommy Shannon played bass and John Turner played drums. There are guest appearances by Edgar Winter, Willie Dixon, Walter "Shakey" Horton, and others.

Second Winter / Columbia / 1969

Second Winter was the last of the classic American blues-rock albums recorded in the sixties. In this two-record, three-sided set, Winter deftly turns Dylan's "Highway 61 Revisited," Chuck Berry's "Johnny B. Goode," and Percy Mayfield's "Memory Pain" into blistering blues rockers that lose none of their driving energy. Highly recommended.

The Electric Flag

The Electric Flag was a noble blues-rock experiment that fell apart before it could ever get off the ground. The idea was to play the blues backed by a three-piece horn section that would give the Flag a full, brassy, driving sound unlike other blues-rock bands of the day. The lineup of first-rate musicians included Mike Bloomfield on guitar, Harvey Brooks on bass, Buddy Miles on drums, Barry Goldberg on keyboards, and Nick Gravenites singing lead. The brass section was made up of Peter Strazz on tenor sax, Herbie Rich on baritone, and Marcus Doubleday on trumpet.

One year after an acclaimed debut at the Monterey Pop Festival in 1967, the Electric Flag released its first album, *A Long Time Comin'*. Although the playing was excellent and the arrangements were on the mark, the songwriting was weak. Intragroup squabbles caused Bloomfield to leave before the next album. *The Electric Flag* was terribly disjointed and flopped, causing the band to break up.

A Long Time Comin' / Columbia / 1968

Despite its flaws, this album contains some exciting blues-rock musicianship. Miles's drums snap like a whip, Brooks's bass is as steady as basses got in the sixties, and the horn section fills out the sound. There's lots of potential. With the right batch of songs, the Electric Flag might have gone far.

Ten Years After

Lead guitarist Alvin Lee's rapid-fire solos were the English blues-rock group Ten Years After's calling card. Lee and the band went over particularly well at Woodstock; their success at the festival, in the documentary movie, and on the soundtrack album was enough to bring them just a few steps from superstardom. Lee played his guitar as if only speed mattered. His fingers flew up and down the neck of his guitar as he tried—usually with success—to overwhelm with a blitzkrieg of power and volume. The live version of "Goin' Home" from *Woodstock* may be the fastest rock guitar solo recorded in the sixties.

Ten Years After used a blend of blues, jazz, and rock to showcase Lee's guitar wizardry. Such early LPs as *Ten Years After, Undead, Stonedhenge,* and *Sssh* offer interesting approaches to jazz rock with a blues core. Alvin Lee was as comfortable playing Willie Dixon's "Spoonful" as he was playing Woody Herman's "Woodchopper's Ball."

But dependence on Alvin Lee's speedy licks eventually gave the band a weary sound, and after *Cricklewood Green* the band began to fade. Ten Years After and Alvin Lee continued to record in the seventies but with less success.

Stonedhenge / London / 1969

Stonedhenge doesn't contain any of the most popular Ten Years After songs, but it's the best example of the group's jazz and blues flavor. "Going to Try" and "Hear Me Calling" are intriguing tracks since they incorporate an odd assortment of blues and jazz riffs that never really settle into one mold.

Greatest Hits / London / 1975

A decent if incomplete collection of Ten Years After's notable tunes. The highlight of this record is the live Woodstock version of "Goin' Home." Also included are Lee's interesting remake of "Wood-chopper's Ball" and "I Woke Up This Morning" from *Sssh*. Also here, from *Cricklewood Green,* is "Love Like a Man," the group's best single.

13
THE L.A. SCENE

The Los Angeles music scene in the mid- and late sixties was actually a hodgepodge of mini-scenes and cliques; some were plugged into the city's music industry establishment, others were not. The scene was rootless, yet it thrived. Somehow every kind of rock music was represented, yet no single style much influenced or dominated the others. Folk rock had certainly come the closest (before that, surf music had), but by the time it had settled in, bands like the Doors, Love, and Spirit swept past folk rock in a flurry of excitement, as did Frank Zappa and the Mothers of Invention and Captain Beefheart and His Magic Band.

One of the main reasons why things weren't as tight in Los Angeles as they were in, say, San Francisco was the demise of Sunset Strip as the hub of activity. Sunset Boulevard was L.A.'s only real meeting ground; it was where the clubs and the bars were, where the musicians played and hung out, and where new groups and the city's music people congregated. But the police decided that the crowds of hippies and the passing of drugs were getting out of hand, so they came down hard on street people and places that catered to rock crowds. This action helped turn the music scene even more inward.

Nevertheless, L.A. did give birth to some very fine groups in the second half of the decade. The Doors, Spirit, and Love all recorded memorable albums delivered with a detached originality that made the music all the more interesting. The Byrds, remnants of the Buffalo Springfield, and Neil Young helped transform the local folk-rock movement into country rock. Crosby, Stills and Nash unveiled an acoustic style of rock that was in sharp contrast to the heavy music coming from England and the East Coast. Frank Zappa and Don Van Vliet (a.k.a. Captain Beefheart) tore rock apart with vastly effective parodies and insults and bizarre thrusts into the realm of jazz rock. Intelligent, artsy, absurd, and musically stimulating, Zappa and the Mothers of Invention and Beefheart's Magic Band turned out to be two of L.A.'s best bands.

With the obvious exception of the surf-music craze in the early sixties and the rise of the Beach Boys, Los Angeles and the rest of Southern California had always suffered from a lack of musical identity. It didn't matter that the city was as important as New York when it came to the business and production of music. And it didn't matter that a number of great bands and artists lived and worked in and around L.A. Before the mid-sixties, simply nothing firmed up what went on musically and pulled it all together.

The city's music reputation, fragmented and loose as it was, endured, however, and finally got its due in the seventies with the rise of Linda Ronstadt, the Eagles, Jackson Browne, Warren Zevon, Randy Newman, and others. From that point on Los Angeles nurtured a fairly healthy musical identity. Later on, in the late seventies and early eighties, it even sprouted strong new wave and punk scenes.

RECOMMENDED ARTISTS

Sonny and Cher

L.A. songwriter Sonny Bono took much of what he learned working as an assistant to Phil Spector and used it on the records he and his wife, Cher, made in the sixties. It wasn't a bad imitation of the Spector sound, but it *was* an imitation.

Bono and Cher had been in the music business a few years before their first big hit, a Bono original, "I Got You Babe" (1965). Bono was a songwriter who had known only occasional success (he cowrote the Searchers' "Needles and Pins" with Jack Nitzsche). He also played percussion on a number of Spector recording sessions. Cher was primarily a back up vocalist when she met Bono. After "I Got You Babe," the duo became the first flower-power couple. Sometimes the bit got a little excessive, especially in the wardrobe department when furry vests were in. But during all this, the duo did make some good pop love songs. "The Beat Goes On" and Sonny's solo record, "Laugh at Me," however, stand out above the others.

Look at Us / Atco / 1965

Each one of these twelve tracks pay homage to Phil Spector. In addition to "I Got You Babe," Sonny and Cher recorded two songs that Spector cowrote, "Then He Kissed Me" and "Why Don't They Let Us Fall in Love." Another Bono original, "Just You," and a surprisingly decent rendition of "Unchained Melody" make this the best of Sonny and Cher's sixties LPs. Out of print, but available. There are also a number of best-of LPs floating around that include these top songs.

The Mamas and the Papas

Few L.A. outfits were as commercially successful as the Mamas and the Papas. In 1966 and 1967, "California Dreamin'," "Monday, Monday," "Words of Love," "I Saw Her Again," "Dedicated to the One I Love," and "Creeque Alley" were Top Ten hits, and *If You Can Believe Your Eyes and Ears* and *The Mamas and the Papas* were commercial and critical successes.

There were several reasons why Cass Elliot (Mama Cass), John Phillips, Michelle Phillips, and Denny Doherty made such a splash. For one, they capitalized on folk rock when it was fresh and used it as the basic sound for all their records. Also, John Phillips wrote genuinely good pop songs that fit the group's vocal style and accented their harmonies. Finally, the Mamas and the Papas had marketable personalities. They were hippies—flower children the public could accept before the Summer of Love in 1967—and so they became celebrities. Mama Cass was the counterculture's first Earth Mother; Michelle Phillips, its Aphrodite; John Phillips, its philosophical truth seeker; and Denny Doherty, the fun-loving punster.

Although the Mamas and the Papas had New York roots, their sound was strictly West Coast. There was a bright, breezy consistency to their records, and their production sounded sunny and warm. But after the Monterey Pop Festival the group's music began to seem too pop-oriented to be taken seriously. Ironically, had John Phillips not organized the Monterey Pop Festival with producer Lou Adler, and had he not given a song called "San Francisco (Be Sure To Wear Flowers in your Hair)" to old friend Scott McKenzie, which inspired thousands to journey to Haight-Ashbury in 1967, the San Francisco music scene might never have taken off the way it did.

When the Mamas and the Papas broke up in 1968, Mama Cass Elliot began a semisuccessful solo career. She died in 1974 of a heart attack. The other members of the group, including John Phillips, were in and out of the music business.

The Mamas and the Papas / Dunhill / 1966

If You Can Believe Your Eyes and Ears, the group's first album, is out of print. But this, its second, is available and gives just as good an indication of the group's glossy folk-rock style as the debut. Two hits, "Words of Love" and "I Saw Her Again," highlight the LP, but "No Salt on Her Tail," "Trip, Stumble and Fall," plus an interesting version of the Motown classic "Dancin' in the Street" make this record a worthy representation of the mid-sixties L.A. pop-rock style.

Sixteen of Their Greatest Hits / Dunhill / 1969

There's more than enough music here to demonstrate why the Mamas and the Papas were a pivotal group. The hits and tracks from the group's best studio albums are included. Perhaps the most important song on this record is "California Dreamin'," the tune that helped redefine the California Dream.

The Doors

One of rock & roll's bigger ironies concerns the Doors' Jim Morrison. For the past few years he's been much more popular dead than he ever was alive. Morrison died in Paris in 1971; mystery still shrouds the details of his death. Even though the band was on the decline at the time of his passing, the late seventies and early eighties have witnessed an explosion of Doorsmania. Much of it was initiated by the best-selling Morrison biography *No One Here Gets Out Alive* by Jerry Hopkins and Danny Sugarman.

Morrison was one of the decade's most arrogant, provocative, sexually direct, and belligerent performers. On stage he was a striking character, to be sure. He seemed to crave confrontation, and when he got it he often lost his class. He was arrested numerous times, mostly for indecency and drunkenness. Whether it was because he drank excessively (he did) or because he had dropped acid too much (he probably did that, too), or because there was something inside him that ached to be let free, Morrison demanded and usually received total attention, both on stage and on record. In the end, his outlandish behavior overshadowed the Doors' musical accomplishments.

The Doors were one of the few groups that could be a Top Forty sensation and the darling of the underground at the same time. "Light My Fire" and "Hello, I Love You" both went to number one. "Touch Me" peaked at number three, "People Are Strange," at number twelve. *The Doors*, the band's 1967 debut album, was a big seller. While AM radio played the short version of "Light My Fire," a song obviously about sex, FM stations were playing the longer one with organist Ray Manzarek's and guitarist Robby Krieger's extended solos. They were also playing "The End," an eerie, Oedipal fantasy which presented Morrison at his manic, depraved best (in it he kills his father and then rapes his mother). The Doors—Morrison, Manzarek, Krieger, and drummer John Densmore—started out as a psychedelic blues band. Despite Morrison's pretentiousness and the band's forays into the musical hinterlands, the blues was the basis of many of its songs.

The Doors' best years were 1967 and 1968; by 1969 Morrison's overindulgences, bad behavior, and the pressure to contain the artistic experiments within the bounds of AM pop began to take their toll. After the huge success of *The Doors* and *Strange Days*, the band's last two sixties LPs, *Waiting for the Sun* and *The Soft Parade*, seemed uninspired. Morrison's drinking and hassles with the law and concert promoters added to the band's problems. In 1971 Morrison decided to go to Paris, where he died of a heart attack at the ripe old age of twenty-seven. The Doors futilely attempted to carry on without him.

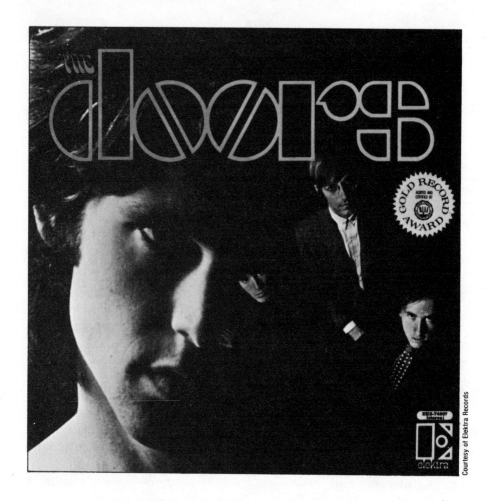

Courtesy of Elektra Records

The Doors / Elektra / 1967

Although "Light My Fire" is the hit, the LP was good enough to become one of the biggest-selling albums of 1967. "Break on Through" is one of the greatest opening album tracks in rock history. "The End" was an FM radio classic. "Twentieth Century Fox"—sassy and sexy—remains one of the group's most durable songs, while "Soul Kitchen" and "The Crystal Ship" demonstrate how sexually charismatic Morrison could be. A superb sixties album and the Doors' best.

Strange Days / Elektra / 1967

This album, rushed out to capitalize on the success of "Light My

Fire" and *The Doors*, would be disappointing were it not for the weirdly appealing single, "People Are Strange," and the next episode of Morrison's obsession with sex and death on "When the Music's Over."

Thirteen / Elektra / 1970
Weird Scenes inside the Gold Mine / Elektra / 1972

Both of these best-of collections contain the Doors' most important material. *Thirteen* includes "Light My Fire," "People Are Strange," "Hello, I Love You," and other assorted early gems. *Weird Scenes inside the Gold Mine* is a double album and contains many of the group's better album tracks, including "Break on Through," "Shaman's Blues," and "The End."

Spirit

Some of the most innovative rock to surface in L.A. came from Spirit. The group was not bound by any preconceived notions; most of the material on *The Family That Plays Together*, *Spirit*, and *The Twelve Dreams of Dr. Sardonicus* is wonderfully diverse. Critics loved the band and its odd yet thoroughly engaging music. But most listeners outside the L.A. area knew of Spirit only from its hit single "I Got a Line on You."

Spirit was guitarist Randy California, guitarist/keyboardist Jay Ferguson, keyboardist John Locke, bassist Mark Andes, and drummer Ed Cassidy. Cassidy, California's step father, came from a jazz background. Ferguson, the band's chief vocalist and one of its songwriters, possessed a mostly folk background. California, Andes, and Locke grew up listening to rock & roll.

"Animal Zoo," "Mr. Skin," and "Nature's Way" from *Dr. Sardonicus*, "Dream within a Dream" and "Jewish" on *The Family That Plays Together*, and "Fresh Garbage" from the self-titled record possess unorthodox chord changes and unusual melody lines that make listening as challenging as it is enjoyable. Although it was Ferguson who was the backbone of Spirit, California garnered much praise for his emphatic guitar skills. *Dr. Sardonicus*'s "Street Worm," where California lets go, is a good example of his style.

The band broke up in 1971, due mostly to frustration and the inability to reach a larger audience. Ferguson went on to form the underrated Jo Jo Gunne with Mark Andes. California did some solo work, and Cassidy and Locke unsuccessfully attempted to bring Spirit back to life with new blood.

Spirit / Ode / 1968

Had this record been promoted properly, it undoubtedly would have made a greater impact than it did. The songwriting is ambitious and zesty, the playing brazen and uninhibited. "Fresh Garbage," "Uncle Jack," and "The Great Canyon Fire in General" are terrific tracks. *Spirit* set the direction that the group's remaining LPs would take.

The Family That Plays Together / Ode / 1968

This album contains the sweeping "I Got a Line on You," the best song California ever wrote for the group. Cassidy has been tragically overlooked as one of the sixties' great drummers, as his work on "I Got a Line on You" demonstrates. "Jewish" is as out there as California and Spirit ever got; the song sounds like a bunch of Hassidic Jews discovering rock the day after they discovered acid.

The Twelve Dreams of Dr. Sardonicus / Epic / 1970

Spirit was a true sixties band and, since this record was its best, it's included here. Ferguson's songwriting on *Dr. Sardonicus* is simply fascinating. "Mr. Skin" is as good as he got; it's full of all the clever hooks and nuances he would bring to Jo Jo Gunne. California's songs show much maturity and progress. But it's the manner in which Spirit pulls everything together—the oddball riff, the nearly schizophrenic melodies, the spontaneous precision—that is most impressive.

Love

Love was another innovative L.A. band. As a group forging its own direction in the mid- and late sixties, its music easily matched the best music from San Francisco. Yet, because of the Haight-Ashbury attraction and the proliferation of the new music, Love, like Spirit, was little known outside L.A.

Love was the brainchild of Arthur Lee. Influenced by the British invasion groups, especially the Beatles during their *Rubber Soul/*

Revolver era, plus San Francisco acid rock and the folk rock from L.A. bands like the Byrds and Buffalo Springfield, Lee could pen a passive, gentle number as easily as an obtrusive rocker. In either case his compositions revealed little of his Memphis roots except on the band's self-titled debut LP. Lee was Love's guitarist and lead singer in addition to its producer and arranger on later albums. As a producer/arranger Lee seemed to prefer a subtle approach. On *Forever Changes*, widely considered Love's finest record, some of the songs sound deliberately hazy and restrained. Much of the guitar work was done with acoustic guitars, and strings and horns tempered the backdrop for his equally hazy vocals. But it was an unusually appealing sound, one that turns up new surprises and delights with each listen.

Even though Lee was, far and away, the group's driving force, Love never really clicked after 1968 with its revolving-door personnel changes. There have since been a few reincarnations of Love, and Lee has released a couple of solo efforts, but nothing much has come of any of this.

Love / Elektra / 1966

Like the Mamas and the Papas, Love could just as easily be in Chapter 10, "Folk Rock," especially with this, Love's first album. The record begins with one of the group's most popular tunes, "My Little Red Book," complete with throbbing bass and no-nonsense vocals. But the rest of the album is full of Byrds-like guitar ("Can't Explain," "A Message to Pretty," "You'll Be Following," and others) and a folk-rock version of the Seeds' "Hey Joe."

Forever Changes / Elektra / 1968

There's a big difference in style and spirit between *Love* and this, the band's third record. (Album number two was 1967's *da capo*, of interest only to those with a deep-seated interest in Love or L.A. rock or both.) Each of *Forever Changes'* eleven songs is thick with poetic imagery. It is Lee's finest moment, as close to a masterpiece as Arthur Lee and Love ever came.

Frank Zappa and the Mothers of Invention

Frank Zappa was—and remains—rock's greatest satirist and one of its most daring technical wizards. His penchant for writing lyrics that drained the propriety, respect, and paradox out of all that was considered good and decent in sixties America, plus his truly amazing talents as a musician, songwriter, bandleader, and studio technician, made Zappa's first few albums genuine classics. Musically, Zappa used a montage of rock, jazz, and classical elements to bolster his biting satire. Zappa's lyrical and musical vision in the late sixties seemed infinite as he probed areas never thought fit for rock and coated the results with a layer of vulgarity and crudeness that some people rejected.

Zappa always surrounded himself with quality musicians. Some of the Mothers have included Lowell George and Roy Estrada, who would form Little Feat; Jean-Luc Ponty, the jazz violinist; Howard Kaylan and Mark Volman (a.k.a. Flo and Eddie), former Turtles; British drummer Aynsley Dunbar; and the jazz-fusion keyboard player George Duke.

Early Zappa and Mothers LPs such as *Freak Out, Absolutely Free, We're Only in It for the Money,* and *Lumpy Gravy* contain many of his more deriding and unrestrained attacks on straight America and conventional pop-music traditions. In those days you either loved or hated Zappa, his music, and, most importantly, what he stood for; there was no middle ground with him. There still isn't.

Freak Out / Verve / 1966
Absolutely Free / Verve / 1967
We're Only in It for the Money / Verve / 1968
Lumpy Gravy / Verve / 1968

Incredibly, not one of these albums is in print. They're easy enough to find secondhand, but the price you're apt to pay for them—forty or fifty dollars apiece—is no bargain. Zappa has a full selection of other Mothers LPs and solo records from the seventies that are still accessible, plus the ones listed below. Check into these; if they fit your fancy and you find you can't get enough of Zappa, then invest in used copies of these. Better yet, borrow copies from someone you know and tape them.

Uncle Meat / Bizarre / 1969

The song titles tell all: "The Voice of Cheese," "Dog Breath in the Year of the Plague," "Sleeping in a Jar," "Ian Underwood Whips It Out," "Zolar Czakl," "Nine Types of Industrial Pollution," and others. Enough said?

Hot Rats / Bizarre / 1969

A Zappa solo album, *Hot Rats* features guest appearances by Captain Beefheart, Shuggie Otis, Jean-Luc Ponty, and Don "Sugar-cane" Harris, among others. It's a fabulous display of Zappa's instrumental genius and awesome guitar talents. "Peaches En Regalia" and "Son of Mr. Green Genes" are both richly melodic, multilayered instrumental tracks. "Willie the Pimp" features Captain Beefheart's vocals and some of the best guitar work Zappa recorded in the sixties. Those who can't stomach much of Zappa's offensive satire but want to appreciate his virtuosity will find *Hot Rats* immensely rewarding.

Captain Beefheart

How does one describe Don Van Vliet, a.k.a. Captain Beefheart? To say that he's outrageously bizarre (more so than Zappa) and far outside the realm of conventional rock & roll would be a start. Actually, what Beefheart created in the late sixties was an avant-garde synthesis of rock, jazz, and mostly blues idioms turned upside down and inside out. The results were then manipulated to carry his achingly poetic interpretation of art, man, and Mother Nature to those brave enough to listen.

Beefheart fell in with Frank Zappa during high school. They later worked on a number of album projects in the sixties and seventies, and Beefheart took advantage of his unlimited freedom in the studio and recorded the classic *Trout Mask Replica* with his Magic Band. The double-record set was a triumph of mind over music, and the critical applause it garnered on both sides of the Atlantic led Beefheart to be revered as Zappa's only rival in free-form rock. Beefheart's records, however, never really sold many copies; his loyal and intensely devoted fans bought whatever he released on vinyl. Beefheart, along with Zappa, represents the underbelly of rock in the late sixties.

Trout Mask Replica / Reprise / 1969

Trout Mask Replica will be the strangest album you've ever placed on your turntable. But have no fear. Repeated listenings bring out all sorts of joys and wonders. There's lots of shapeless soloing going on, courtesy of Beefheart and his saxophone and Magic Band musicians such as Zoot Horn Rollo, Antennae Jimmy Semens, the Mascara Snake, and Rockette Morton. Beefheart's crusty, weather-beaten vocals often belie his seven-octave vocal range. Pieces like "Dachau Blues," "Hair Pie, Bake 1 and 2," "Sugar 'n' Spikes," "China Pig," and "Old Fart at Play" are ceaselessly entertaining. Filling out the songs are various shades of desert-dried grunts and whines and lyrics that reveal Beefheart's power of the pen.

Courtesy of Atlantic Records

Crosby, Stills and Nash

Perhaps no single group captured the airy, utopian spirit of the Woodstock Nation in the summer of 1969 better than Crosby, Stills and Nash. Their soothing angelic harmonies, romantic lyrics, and vibrant acoustic guitar work provided a sharp contrast to the cries of revolution echoed by groups like the Jefferson Airplane, the MC5, and the Rolling Stones.

David Crosby had previously been a member of the Byrds, Stephen Stills came from Buffalo Springfield, and Graham Nash had belonged to the Hollies. They were a supergroup of sorts and, after their appearance at Woodstock in August, record sales and media attention made them worthy of the title. Crosby and Nash were primarily responsible for the delicate harmonies, while Stills wrote the trio's best songs and provided its instrumental focus. By year's end, Buffalo Springfield member Neil Young joined the group, and Crosby, Stills and Nash became Crosby, Stills, Nash and Young.

Young gave the group an added dimension; his probing songs and soaring guitar work helped make *Déjà Vu* the quartet's most noteworthy album. Despite the group's overwhelming success, however, the problems that plagued the Buffalo Springfield and the Byrds plagued Crosby, Stills, Nash and Young. Internal squabbles erupted, egos were bruised, and the pressures of superstardom caught up with the group so that by its third album, *4 Way Street* (recorded live), Crosby, Stills, Nash and Young were disbanding.

Throughout the seventies, though, Crosby, Stills and Nash again performed and recorded together. Crosby and Nash also recorded a few albums on their own in the mid-seventies, and in 1976 Stills and Young got together one more time to record the surprisingly potent *Long May You Run.*

Crosby, Stills and Nash / Atlantic / 1969

Virtually all the tracks on this LP blend acoustic and electric guitars and gorgeous harmonies in near-flawless fashion. "Suite: Judy Blue Eyes," a song written by Stills about folksinger Judy Collins, epitomized the trio's vocal strengths. Other tunes, Nash's "Marrakesh Express," Crosby's "Long Time Gone," and the excellent "Wooden Ships," helped make this record a sixties classic.

Déjà Vu / Atlantic / 1970

On *Déjà Vu,* Crosby, Stills, Nash and Young's only studio album, Young's impact was considerable. His "Helpless" and "Country Girl" were two of the three top cuts (the other was Stills's "Carry On"). On "Helpless," a song that fit Young's weepy, thin voice perfectly, he demonstrated an amazing vocal capacity.

Neil Young

After Buffalo Springfield broke up and during the time he was with Crosby, Stills and Nash, Neil Young recorded two exceptional sixties solo albums. *Neil Young* and *Everybody Knows This Is Nowhere* established him as a compelling songwriter.

Neil Young was very folk-rockish and contained a number of different musical ideas that seemed to sum up his past fascination with acoustic montages and Dylan-influenced lyrics ("The Last Trip to Tulsa"). *Everybody Knows This Is Nowhere,* on the other hand, was a guitar-dominated rock & roll album on which Young incorporated the band Crazy Horse. Of the two, this received the most attention and sold the most copies.

Neil Young / Reprise / 1968

Produced by Jack Nitzsche, *Neil Young* is the most interesting of Young's early solo albums. "The Loner," "I've Been Waiting for You," and "I've Loved Her So Long" reveal Young's fascination with love, isolation, and personal doubt. "The Emperor of Wyoming" is a terrific little instrumental complete with country-style strings and warmth. But the most striking song on the album is the nine-minute-plus narrative, "The Last Trip to Tulsa."

Everybody Knows This Is Nowhere / Reprise / 1969

This contains Young's "Down by the River," a long, self-indulgent number that became an underground favorite and opened up a whole new audience for Young. But the album had better, more convincing songs: "Cowgirl in the Sand" and "Cinnamon Girl." The former, another marathon cut, tracking at a hair over ten minutes, contains a better guitar solo, and "Cinnamon Girl" is the strongest rocker contained on *any* of Young's early solo albums.

14
THE SOUL SOUND

In the mid- and late sixties, soul came primarily from three places: New York, Memphis, and Muscle Shoals, Alabama. Outside of James Brown and, later, Sly and the Family Stone, all the major soul artists of the sixties (except the Motown artists, of course) were connected with one, two, or all three areas in one way or another.

Stylistic differences among the soul records made in New York, Memphis, and Muscle Shoals were minor; although the three locations were competitive with each other, the basic soul style christened in the early sixties was used in all three. Two noticeable differences in the production *sound* of the records, however, could be heard: Memphis and Muscle Shoals records contained sharper, brighter instrumentation than those made in New York at the Atlantic Studios. And Memphis, far more than the other two, had *the* horn section.

While both Memphis/Muscle Shoals/New York soul and Motown music were almost exclusively black music forms of the sixties, the stylistic differences betweeen the two forms were significant. Whereas Motown actively catered to white pop tastes, and its records were polished and glossy, Memphis, Muscle Shoals, and New York retained soul's inherent "blackness" and courted pop listeners on their own terms. The gospel roots of soul were more pronounced in the three other cities than they were in Detroit. Also, a rural quality can be found on Memphis and, especially, Muscle Shoals records that cannot be found on those made in the Motor City.

The golden era of soul was 1966–68. During that time Aretha Franklin, Otis Redding, James Brown, Wilson Pickett, and Sam and Dave made their greatest records. Also, Stax Records enjoyed its greatest success in these three years and had an impact on popular music as deep and as strong as Motown did in its heyday.

RECOMMENDED ARTISTS

Aretha Franklin

In 1967 Atlantic Records released Aretha Franklin's version of Otis Redding's "Respect" as the follow-up to "I Never Loved a Man (The Way I Love You)," her first hit single. "Respect" shot to number one, sold more than a million copies, included Franklin's most stirring vocal output, and almost at once became a black American anthem. Racial tension was in the streets that spring and summer. Watts had burned two years earlier. Detroit and Newark were set to blow. And on the airwaves Aretha was singing about respect. The record said it all.

"Respect" could very easily be considered the greatest soul record of the sixties. The song was a classic to begin with, and Franklin's vocal style, which maximized her own gospel roots, commanded attention. When she cried out for respect, there was not a molecule of doubt about what she wanted.

Queen of Soul, First Lady of Soul, Soul Sister Number One: All these were tagged on Franklin in the sixties. Yet it was only in 1967 and 1968 that Franklin owned the soul charts. Before that she had been with Columbia Records, where producers mismatched her voice to light, jazzy tunes. Very few of her recordings from 1960 to 1965 are worth recalling. But later at Atlantic, under the direction of Jerry Wexler, Franklin drove home notes and feelings that other soul singers could only marvel at.

The results speak for themselves: "I Never Loved a Man (The Way I Love You)," a million-seller, reached number nine in 1967. "Respect" was next. Three months later "Baby I Love You" peaked at

Aretha Franklin
I Never Loved A Man
The Way
I Love You

number four and was another million-seller. "A Natural Woman" stopped at number eight. "Chain of Fools," another million-seller, topped at number two. "(Sweet Sweet Baby) Since You've Been Gone" was her first hit of 1968, another million-seller. "Think," "I Say a Little Prayer," and "See Saw" were all million-sellers.

Few artists in any genre could boast a better two-year track record than Franklin's in 1967 and 1968. But the pace was too fast, the pressure too demanding. Wexler, it seemed, could go on forever. With people like Tom Dowd and Arif Mardin helping him along in the studio, and musicians such as Roger Hawkins, Jerry Jammott, and Duane Allman down at Muscle Shoals, and the Atlantic studios New York crew backing up Franklin, soul was enjoying its finest hour and no one, least of all Wexler, wanted the party to end.

And it didn't exactly end musically. There were no million-sellers in 1969, but there were hits nevertheless ("Share Your Love with Me," "The Weight"). Aretha's personal life, however, was a mess. In 1970 she launched the third phase of her career with four million-sellers in 1971 and 1972 and such wonderful albums as *Spirit in the Dark, Live at the Fillmore West,* and *Amazing Grace.* The respect she had earned in 1967 stayed with her, and rightfully so.

I Never Loved a Man (The Way I Love You) / Atlantic / 1967

Aretha's masterpiece. Recorded in both New York and Muscle Shoals, every track overflows with a gripping soul intensity. Her vocals on "Respect," "Baby Baby Baby," "Do Right Woman—Do Right Man," and the title track are as good as soul ever got. In addition, her piano playing is as sharp as some of the best things Ray Charles ever laid down in the studio. This is one of the few Franklin albums from the sixties that's still in print, and an absolutely essential soul album.

Aretha Now / Atlantic / 1968

Aside from *I Never Loved a Man . . .* , this is Franklin's best sixties studio album. The LP is spearheaded by such tracks as "Think," "You Send Me," "I Say a Little Prayer," and "See Saw." Franklin displays all sides of her vocal gift and Wexler all sides of his production genius.

Aretha's Gold / Atlantic / 1969

An equally essential album. *All* the 1967–68 hits mentioned above are included here (eleven in all) plus three selected album tracks, "Do Right Woman—Do Right Man," "Dr. Feelgood," and Franklin's version of Sam Cooke's "You Send Me." Franklin's vocals cut like a razor. The arrangements, precise and wonderfully effective, are classic soul; the musicianship is impeccable.

Soul '69 / Atlantic / 1969

There's more blues and jazz and a combination of the two on this record, all presented in a pop context. Aretha sings "Gentle on My Mind," "Elusive Butterfly," and Smokey Robinson's "Tracks of My

Tears," among others, but don't let the song titles throw you. *Soul '69* is an excellent indication of Franklin's ability to go beyond the soul idiom and remain every bit as convincing.

Otis Redding

If Aretha Franklin was Queen of Soul, then Otis Redding was King. There were two reasons for this, neither of which was that he packed the charts with hits. As a matter of fact, not one of his songs even made it to the Top Twenty until after his death. But Redding had triumphed at the Monterey Pop Festival in June 1967 and tapped into a whole new hip white audience. Even more important, he had finally perfected his vocal style and delivery so that he seriously rivaled the great James Brown, both onstage and in the recording studio.

But 1967 was also a year of tragedy. In December, Redding and four of six members of the Bar-Kays, his back up band, were killed in a plane crash. "Sittin' on the Dock of the Bay," released posthumously, went on to sell more than a million copies and was Redding's only number-one single.

Redding was the artist to bridge the pop music gap between blacks and whites. Whites could admire and enjoy James Brown—but from a distance. Redding, however, had a commanding warmth and expressed a universality through his music. The proof was at Monterey when he took the stage late and overwhelmed an exhausted crowd with inspiring versions of Sam Cooke's "Shake," "Respect," and "I've Been Loving You Too Long."

Redding began recording in 1962. Being from Georgia, he was greatly influenced by two other Georgians, Little Richard and James Brown. He was especially taken by the vocal acrobatics of Little Richard and incorporated Richard's style into his own. Early Redding records, however, weren't the shouters one might think they'd be; songs like "These Arms of Mine" and "Pain in My Heart" (which the Rolling Stones later covered) were ballads. Redding was never a pop-chart king; his popularity stemmed from his live performances and superbly constructed albums.

Redding also managed, wrote for, and produced other artists, among them Arthur Conley, and he owned a publishing company and record label.

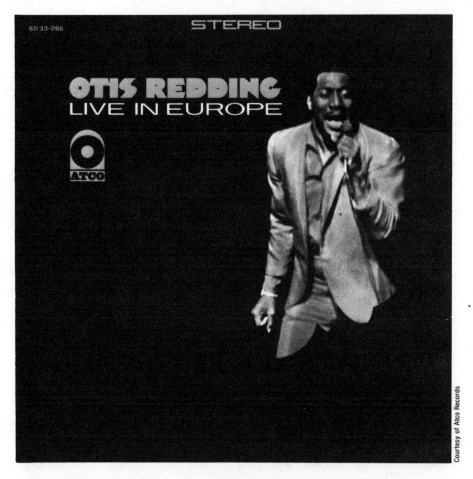

Had Otis Redding lived he might very well have exceeded all expectations. But whatever Redding could have been, it's what he *was* that really counts—a master soul singer.

The Best of Otis Redding / Atco / 1972

This two-record set sums up Redding's achievements in particularly grand fashion. "Shake," "I Can't Turn You Loose," "These Arms of Mine," "Try a Little Tenderness," the Stones' "Satisfaction," and his own "Respect" highlight the collection, and sound as exhilarating today as they did the day he recorded them. An essential album, especially since many of Redding's studio albums are out of print.

Live in Europe / Atco / 1967

Live in Europe ranks with James Brown's *Live at the Apollo* as the two most stimulating live R&B/soul LPs of the sixties. Recorded in France and England when Redding headlined the Stax/Volt Revue, the LP is a stunning reflection of just how good Redding was in concert. "Respect," "Shake," and "Can't Turn You Loose" explode with energy and exuberance. Redding also makes good use of the Beatles' "Day Tripper" and Smokey Robinson's "My Girl."

Otis Redding, Jimi Hendrix Experience / Reprise / 1970

This record was made from the performances of Redding and the Jimi Hendrix Experience at the Monterey Pop Festival in 1967. Side one is all Hendrix; side two is Redding. It's a historically important record, since the performances of both artists at the fest unleashed a wave of media attention on them and their music.

Arthur Conley

That Arthur Conley bore a strong resemblance to Otis Redding was no coincidence. Redding discovered and managed Conley and produced his records. Together they wrote "Sweet Soul Music," Conley's only Top Ten hit.

Redding's death had a disastrous effect on Conley's career. Without Redding's guidance, Conley had problems selecting the right material to record, and when he turned increasingly back to Redding's catalog for songs, some critics accused him of being a rip-off. Conley's last charted single was a sprightly version of the Beatles' "Ob-La-Di, Ob-La-Da" in 1969; it made it to number fifty-one, and that's all anyone has heard from him since.

Arthur Conley / Atlantic / 1981

This British import is about the only LP available that gives Conley his due. (The sixties album *Sweet Soul Music*, which included the hit single, is better, but out of print.) This is a best-of collection and contains "Funky Street," his second most popular single, and his impressive renditions of Redding's "Ha! Ha! Ha!," "Let Nothing Separate Us," and "I've Been Loving You Too Long." Conley is a perfect example of a truly fine singer who lacks his own identity. If Conley somehow could have broken free of his overreliance on Redding, he might be better remembered today.

Wilson Pickett

When it came to sweaty, screeching soul vocals and records that practically exploded with frenzy, James Brown and Otis Redding's chief rival was Wilson Pickett. Pickett's manly brand of soul—rough-edged, gritty, raw—was just a notch or two below Brown when it came to live performances, but it was equally as strong on record. Songs such as "In the Midnight Hour," "634-5789," and "Mustang Sally" are soul standards.

Pickett was born in Alabama but raised in Detroit with a firm foundation in gospel and R&B. In the early sixties he signed a recording contract with Lloyd Price's Double L Records and released "If You Need Me." Solomon Burke's version sold better and charted higher, and soon thereafter Pickett signed with Burke's record company, Atlantic.

Pickett's first Atlantic singles stiffed. It was then decided that Pickett would record in Memphis, and from there came "In the Midnight Hour," which Pickett cowrote with session guitarist Steve Cropper. The cool, shuffling beat was built around a line Pickett frequently used live, something about "waiting for the midnight hour." In 1965 the song just missed breaking into the Top Twenty, but it remained popular throughout the soul era and is considered one of the era's most influential recordings.

From Memphis, Pickett moved down to Muscle Shoals where he recorded a sweltering remake of "Land of 1000 Dances," his biggest-selling single (number six in 1966), plus "Mustang Sally" and "Funky Broadway."

As soul began to cool in 1969, Pickett turned to more melodic songs. A rousing interpretation of the Beatles' "Hey Jude," which session guitarist Duane Allman convinced him to cut, fit the "new" Wilson Pickett well. Two years later, in 1971, Pickett had his first two million-sellers, "Don't Let the Green Grass Fool You" and "Don't Knock My Love—Pt. 1." Pickett later slipped from the charts.

The Best of Wilson Pickett / Brookville / 1977

This two-record set is a good anthology of Pickett's sixties and early-seventies career. All the hits are here as well as a great rendition of "Stagger Lee" and Pickett's tribute to bubblegum soul, "Sugar Sugar." Other Pickett greatest-hits collections worth checking out are *The Best of Wilson Pickett* (Atlantic / 1967) and *The Best of Wilson Pickett, Volume 2* (Atlantic / 1971) or *Wilson Pickett's Greatest Hits* (Atlantic / 1973). His sixties studio albums are out of print.

Sam and Dave

Sam (Moore) and Dave (Prater) brought their gospel and church roots to Stax Studios in 1966. The outcome was a series of soul records—"Hold On! I'm Comin'," "Soul Man," and "I Thank You"—that were structured around gospel's traditional call-and-response vocal pattern and included the same Memphis rhythms and production techniques that made Wilson Pickett's records successful.

Sam and Dave had been together some six years and made some uneventful records for Roulette before being signed by Jerry Wexler. Wexler noted the similarity between the duo's and Wilson Pickett's styles and figured that if Pickett could score with the Memphis crew, then so might Sam and Dave. From 1966 to 1969 Sam and Dave released a number of singles. Most of the better ones were written by the team of Isaac Hayes (melody) and David Porter (lyrics), and produced by either Jim Stewart or Hayes and Porter. Steve Cropper (guitar), Duck Dunn (bass), and Al Jackson, Jr., (drums) played on the records and gave them a cutting edge that was just as sharp and rousing as that of any of the solo singers of the day. Sam Moore was responsible for the upper vocal register while Prater handled the bottom.

Things ground to a halt when Hayes and Porter, and Sam and Dave, parted ways in 1969 after Stax was sold to Gulf & Western. Sam and Dave had problems finding suitable material to record, and a year later they separated. Throughout the seventies and eighties, despite intense personality conflicts, the two have continued to perform on and off, mostly rehashing old songs and living on past glories—of which, fortunately, there are many.

The Best of Sam and Dave / Atlantic / 1969

As is evidenced on these fourteen tracks, Sam and Dave demonstrated the full influence of gospel on sixties soul. The duo took the classic call-and-response pattern and filled it with the kind of vocal tradeoffs that fit perfectly with the soul sound. The pulse of the songs "Soul Man," "I Thank You," "You Don't Know Like I Know," and "Hold On! I'm Comin'" give them soul music's strength and drive. Even the lesser-known tracks—"Small Portion of Your Love," "Wrap It Up," and "I Take What I Want"—pack the same wallop as the hits. A must LP because none of Sam and Dave's original sixties albums, gems like *Soul Dynamite, Soul Man,* and *Hold On, I'm Comin',* is in print.

Percy Sledge

Before Percy Sledge recorded "When a Man Loves a Woman", he was an unknown R&B/gospel singer from Alabama. But with the aid of producer Marlin Greene, Sledge became one of the sixties' most respected soul balladeers.

"When a Man Loves a Woman" is the quintessential soul ballad. Its simple yet immensely poignant arrangement gave Sledge all the room he needed to unleash his powerful voice and make the song a number-one single in 1966. Just about all of Sledge's follow-ups were produced in the same manner—slow, emotional displays of tenderness that could just as easily have been heard in a church as on a car radio. "Take Time to Know Her," "Cover Me," and "It Tears Me Up" were also hits in the late sixties.

Sledge, however, had a difficult time extending beyond his gospelized soul realm and, as black music got funkier, he lost his audience. Still, for those who appreciate the gospel-and-church-influenced side of sixties soul music, Sledge cannot be ignored.

The Best of Percy Sledge / Atlantic / 1969

All the tracks included here were produced by Quin Ivy and Marlin Greene and recorded at Muscle Shoals between 1966 and 1969. Nothing but ballads, the LP's pace is slow and sometimes ponderous. But Sledge is such a compelling vocalist that "Warm and Tender Love," "Take Time to Know Her," and of course "When a Man Loves a Woman" leave a mark in one's heart as few other soul ballads can.

James Brown (Part II)

Sometime around 1963 James Brown realized that if he was to expand his popularity and enlarge his clout, he had to switch gears. There was no question that Brown's power as a live performer was awesome and that his records were eagerly anticipated by most blacks. But Brown wanted to touch white folks, too.

Brown secured full control of his music from King Records. Next he told band leader Nat James to restructure the JB's (Brown's backup band) to give them a funkier sound. In 1965 "Papa's Got a Brand New Bag" put Brown on the top of the pop charts. For the first time he had a record whites felt comfortable enough with to go out and buy. What Brown did differently on this song and the bunch that followed was emphasize the new funk in his music with a basic, repetitive rhythm that gave Brown more vocal freedom. With a minimal melody line that could verge on being monotonous, Brown grabbed the listener's attention with funkified vocal escapades that couldn't be ignored.

Brown used the same formula for "I Got You (I Feel Good)," "It's a Man's Man's Man's World," "Cold Sweat—Part 1," and "I Got the Feelin' "—all Top Ten hits. But it was more than this that made Brown so popular and his music so successful in the years from 1965 to 1968. Not only did he tour continuously, but he became one of black America's chief spokesmen, its chief soul dignitary. His work defusing the anger of blacks when Martin Luther King, Jr., was assassinated earned him the public gratitude of Vice President Hubert Humphrey. Brown made special appearances in ghetto areas and was accepted by most blacks in his role of diplomat. Whites thought him sincere and honest, and this unquestionably had a significant impact on his record sales.

But as the soul era began to ebb, Brown's music began to sound weary. There was a new sound in black music in 1969, and it was coming from the likes of Norman Whitfield and the "new" Temptations and from a San Francisco outfit called Sly and the Family Stone.

Papa's Got a Brand New Bag / King / 1965

This record and the other James Brown LPs mentioned below have

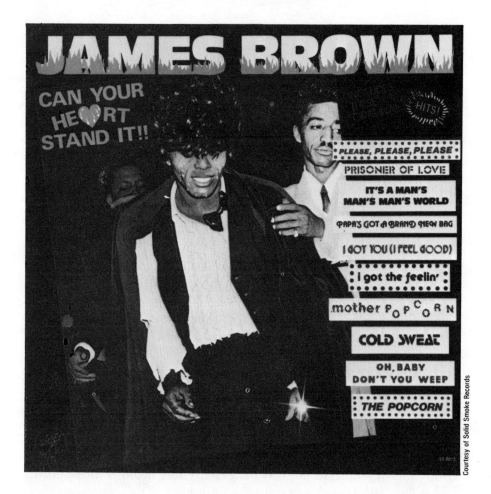

CAN YOUR HEART STAND IT!!

INCLUDES THESE GREAT HITS!

PLEASE, PLEASE, PLEASE
PRISONER OF LOVE
IT'S A MAN'S MAN'S MAN'S WORLD
PAPA'S GOT A BRAND NEW BAG
I GOT YOU (I FEEL GOOD)
i got the feelin'
mother POPCORN
COLD SWEAT
OH, BABY DON'T YOU WEEP
THE POPCORN

Courtesy of Solid Smoke Records

all been rereleased by Polydor Records. Prior to this, *all* of Brown's sixties records were out of print and no adequate anthology existed. *Papa's Got a Brand New Bag* is the first real example of Brown's new emphasis on funk and sparse rhythms. Most of the tracks are basic dance tunes with sexy background riffs and Brown's great vocals up front.

I Got You (I Feel Good) / King / 1965

More of the same funky bass runs and spicy horn parts, except that the song selection here is somewhat better than on the above record. The title track and "Night Train" highlight the LP.

Soul Brother #1 / King / 1966

The production, arrangement, riffs, and rhythms are pretty much the same here as they are on the above two albums. Had Brown not been such an exciting vocalist, these records might not have withstood the test of time due to their repetiveness.

Cold Sweat / King / 1967

Of the four James Brown albums rereleased by Polydor from Brown's mid- and late-sixties period, this one holds up best. It contains one of Brown's more titillating tracks, "Cold Sweat," plus versions of "Stagger Lee," "Kansas City," "Fever," and "Good Rockin' Tonight."

Sly and the Family Stone

At a time when rock and soul sought something to carry them further, along came Sly Stewart. Rock was dangerously close to spreading itself too thin (acid rock, folk rock, blues rock, British rock) and taking itself a mite too seriously. Soul, on the other hand, had just lost one of its greatest artists, Otis Redding, and the original Motown sound was on the wane.

What happened was Sly and the Family Stone. Well versed in the intricacies of rock from days spent as a San Francisco record producer, disc jockey, and scenemaker, Sly Stewart also had a firm command of soul. He meshed his experiences in both music forms and boldly showcased a brand-new sound.

Sly and the Family Stone simply defied categorization. What they played was a free-form synthesis of contemporary music. Sly's songs and arrangements signaled a radical departure from pop, rock, and soul conventions. He uncorked a potpourri of bubbly soul energy, inner-city cool, Haight-Ashbury hipness, and a delightfully new rhythm that culminated in one of the more influential musical progressions of the late sixties.

Sly had been involved in music all his life. First it was gospel, then rhythm & blues. He studied music theory and became proficient on a number of instruments. He worked as a producer under San Francisco music kingpin Tom Donahue and his Autumn Records and produced the Beau Brummels, among others. He was a DJ on KSOL and a member of various bar bands in the Bay Area. Finally, he formed the Family Stone, which combined brothers, sisters, cousins, and friends.

Sly and the band's 1967 debut album, *A Whole New Thing*, was pretty much a warm-up for what would follow. Their direction wasn't altogether clear, and Sly's ambitious merger of rock and soul lacked depth. The next two LPs, *Dance to the Music* and *Life*, realized the promise of the first record. "Dance to the Music" broke into the Top Ten with its uplifting lyrics and bassy drive. But it was *Stand!* in 1969 that fully defined the new psychedelic soul music, as it was called. The LP yielded two more hit singles, one of which clocked in at number one ("Everyday People"). The most invigorating song on the record, though, and the one that summed up Stewart's "new" music, was "I Want to Take You Higher."

Stewart, though, could go no higher. He enjoyed his stardom too much; he quickly gained a reputation for showing up at concerts late, or worse, not at all. He grew lazy and took two years to record a follow-up to *Stand!* He also indulged in heavy drugs. All these factors contributed to a downfall from which he's yet to recover.

Stand! / Epic / 1969

With songs like "Stand!," "I Want to Take You Higher," "Don't Call Me Nigger Whitey," "Sing a Simple Song," and "Everyday People," this resembles a greatest-hits album. Precious few rock albums from the late sixties possess the underlying perfection of *Stand!* Psychedelic soul at its all-time finest.

Anthology / Epic / 1981

This two-record set sums up Stone's career with remarkable insight. The tunes cover all aspects of his reign atop the psychedelic soul heap. "Dance to the Music," "Stand!," "Thank You (Falettinme Be Mice Elf Agin)," and "Thank You for Talkin' to Me Africa" are here. Too bad the rhapsodic liner notes offer so little hard information.

15
THE SECOND BRITISH INVASION

The history of sixties rock is really the story of how American artists (Elvis, Ray Charles, Roy Orbison, etc.) influenced British bands (the Beatles, the Stones, the Animals), who, in turn influenced American bands and artists (the Rascals, the Byrds, the San Francisco bands), who then turned around and influenced the British all over again.

After the Beatles and the rest of the British Invasion groups had thoroughly inundated America, what occurred in San Francisco was a sort of reaction to it all rather than a response. The response, as already noted (see Chapter 7), came mostly from American pop groups bent on imitation. But what came out of San Francisco was *inspired* by the first British Invasion. And it was the Beatles who were the primary stimulators of the wealth of rock enthusiasm and innovation that took root in San Francisco.

By 1967 the same fascination with psychedelia and mind-expanding drugs found its way into British rock as had found its way into San Francisco rock the previous year. No single British album represented this influence better than the Beatles' *Sgt. Pepper's Lonely Hearts' Club Band.* By the end of that summer, a number of British bands (and American too) had gone into the studio and recorded albums greatly influenced by *Sgt. Pepper*. Some set about merely to copy what the Beatles did, but others delved into previously uncharted territories. The results were diverse, progressive, and quite exciting, not to mention totally unpredictable. Once again the Beatles led the way. Behind them were new bands like the Moody Blues, Traffic, Jethro Tull, Pink Floyd, and Procol Harum, and veterans the Who and the Rolling Stones.

Although virtually all the music from Britain in 1968 and 1969 was album-oriented rock, many groups did place singles high on American charts. But were it not for the rise of FM radio here and pirate radio stations off the coast of England, the "new" rock would have stood little chance. Radio had always played a large role in the development of rock, but before 1967 it catered to singles.

There was also a flurry of concert halls and mid-sized venues opening their doors to rock in major cities across the United States. The promoters who booked many of the new British bands to play in them often had them open for better-known acts. Linked to this phenomenon was the proliferation of rock festivals. Through the Monterey Pop, Woodstock, and the Isle of Wight festivals, many British (and American) bands gained valuable exposure. The Who was one of the first British bands to profit from a festival appearance. The group's incredible set at the Monterey Pop Festival attracted the media's attention in the United States and won over a whole new audience.

The second wave of British music borrowed from many sources. Cream and Fleetwood Mac stayed within traditional blues realms. The Small Faces stuck pretty closely to R&B. But the Moody Blues and Procol Harum toyed with strains of classical and symphonic music. Jethro Tull took from English folk ballads. Blodwyn Pig stressed a jazz-rock blend. Pink Floyd became obsessed with esoteric psychedelic rock. The Who experimented with a rock opera. The Beatles, as usual, continued to be their own influence, and the Stones rebelled against psychedelia after realizing they could never become part of it.

One thing nearly all the bands had in common was an awareness of the subtleties and sophistication of the music. The trend was to dress up the music, make it more elaborate, more cerebral, more artsy, and more visionary. With a tremendous rise in the quality of musicianship and the studio proficiency exhibited by many British bands, it *was* possible to take rock to a new plane, a higher level of consciousness. Some who took it *too* high lost sight of rock's original intentions. But most of the bands discussed here made solid contributions to a new rock sound. You only have to compare the Beatles' "She Loves You" (1964) with their "A Day in the Life" (1967) to realize just how far this new sound was from what the British Invasion bands of 1964 and 1965 were calling rock.

RECOMMENDED ARTISTS
The Beatles (Part II)

The story of the Beatles from 1967 to their break-up three years later is one of fast-paced confusion, Indian mysticism, drugs, and the unmanageable pressures of phenomenal commercial success. Still, creative brilliance shown through on virtually every album and single the group produced during this period.

The release of *Sgt. Pepper's Lonely Hearts Club Band* in 1967 signaled a new era for all of rock. *Sgt. Pepper* may or may not be the best rock record ever made, but it unquestionably is one of the most significant. *Sgt. Pepper* revolutionized the art of recording with its complexities and innovative studio technology. It was rock's first important "concept" album—which meant, essentially, that the songs were all interrelated. *Sgt. Pepper* was a grand celebration of psychedelia and the use of drugs for the purpose of art.

The group was dropping acid, practicing transcendental meditation, embracing the Summer of Love, dressing differently, acting differently. The Beatles' group image was shattered. They weren't the Fab Four but four individuals who came together in the recording studio to record great albums. And they made some mistakes: The film *Magical Mystery Tour* was a disappointment, and the utopian Apple empire (clothing boutique, record company, publishing company, etc.) failed. It was also realized that manager Brian Epstein, who died in 1967, had made some serious blunders in marketing. And without his paternal guidance the petty bickering between Beatles got worse and eventually led to serious rifts.

One of the biggest sources of irritation was John Lennon's relationship with Yoko Ono. John became increasingly alienated from the rest of the group, and it showed. *The Beatles* (better known as the White Album) consisted of Paul singing the sweetly effective pop songs and John, the more striking rockers. There was a difference of opinion about the focus of the *Abbey Road* album. As a result, side one goes in one direction and side two in another. In spite of this both albums stand among the best records the Beatles ever made.

In 1969 and 1970 the Beatles released three more albums before disbanding. *Yellow Submarine* was the soundtrack to their animated movie of the same name. *Hey Jude* was a collection of songs that never made it on previous Beatles records. A third, *Let It Be*, was produced by Phil Spector after the Beatles failed to make any sense of what they recorded in the studio.

With the creative artistry of *Sgt. Pepper*, the White Album, and *Abbey Road*, the final phase of the Beatles' recording career turned out to be its best. In April 1970 the Beatles quit being the Beatles, and a chapter of rock history—and twentieth-century music history—ended.

Sgt. Pepper's Lonely Hearts Club Band / Capitol / 1967

A truly remarkable album, *Sgt. Pepper* contained more art than any previous rock album. Each of the thirteen tracks is a goldmine. The lyrics have a ringing, poetic brilliance and often deal with drug-inspired fantasies. And then there's Ringo singing about getting high with a little help from his friends. Musically, the instrumentation and production are impeccable. "A Day in the Life" is a mesmerizing piece: Although it's actually two incomplete songs sewn into one, the end product is a seamless and haunting spectacle and the greatest of all Beatles studio accomplishments. *Sgt. Pepper* is simply indispensable.

Magical Mystery Tour / Capitol / 1967

The LP *Magical Mystery Tour* was a greater success than the disjointed Beatles-produced movie it accompanied. Both the songs and their studio production are a continuation of what was heard on *Sgt. Pepper*. "Strawberry Fields Forever," for example, is as innovative and important as "A Day in the Life." The LP has suffered from being compared with *Sgt. Pepper* and associated with the movie, but when one considers the songs, it's impossible not to recognize it as a great album. A sampling of tunes: "All You Need Is Love," "Hello Goodbye," "I Am the Walrus," "Penny Lane," and "Strawberry Fields Forever." Case closed.

Courtesy of Capitol Records

The Beatles (The White Album) / Capitol / 1968

The White Album, as it's more commonly called, was the only double record the Beatles ever made. It's a potpourri of light and heavy, fun and serious ballads and rockers, very few of which fail to impress. George Harrison's "While My Guitar Gently Weeps" is one of the album's best tracks. It's amazing that the record turned out so beautifully, considering the disarray of the Beatles: friction between Lennon and McCartney was growing, Ringo actually quit the band for a week; and in the studio one Beatle would work on his contribution to a song and leave, and then another would come in and work on his. The result was a surprisingly superb record.

Abbey Road / Capitol / 1969

The production of *Abbey Road*'s side two ranks with the best of *Sgt. Pepper*. The clever, intricate medley of "Sun King," "Mean Mr. Mustard," "Polythene Pam," and "She Came in through the Bathroom Window" is a listening experience to enjoy again and again. Compare these tunes to side one's "Come Together" and "Oh Darling" and it's easy to see Lennon and McCartney's drift apart.

Hey Jude / Capitol / 1970

Fortunately the songs on *Hey Jude* are in some sort of chronological order. Otherwise the LP would surely sound disconnected. The tracks here are those that didn't belong to any previous Beatle LP. Included are "Can't Buy Me Love," "Lady Madonna," "The Ballad of John and Yoko," and the great unsung Beatle track "Rain," which features Ringo's best drumming. Most of the tracks are excellent.

Let It Be / Apple / 1970

Let It Be ended it all. The LP, produced by heavy-handed Phil Spector (as evidenced by "The Long and Winding Road"), depicted the Beatles as a band for the very last time. The film *Let It Be* documented the making of the album. One of the Beatles' finest late-sixties rockers, "Get Back," is included here, as is the outstanding title track. Not really a grand finale, but close enough.

The Beatles 1962–1966 / Capitol / 1973
The Beatles 1967–1970 / Capitol / 1973

For those not inclined to own all the great Beatles albums, these superb compilations will at least give you the necessities. Each album is a double-record set that whets the appetite for the originals.

The Rolling Stones (Part II)

The Rolling Stones passed through the initial British Invasion in fine form. They had established themselves as the best R&B-influenced rock band. The songs "Time Is on My Side," "The Last Time," "Satisfaction," "Get Off of My Cloud," "As Tears Go By," and "19th Nervous Breakdown" were all big hits.

In 1966 the Stones released *Aftermath*, an important LP for them since it marked the first time they were able to present an album not reliant on a couple of singles or covers. Unfortunately, both *Aftermath* and its studio LP follow-up, *Between the Buttons*, though not exactly ignored, failed to drum up the enthusiasm they should have. Both were excellent records loaded with Mick Jagger–Keith Richards songs and Brian Jones's powerful instrumental presence. Yet, due to the changing face of rock in 1966 and 1967, the Stones seemed a bit behind the pack despite the number-one hits "Paint It, Black" and "Ruby Tuesday."

Besides *Between the Buttons*, released in January 1967, two other Rolling Stones albums came out that year. With *Flowers* and *Their Satanic Majesties Request* the Stones tried to force themselves into the spirit of psychedelia and failed. There are decent tracks on both records, but their mood seemed contrived and artificial. A particularly disturbing 3-D cover photo of the band on *Their Satanic Majesties Request* made the Stones look foolish in their obvious imitation of the Beatles' *Sgt. Pepper* cover.

But in 1968 the group got back on track. With *Beggar's Banquet* the Stones renounced the direction they had taken on *Flowers* and *Their Satanic Majesties Request* and put forth raw, raunchy rock 'n' blues. *Beggar's Banquet* remains one of the most incisive and brutal albums the Stones ever made. "Sympathy for the Devil," "Street Fighting Man," and "Salt of the Earth" bristle with intensity and announced the death of innocence in rock & roll.

The year 1969 found the Rolling Stones, who for three years had kept low profiles after drug busts and a couple of less-than-earth-shattering albums, poised to make up for lost time. After some three years away from the States, a giant U.S. tour was planned; a documentary movie, *Gimme Shelter*, comprised of the tour's best concert footage, followed; and another studio LP, *Let It Bleed*, as well as a live album, *Get Yer Ya-Ya's Out*, would be recorded.

But all was not right. Burned out and bummed out, Brian Jones left the band that year, and a month later he drowned in his swimming pool. The Stones got Mick Taylor, the guitarist from John Mayall's Bluesbreakers, to replace Jones, but his presence was sorely missed.

The Stones missed Woodstock that summer, but that fall their U.S. tour began and *Let It Bleed* was released. Woodstock was a major rock event, perhaps the biggest of the decade. But since the Stones missed it, they decided to have their own Woodstock. In December that year the group performed a free concert at the Altamont Speedway in Livermore, California. The results were hardly Woodstockian: one murder not fifty feet from the stage and in full view of movie cameras and Mick Jagger, three other fatal accidents, tons of bad trips from bad drugs, and a scary domination of the scene by the Hell's Angels motorcycle club. Although the Stones were not entirely to blame, they were forced to shoulder the responsibility for what happened. It wasn't something the Stones would get over quickly.

Aftermath / London / 1966

The Rolling Stones didn't include any R&B or blues cover songs on *Aftermath*, but it still is very much an R&B/blues LP. "Doncha Bother Me" and the eleven-and-a-half minute "Coming Home" are solid indications of that. "Stupid Girl," "High and Dry," and "Flight 505" reaffirmed the Stones's connection with American music, although "Paint It, Black" and "Lady Jane" were definite hints of things to come. Musically, Brian Jones's experimentation with the dulcimer and sitar opened up the Stones' sound. However, producer Andrew Loog Oldham's inability to make the songs more raspy and real especially hindered *Aftermath*'s best song, "Under My Thumb."

Between the Buttons / London / 1967

Between the Buttons contains the number-one hit single "Ruby Tuesday" and the controversial "Let's Spend the Night Together." But what really stands out here is the transformation that was occurring in the Stones' outlook. There's far less R&B here than on *Aftermath* and, considering the sound and style of "Ruby Tuesday" and "Something Happened to Me Yesterday," *Flowers* and *Their Satanic Majesties Request* should have come as no surprise.

Beggar's Banquet / London / 1968

By going back to the biting, ballsy style of their early years, the Rolling Stones came up with the most penetrating LP of 1968 and one of the decade's greatest albums. There's the belligerence of "Street Fighting Man," the demonic suggestion of "Sympathy for the Devil," and the sexy bravado of "Stray Cat Blues" to go with the

blue-collar leanings of "Factory Girl" and "Salt of the Earth." If you thought the Stones stopped being *bad* in 1967, *Beggar's Banquet* set you straight but quick. They say a picture's worth a thousand words: Compare the cover of *Their Satanic Majesties Request* with the inside photo of *Beggar's Banquet*.

Let It Bleed / London / 1969

Let It Bleed is as dramatic as *Beggar's Banquet*, but its songs are sharper and more polished. "Love in Vain" is a typically keen blues tune. "Live with Me," "Gimme Shelter," and "Midnight Rambler" are fabulous rockers and, along with "You Can't Always Get What You Want" and the title track, possess elements that would be elaborated on in the early seventies. To surpass what the Stones accomplished on *Beggar's Banquet* would have been impossible, so the Stones almost pulled off the next best thing—matching it.

Get Yer Ya-Ya's Out! / London / 1970

The songs for this live album came from the Stones' Madison Square Garden concerts in November 1969, considered the best shows of the Stones' U.S. tour. Judging from the tightness of the band and Jagger's powerful and magnetic vocals, they probably were. Songs such as "Jumpin' Jack Flash," "Midnight Rambler," "Sympathy for the Devil," and two Chuck Berry covers, "Carol" and "Little Queenie," highlight the LP.

The Who (Part II)

Despite its success in England, the Who didn't have an impact on America until its triumph at the Monterey Pop Festival in June 1967. The band had just released its second album, *Happy Jack* (called *A Quick One* in England), and the title track was making some progress on the American charts. But it was the band's onstage dynamics—complete with the obliteration of its equipment—that introduced the Who to American audiences (the set was included in the documentary *Monterey Pop*).

Happy Jack was followed by *The Who Sell Out* in late 1967. Although primarily a concept LP that parodied the advertising world, it also contains the Who's biggest-selling single to date, "I Can See for Miles," which made it into the Top Ten.

Both *Happy Jack* and *The Who Sell Out*, however, were warm-ups for Townshend and the Who's grand masterpiece, *Tommy*. While Townshend was still working on rock's first opera, MCA released *Magic Bus* in 1968. The title track was a moderately successful single. The album also included "Pictures of Lily."

Finally, in May 1969, MCA unveiled *Tommy*. Released some three months prior to the Who's second live performance triumph in America, this time at Woodstock, *Tommy* inspired a wave of critical acclaim.

What *Tommy* did for the Who was nothing short of amazing. Almost immediately the Who was a major band to be reckoned with, and Townshend was proclaimed rock's newest genius. Looking back, the actual idea behind *Tommy*—a rock opera—and its music were far more brilliant than its story line. Tommy is a deaf, dumb, and blind boy with an astonishing talent for playing pinball. He becomes a "pinball wizard" and winds up as a spiritual master who abuses his power. The concept worked on record because the emphasis was on the music. When director Ken Russell tried to make a movie out of the opera, *Tommy* fell flat on its face.

Townshend and the Who entered the seventies riding on the success of *Tommy*. But an even greater achievement was just down the road. In 1971 the Who released *Who's Next*, without a doubt one of the two or three perfect rock records ever made.

Happy Jack / MCA / 1967

There's really a treasure chest full of obscure but tasty Who tracks here. The two most noted are the title tune and John Entwistle's "Boris the Spider." But there's also the Mod-ish "Run Run Run," Townshend's "A Quick One, While He's Away," and Entwistle's "Whiskey Man."

Tommy / MCA / 1969

Forget trying to find true meaning in the story line and enjoy the musical extravaganza. Tracks like "Amazing Journey," "Pinball Wizard," "Welcome," "I'm Free," and the best of the lot, "We're Not Gonna Take It," sparkle with originality and flair. A two-record set, *Tommy* certainly isn't typical. But when you put it on your turntable, it's a rewarding experience.

Meaty Beaty Big and Bouncy / MCA / 1971

A best-of collection that's right on target, *Meaty Beaty Big and Bouncy* includes "I Can't Explain," "The Kids Are Alright," "I Can See for Miles," "My Generation," "Magic Bus," "Boris the Spider," and "Pinball Wizard." If you don't own any of the Who's sixties LPs, then you should own this.

The Small Faces

The Small Faces are more important in the States for what resulted from their break-up than their accomplishments while together. The Small Faces were Steve Marriott (guitar, vocals), Ian McLagan (organ), Ronnie Lane (bass guitar, vocals), and Kenney Jones (drums). In 1969, when the Small Faces disbanded Marriott joined with guitarist Peter Frampton to form Humble Pie, a very popular early-seventies blues-influenced rock outfit. McLagan, Lane, and Jones teamed up with Ron Wood and Rod Stewart to become the Faces. McLagan also toured with the Rolling Stones, Ron Wood later became a member of the Stones, and Kenney Jones took over the drum chair for the Who after the death of Keith Moon.

Back in the mid-sixties, the Small Faces and the Who were London's two most popular Mod bands. Brandishing a surprisingly well-cultivated perspective of American R&B, the Small Faces had a number of hits in England from 1965 to 1967. In late 1967 and 1968 the Small Faces, however, felt the pressure to psychedelicize. "Itchycoo Park," from *There Are but Four Small Faces*, was a neat mixture of R&B, pop, and psychedelia and gave the group its only U.S. hit. A bit later in the year the group released *Ogden's Nut Gone Flake*, which contains one of the finest songs that Steve Marriott and Ronnie Lane wrote together, "Afterglow (Of Your Love)." But the album didn't sell well enough, and frustration over its lack of success, among other things, led to the demise of the group.

Ogden's Nut Gone Flake / Abkco / 1968

With the slew of arty concept albums, it's not surprising that this record kind of stalled in the traffic. Despite structural problems it's a very good—and very interesting—album, one of the best blends of psychedelia and R&B recorded in England. "Afterglow (Of Your Love)" should have been a big hit in the States, considering how close it sounds to what the Turtles were doing at the time.

Greatest Hits / Immediate / 1977

An adequate, although by no means thorough, British import collection of a dozen Small Faces songs. Among them: "Itchycoo Park," "Afterglow," "Here Comes the Nice," and "Tin Soldier." The production is authentically muddy, and Marriott often sounds like he sat on a tack, but the musicianship is quite good and the songs exude a delightful sense of originality.

Jeff Beck

After Jeff Beck left the Yardbirds, he formed the Jeff Beck Group. Beck wanted a band that would revolve around his guitar playing, a group that would handle the essential chores while he and his guitar basked in the spotlight. He first got Aynsley Dunbar, then Mickey Waller, to play drums, Ron Wood to play bass, and a young, brash vocalist named Rod Stewart to sing.

The group was terrific from the very beginning. *Truth*, its first album, soared with Beck's vastly imaginative, cutting guitar riffs. As a pure stylist, only Jimi Hendrix was better. Beck's solos were articulate in spite of all the fuzz tones that surrounded them, and his extraordinary technique was as notable as it was unpredictable.

But there was also Rod Stewart's voice. His vocals on *Truth* and the follow-up LP, *Beck-Ola*, are some of his best. Gritty, grainy, and roughneck rowdy, Stewart's vocals never quite stole the show, but they garnered a fair share of attention and praise. It was only a matter of time before the egos of Beck and Stewart would clash. After *Beck-Ola* the group broke up. Stewart and Wood then joined forces with Ian McLagan, Ronnie Lane, and Kenney Jones as the Faces. Beck would form another version of the Jeff Beck Group, this time consisting of unknowns Max Middleton (keyboards), Cozy Powell (drums), Clive Chaman (bass), and Bob Tench (vocals).

Truth / Epic / 1968

There are some killer cuts on *Truth:* "Rock My Plimsoul," "Beck's Bolero," and "I Ain't Superstitious." Much of the record is blues-based but Anglicized in such a way that you'd only vaguely know it. Beck proved that the potential of rock guitar was inexhaustible and that style didn't necessarily have to eclipse substance.

Beck-Ola / Epic / 1969

Beck-Ola is thrown off balance by the unnecessary piano instrumental by newcomer Nicky Hopkins and two Elvis Presley originals, "All Shook Up" and "Jailhouse Rock." But "Plynth (Water Down the Drain)" and "Rice Pudding" give the LP merit, and both Beck and Stewart are as amazing here as they were on *Truth*.

Traffic

Everyone in England's rock circle knew that when Steve Winwood left the Spencer Davis Group it wouldn't be the last time he was heard from—and it wasn't. Shortly thereafter, Winwood and drummer Jim Capaldi, guitarist Dave Mason, and flautist/sax player Chris Wood formed Traffic. The group's first album, *Mr. Fantasy*, has an enticing assortment of gentle rock, lightly seasoned with jazz and some folk strains as well as a trace of psychedelia. Before the album was released Mason left the band. Despite his not appearing on the LP's cover or being mentioned in the credits, Mason's sitar can be heard on "Paper Sun," and two of his songs, the British hit single

"Hole in My Shoe" and "House for Everyone," are included. Mason came back and played a major role in the huge success (at least critically) of *Traffic*, the group's best effort. But then Mason left for good. Winwood too was looking elsewhere and joined a true British supergroup, Blind Faith. After an album and a U.S. tour the Blind Faith project fell apart—a victim of one of rock's greatest enemies, swollen egos. Winwood eventually re-formed Traffic and in 1970 the group cut *John Barleycorn Must Die*, Traffic's best-selling record, which prompted Winwood to move in a jazz direction, something he had originally intended for Traffic from its inception.

Mr. Fantasy / United Artists / 1968

If you listen to *Mr. Fantasy* in a late-sixties frame of mine, the LP still makes wonderful sense and is as enjoyable to listen to today as it was in 1968. If you don't, it will sound quite dated. Whatever the case, four exceptionally fine tunes—"Paper Sun," "Dealer," "Hole in My Shoe," and "Dear Mr. Fantasy"—reveal the gorgeous possibilities of Traffic.

Traffic / United Artists / 1968

An outstanding album on all fronts, *Traffic* vividly portrays how important Dave Mason's contribution to the band actually was. Four songs—the perky "You Can All Join In" and the classic "Feelin' Alright," plus two others—were written solely by Mason; he cowrote another one, "Vagabond Virgin," with Capaldi. "You Can All Join In" is light and upbeat, while the Winwood–Capaldi numbers, "Forty Thousand Headmen" and "Who Knows What Tomorrow May Bring," are strange. *Traffic* turned out to be one of the finest LPs of 1968.

The Moody Blues

One of the bands that matured the most dramatically from its early days as a British Invasion pop group was the Moody Blues. Its 1965 hit "Go Now!" reached the American Top Ten before the group went dry. In 1967 guitarist Denny Laine and bassist Clint Warwick left and were replaced by Justin Hayward and John Lodge, respectively.

The change in personnel inspired a new beginning. The band

charted a radically different course, one that mixed classical music and symphonic instrumentation with rock. Later that year the Moody Blues unveiled *Days of Future Passed*. Recorded with the London Festival Orchestra, the record was much more symphonic than rock, but it was warmly received by rock audiences as yet another adventurous concept album. The album contained "Nights in White Satin," which, when rereleased in 1972, sold well over a million copies and went to number two.

Up next was *In Search of the Lost Chord*, which had *Days of Future Passed*'s classical intonations without all the orchestration. The Moodys attempted to be poetic and philosophical; today the lyrics sound excessive and sophomoric. But in the late sixties many considered them profound.

The Moodys continued in this vein as long as they could. *On the Threshold of a Dream*, *To Our Children's Children's Children*, and *A Question of Balance* took the band into the seventies. With loyal and consistent support, the Moody Blues remained a factor in pop music, albeit a minor one, until its members embarked on solo careers beginning in 1973.

Days of Future Passed / Deram / 1967

The Moodys used a day as a thematic and conceptual springboard from which to launch their grand experiment with orchestrated rock. The tracks are labeled "The Day Begins," "Dawn," "The Morning," "Lunch Break," and so on. There's a warm, dreamy ambience that flows from the record. "Nights in White Satin," a slow-moving and absorbing ballad, and "Peak Hour" highlight a most interesting album.

In Search of the Lost Chord / Deram / 1968

The Moody Blues always made the listener feel as though he or she were embarking on a musical voyage. *In Search of the Lost Chord* opens with departure sound effects, followed by "Ride My See-Saw," one of the very best rockers the Moody Blues ever recorded. "Om" (as in meditation) was a track ideally suited for getting high—metaphysically or with some good Colombian weed. *In Search of the Lost Chord* has become dated, but a few cuts have weathered the passage of time.

Pink Floyd

Of all the major bands to emerge in Britain in the late sixties, none was more wildly experimental and more closely tied to the atmospheric qualities of acid rock than Pink Floyd. The roots of the band were innocent enough: R&B presented with an art-school playfulness. But when guitarist/vocalist/songwriter Syd Barrett joined with Roger Waters (bass), Rick Wright (keyboards), and Nick Mason (drums) and officially became Pink Floyd, the change in musical direction was dramatic and complete.

Barrett set Floyd on a psychedelic course with a strong emphasis on shapeless, experimental swirls of guitars and organ and spacy, surreal lyrical imagery. *The Piper at the Gates of Dawn*, the band's first LP, was released in 1967. Most of the songs were written by Barrett, whose heavy use of LSD definitely affected his writing and later precipitated a nervous breakdown. He was replaced by guitarist David Gilmour in 1968.

The remainder of Floyd's history—up to *The Dark Side of the Moon* in 1973—was one of continued musical experimentation, especially with sounds, sound effects, the more sublime textures of composition, and often fascinating probes into the inner dimensions of what would eventually be labeled space rock.

A Saucer Full of Secrets (1968), *Ummagumma* (1969), *Atom Heart Mother* (1970), and *Meddle* (1971) were comprised of what one might expect from any late-sixties experimental group: dismal failings and swatches of sheer brilliance.

The years of mining the musical unknown paid off, however, with *The Dark Side of the Moon*, the most durable LP in the history of popular music. The LP has been on *Billboard*'s charts for more than ten years.

The Piper at the Gates of Dawn / EMI / 1967

The LP is most important because it displays the encompassing talents of Syd Barrett just prior to his breakdown and eventual seclusion. His mark on Pink Floyd was strong and permanent, and on tracks like "Astronomy Domine," "Lucifer Sam," "The Gnome," and "Interstellar Overdrive" (which was written by the entire band), his creativity flows uninterrupted. *The Piper at the Gates of Dawn* presents rock not in a puffy blast of complexities for the sake of complexity but in a more sparse, striking way that's still challenging today.

A Saucer Full of Secrets / Capitol / 1968
Ummagumma / Capitol / 1969

Both these records have their highs and lows and are recommended mostly to those interested in Pink Floyd or the development of art rock. *A Saucer Full of Secrets* is generally stronger than *Ummagumma*, a double LP of live and studio tracks.

Procol Harum

Procol Harum, another progressive outfit, had more success than Pink Floyd in the late sixties because of its immense hit "A Whiter Shade of Pale," which sold in the millions and is considered one of the genre's great masterpieces. Internal managerial problems, financial disasters, personnel changes, and an inability to record a worthy follow-up plagued Procol Harum for most of its existence.

The group's most noted members were Gary Brooker on piano and other instruments, Matthew Fisher on organ and other instruments, Robin Trower on lead guitar, Barrie Wilson on drums, and David Knights on bass. Lyricist Keith Reid was also an integral member of the band but did not play any instruments. He, Brooker, Fisher, and, to a lesser extent, Trower, wrote Procol Harum's material.

The band explored classical rock and came up with a sound and meaning far different from that of the Moody Blues. Procol Harum used its orchestral arrangements only to complement its somber, sometimes even melancholy songs. At times the instrumentation was economical and simple, but there were other times when a creeping orchestration could be heard filling in the background and finally enveloping the track.

Procol Harum's music took time to appreciate; much of its material was masterfully composed and wonderfully challenging. But patience wasn't an especially strong virtue of rock fans in the late sixties and early seventies (as it's not now), so much of the band's work drifted by largely unnoticed. Procol Harum continued to make imaginative, innovative albums well into the seventies before finally calling it quits in 1977.

A Whiter Shade of Pale / A&M / 1967

This, Procol Harum's greatest album (called simply *Procol Harum* in England) is out of print but easily obtainable in used-record bins or as an import. It contains the classic title song, with its elements of Bach and Ray Charles (how's that for diversity?), and reflects the band at its most focused. "Conquistador" and a few other lesser-known though equally compelling tracks are here, too.

Shine on Brightly / A&M / 1968

Musically, *Shine on Brightly* is more or less a review of the themes explored on *A Whiter Shade of Pale*. The band comes across as tightly knit and confident, and Brooker's compositions reveal a noticeably heightened sophistication.

A Salty Dog / A&M / 1969

Produced by Matthew Fisher (this was the last album he made with Procul Harum), *A Salty Dog*'s brightest moment is the beautifully composed and neatly produced title song. Keith Reid's lyrics here as well as on the rest of the record are expressive and strangely seductive. Songs like "The Milk of Human Kindness," "Wreck of the Hesperus," and "The Devil Came from Kansas" combined with the title track to make *A Salty Dog* one of the great unsung albums of 1969.

King Crimson

King Crimson, which formed and recorded *In the Court of the Crimson King* in 1969, made a substantial impact on progressive rock. The band consisted of Robert Fripp, an astounding guitarist and songwriter; bass player and lead vocalist Greg Lake; Ian McDonald on reeds, woodwinds, vibes, and keyboards; and Michael Giles on drums. Pete Sinfield was King Crimson's lyricist. *In the Court of the Crimson King*, a highly regarded LP (and deservedly so), was lush with instrumentation and full of acute guitar riffs from Fripp.

Had King Crimson retained its original lineup and matured, it might have become the greatest band of early-seventies progressive rock. But Lake left to form Emerson, Lake and Palmer in 1970, and McDonald and Giles split to record *McDonald and Giles*. Although Fripp acquired competent replacements—Bill Bruford (drums), John Wetton (bass) and, later, Adrian Belew (guitar), to name some—King Crimson never quite regained its early momentum.

In the Court of the Crimson King / Atlantic / 1969

There are only five tracks on this album but they contain more than enough music for any listener to digest. Each composition, especially "21st Century Schizoid Man" and the title track, is a full-course meal, a wealth of eloquent phrasing and instrumentation. Sinfield's poetic lyrics add further drama and sophistication. A magnificent, full-bodied record, it broke new ground in sound and production.

Jethro Tull

Jethro Tull dealt not so much with classical influences as a collage of jazz, rock, and traditional British folk music set together with the sometimes soothing but sometimes frenetic lead singer/songwriter Ian Anderson's flute. Although the group's greatest success came after the release of the hugely popular *Aqualung* in 1971, Jethro Tull's engaging sixties LPs, *This Was* and *Stand Up*, are gems too.

In an era ripe with the first harvest of truly great rock guitarists, Tull hinged its style on Anderson's flute. Early Tull was a study of contrasts: One moment Anderson's flute would echo sweet folkish lines against a backdrop of acoustic guitar, then the band would tear off on a musical tangent with electric guitars and bold, bassy bass lines.

Much of the group's popularity was due to its rather uncompromising originality. Formed in 1967 its members were Anderson, who also played guitar and sang; Mick Abrahams, guitar; Glenn Cornick, bass; and Clive Bunker, drums. From the beginning Anderson and Abrahams both agreed that Tull would explore some of the jazz possibilities inherent in the rock format, and *This Was* was firm testament to this. Borrowing extensively from Rahsaan Roland Kirk in terms of technique as well as song—Kirk's "Serenade to a Cuckoo" was one of *This Was*'s more popular tracks—Anderson's flute gave the record a delightful jazzy feel.

Anderson soon found other interests. He grew increasingly keen on meshing strains of British folk with rock and using both the acoustic guitar and flute as primary instruments. Abrahams, however, left the band before work was begun on *Stand Up* and was replaced by Martin Barre. Jethro Tull went on to become one of the more commercially successful progressive bands of the seventies—with Anderson firmly at the controls.

This Was / Chrysalis / 1968

With a sound altogether fresh and distinctive, *This Was* is as sturdy a record to come out of England in the late sixties as you're apt to find. The jazz-rock merger comes off beautifully even though one or two cuts weren't as convincingly executed as the others.

Stand Up / Chrysalis / 1969

Stand Up hinted of things to come. Without Abrahams in the group Anderson began to exercise full control; the songs are all his, as is the production, and he played a multitude of instruments on the record. The best songs on *Stand Up*—"A New Day Yesterday," "Nothing Is Easy," and the especially delightful "Fat Man"—are irresistible.

Blodwyn Pig

After Mick Abrahams left Jethro Tull, he formed Blodwyn Pig. Short-lived and nowhere as popular as Jethro Tull, Blodwyn Pig nonetheless made a pair of fine albums, *Ahead Rings Out* and *Getting to This*. Abrahams's goal was to stretch out even further into jazz than Tull did and to create a sound that was even more progressive and texturally diverse. Abrahams got saxophonist Jack Lancaster, who played both alto and soprano—often simultaneously—to give the group part of its jazzy edge. Together the two musicians inspired Blodwyn Pig's invigorating probe into British jazz-rock.

The group's debut record was released in 1969 but, despite considerable acclaim, it didn't catch on with the public. *Getting to This* followed the same formula, but that too was lost somewhere along the line. Abrahams, however, had left the band by this time. His departure caused Pig's early demise.

Ahead Rings Out / A&M / 1969

Some of the chord changes and riffs heard on tunes like "The Modern Alchemist," "See My Way," and "Dear Jill" possess a delectable jazzy pitch. There's also a lot of hard rock included. Abrahams comes across as an odd fellow (even odder after you read the liner notes), but he's creative and versatile in his approach to songwriting. "Summer Day" has one of the most bizarre endings ever heard on a rock tune.

Joe Cocker

Joe Cocker burst upon the scene in 1969 after a triumphant performance at Woodstock. A singer and performer long before the festival, Cocker recorded little and was generally an obscure English pub soul shouter prior to his debut album, *With a Little Help from My Friends.*

Cocker's leathery, rough-up voice sounded like it came from a gravel pit. Despite its incredible coarseness, it was strangely appealing. His raving vocal deliveries and weird robotic motions onstage made him seem unique. His appearance in the film *Woodstock* and a spot on the soundtrack furthered his popularity.

A grand tour in 1970, featuring the talents of keyboards ace Leon Russell, led to the live LP *Mad Dogs and Englishmen.* But fascination with Cocker began to wear thin when he let a heavy booze and drug indulgence overwhelm his ability to perform effectively. Little else of substance was recorded by Cocker until he teamed up with Jennifer Warnes on the number-one hit single "Up Where We Belong" in 1982.

Joe Cocker / A&M / 1969

Undoubtedly Cocker's best album, it includes such songs as the Beatles' "She Came in through the Bathroom Window," John Sebastian's "Darling Be Home Soon," and Leon Russell's "Delta Lady." Few late-sixties artists had as much success interpreting other people's songs as Cocker, and none so thoroughly overhauled them as he did.

Mad Dogs and Englishmen / A&M / 1970

This double-record LP is an excellent account of Cocker's celebrated 1970 tour which featured keyboards players Leon Russell and Chris Stainton, bassist Carl Radle, drummers Jim Gordon and Jim Keltner, back up vocalists Rita Coolidge and Claudia Linnear, and a slew of others. Each song is packed with loads of energy and excitement. Only a handful of live albums recorded in the late sixties and early seventies are as successful as this one.

16
THE ORIGINS OF HEAVY METAL

Although heavy-metal music didn't fully come to the fore until the seventies, its roots are firmly embedded in the sixties. The earliest indications of heavy metal came from mid-sixties bands like the Yardbirds and the Who. Then in 1967 the Jimi Hendrix Experience in England and Blue Cheer in the States began basing songs around a "heavy" guitar sound. By the end of the decade Led Zeppelin, Steppenwolf, Iron Butterfly, Mountain, and others were doing the same.

As a distinct rock-music form, heavy metal borrowed considerably from electric blues. Since its inception heavy metal has been a guitar-dominated form, and since most of the best guitarists of the late sixties either had blues backgrounds or played at one time or another in blues-rock bands, the link was natural. Also, the blues lent itself quite nicely to heavy metal. Guitarists could stretch out in heavy-metal songs much the same as they could when they played the blues. Sixties heavy-metal albums almost always contain a standard blues song or two. There were also definite acid rock and psychedelic tie-ins. Blue Cheer's very name came from a particular brand of LSD; "In-A-Gadda-Da-Vida," Iron Butterfly's heavy-metal epic, was steeped in psychedelia.

Almost from the start, heavy metal possessed the stentorian blasts of fuzzed-out guitar chords and screeching guitar solos. Guitarists such as Jimi Hendrix, Jimmy Page (Led Zeppelin), Leslie West (Mountain), and John Kay (Steppenwolf) also relied on feedback and distortion. Busy and loud drummers provided balance. The great drummers—John Bonham (Led Zeppelin), Mitch Mitchell (Experience), Ginger Baker (Cream and Blind Faith), and Keith Moon (the Who)—did their own soloing onstage and in the studio.

The two sixties groups that did the most to set heavy metal rolling were the Jimi Hendrix Experience and Led Zeppelin. As guitar stylists both Hendrix and Led Zep's Jimmy Page were extremely influential on future metal guitarists. Hendrix died in 1970, but the vast amount of work he left behind, first with the Experience and then with his Band of Gypsys, is breathtaking. Hendrix did more things with a guitar and pulled out of it more varied sounds than anyone else in the history of rock. Page's influence, on the other hand, extended throughout the seventies as Led Zeppelin was *the* heavy-metal group of the decade, and quite possibly the best the genre ever produced.

RECOMMENDED ARTISTS

Blue Cheer

One of the earliest and heaviest of the American heavy-metal bands was Blue Cheer. A trio from California, Blue Cheer dealt almost exclusively with deafening power chords soaked in fuzz and distorted feedback. Leigh Stephens's guitar work was crude and basic; he couldn't play lead worth spit. But it was the group's blunt amplified power that mattered. And it was unbearable.

Heavy metal was made to be played loud; that's why *Vincebus Eruptum*, the band's debut album, didn't sound as full as it did live, where Blue Cheer—and not you—determined the volume. As strange as it may seem, Blue Cheer actually had a hit single in 1968. The band's cover version of Eddie Cochran's "Summertime Blues" went to number fourteen.

Vincebus Eruptum / Philips / 1968

For all its crudity *Vincebus Eruptum* has become an American heavy-metal classic. "Summertime Blues" is on the LP, as is the agonizing "Doctor Please" and renditions of "Rock Me Baby" and "Parchman Farm," two popular blues standards. The songs are simply shellacked with a bellowing round of feedback.

The MC5

The MC5 (short for Motor City Five) was perhaps the most outrageous band to adopt a heavy-metal edge in the late sixties. The band could play as loud as (or louder than) Blue Cheer, but unlike Cheer the MC5 coupled its blasts of power chords with lyrics that boldly espoused radical politics, the kind advanced by organizations such as the White Panther Party and the Students for a Democratic Society.

The MC5 wasn't the commercial success other late-sixties heavy-metal acts were, primarily because of its blunt, confrontation-style songs of revolution. Its creed: "Kick out the jams, motherfuckers!" This quickly got the MC5 in trouble with its record company and those radio stations that sought to promote rock which was underground, but not *that* low.

The MC5 unraveled in the early seventies, a victim of its own political excess. But its influence was felt for the remainder of the decade through punk.

Kick Out the Jams / Elektra / 1969

Recorded live, *Kick Out the Jams* is the best example of the MC5's reckless attempt to politicize rock. Songs such as "Motor City Is Burning" and the title track practically bowl over the listener with fury. These guys believed in the revolutionary rhetoric of the day. If you can't hear it in the music, then listen to lead singer Rob Tyner's speech that precedes "Ramblin' Rose." Much of what's between the grooves, though, sounds like ancient history today.

Jimi Hendrix

It's practically impossible to overstate Jimi Hendrix's talent. No one was better equipped to revolutionize the rock guitar. His intimate, almost sexual relationship with his instrument, plus his uncanny feel for the strange notes and sounds he could get out of it, and his knack for somehow putting them into focus all served to define the guitar's (and rock's) potential.

Hendrix first came on the scene as a headliner in 1967 with his band, the Jimi Hendrix Experience (Mitch Mitchell on drums, Noel Redding on bass). Although Hendrix was an American and had played in American groups, his psychedelic roots were as British as his band. It was ex-Animal Chas Chandler who brought Hendrix to England, managed him, and helped him form the Experience.

Hendrix made his American debut at the Monterey Pop Festival. After playing some of the most outrageous licks heard during the three-day event, he culminated his set by setting his guitar on fire. It was a musical *and* visual spectacle that shocked the audience as much as it entertained them. From that point on Jimi Hendrix never looked back.

Hendrix recorded three studio albums with the Experience—*Are You Experienced, Axis: Bold as Love,* and *Electric Ladyland*—and one live album, *Band of Gypsys,* with his second trio (Billy Cox on bass and Buddy Miles on drums). It's hard to pinpoint the origins of his amazing guitar style. If you dissected his style, you'd find strands of standard Memphis soul guitar, a swatch or two of Dick Dale (whom Hendrix listened to in the early sixties), layers of blues guitar inspired by B. B. King and others, plus everything he picked up backing such rockers as Little Richard, King Curtis, the Isley Brothers, and Wilson Pickett. Hendrix was unique in that he had the improvisational attitude of a jazz guitarist and the daring of an avant-garde artist. He simply erased any limitations or restrictions.

Not everything Hendrix played was brilliant. The vast majority of it bordered on excellent, but when Hendrix let his personal problems intrude, what he played often sounded confused or panicked.

Hendrix never considered himself a good vocalist, and he wasn't. But his voice was good enough to carry the lyrics to a point at which they could be supplemented by his guitar riffs. And as for his songwriting skills, virtually all the songs he wrote were wrapped around guitar ideas he had in mind.

Like all great artists, Hendrix suffered periods of intense frustration and self-doubt. The pressures that he himself had helped to create stemmed from his need to push further and dig deeper. Hendrix would frequently escape these agonizing periods with drugs or incessant jamming, or both. But it was impossible to run away from the outside demands without becoming a recluse. There were those who wanted Hendrix to be more politically active or to fully

exploit his commercial potential. Given all these factors, it's as easy to consider his death a suicide as an accident. In any case, Jimi Hendrix became a rock & roll casualty in 1970.

Are You Experienced / Reprise / 1967

Are You Experienced introduced Jimi Hendrix in a big way. From the opening salvos of "Purple Haze" to the crashing guitar heard on the title track, Hendrix came on like he owned the rock world. The frantic notions that race in and out of "Fire," "Love or Confusion," and "Manic Depression" are not real; Hendrix was in control throughout, even though he teases us with the impression of reckless abandon. This LP left no doubt that an incredible new talent was on

the scene. The best tracts: "Purple Haze," "The Wind Cries Mary," "Fire," and "Third Stone from the Sun."

Axis: Bold as Love / Reprise / 1968

On *Axis: Bold as Love* Hendrix sought to advance everything on *Are You Experienced* to another dimension. The guitar work is as engaging and expressive as anything he'd ever record, but it's all shot into a swirl of psychedelic sounds and heavy feedback frenzies. It takes a while to digest all that happens here. Two great tracks came from *Axis*: "Little Wing," which would be covered by Eric Clapton on Derek and the Dominos' *Layla* in 1972 with splendid results, and "Castles Made of Sand."

Electric Ladyland / Reprise / 1968

What Hendrix had hinted at all along came to be on *Electric Ladyland*. Such tracks as "Crosstown Traffic," "Voodoo Child" (with Jack Casady from the Jefferson Airplane on bass and Steve Winwood from Traffic on organ), "Little Miss Strange," and Hendrix's greatest studio achievement, a stunning reworking of Dylan's "All Along the Watchtower," reveal Hendrix to be not only a master guitarist but a musical genius. Produced by Hendrix, the *sound* of the two-record set is superior to that of both *Are You Experienced* and *Axis: Bold as Love*, and the Experience delivers its most inspirational performances ever.

Band of Gypsys / Capitol / 1970

Recorded live at the Fillmore East on New Year's Eve 1969–70, the music on this album is a striking departure from *Electric Ladyland*. The songs and deliveries are both toned down and tend more toward jazz than psychedelia. Still, the guitar playing is exquisite. "Machine Gun" is a riveting guitar epic; "Changes" features drummer Buddy Miles singing lead; and "Power of Soul" sees Hendrix exploring his black roots in a new, inventive fashion.

Steppenwolf

Steppenwolf was responsible for one of heavy metal's first anthems, "Born to Be Wild." The song began with an intimidating guitar run helped along with a cracking snare. Then the bass and organ chipped in and John Kay shifted the song about motorcycles and freedom into full gear with his gravelly vocals. Steppenwolf rode the tune all the way to number two in the summer of 1968.

The band is most remembered for that song and its follow-up, "Magic Carpet Ride," although other songs such as "Rock Me Baby" (a Kay original), "The Pusher" (penned by Hoyt Axton), and the politicized "Monster" (cowritten by Kay and drummer Jerry Edmonton) were indicative of Steppenwolf's pop/heavy-metal slant.

Steppenwolf recorded a number of albums from 1968 to 1972, when the band broke up. The earlier albums are better than the later ones, with the group's first being the best. *Monster* was an ambitious attempt to make a strong metal comment, but only the title song succeeded.

Steppenwolf / Dunhill / 1968

"Born to Be Wild" and "The Pusher" highlight this, the band's debut record. While the former tune became an AM-radio favorite, "The Pusher," with its sordid antidrug lyrics, became an underground hit.

Sixteen Greatest Hits / MCA / 1973

A typical best-of collection with flimsy liner notes and a cheap packaging job. But all the essential Steppenwolf tracks are included. This LP and the debut together present the group's best moments.

Mountain

In the wake of Cream's huge success, producer Felix Pappalardi set about incorporating the ingredients that went into the English trio into his own band. What resulted was Mountain. On guitar was Leslie West, who, although not nearly as proficient as Eric Clapton, was a powerful heavy-metal guitarist. Pappalardi was an exact replica of Jack Bruce both when he played bass and sang, and drummer Corky Laing was similar to Ginger Baker if only on heavy pounding and tommy-gun rolls. The fourth player was organist Steve Knight.

A short time after forming, Mountain played Woodstock. By taking advantage of all the notoriety it received from what was only its third full gig as a band, Mountain instantly became America's most popular heavy-metal outfit and remained so into the early seventies. There was nothing that came out of Mountain that hadn't been done before by Cream, but by writing such weighty songs as "Mississippi Queen," "Nantucket Sleighride," and "Never in My Life," the group was able to capitalize on the craving for Cream and Cream-style rockers until 1973.

Mountain Climbing! / Windfall / 1970

With tracks such as "Never in My Life," "Mississippi Queen," and "Silver Paper," *Mountain Climbing!* showed just how heavy Mountain could be. Yet the LP's class cut was the Jack Bruce–penned "Theme for an Imaginary Western." Pappalardi's vocals evoked the very best qualities of Bruce. "Never in My Life" showed off West's and Laing's talents better than any other cut they recorded. All this adds up to one of the best early heavy-metal albums by an American group.

Iron Butterfly

The story of Iron Butterfly is really the story of *In-A-Gadda-Da-Vida*, one of the biggest-selling albums of the late sixties. By taking psychedelia and the nascent sound of heavy metal, keyboard player Doug Ingle stumbled upon a perfect blend and demonstrated that: (1) not all popular songs had to be less than three or four minutes long (the title track was seventeen minutes long and took up all of side two of the album), and (2) psychedelia and heavy metal were really one and the same thing in 1968.

Iron Butterfly hailed from San Diego and recorded two other sixties albums, *Heavy* and *Ball*, neither of which contained anything of substance, but sold well nevertheless. The band was a top concert draw in 1968 and 1969, mostly on the strength of "In-A-Gadda-Da-Vida," which the band was obliged to play at every gig. The instrumentation was quite basic, but Iron Butterfly endured until 1971 and even managed a revival a couple of years later.

In-A-Gadda-Da-Vida / Atco / 1968

Of all the heavy-metal albums that mean anything in terms of historical significance and evolution of sound, this one is the most dated. Side one consists of a few throwaway tunes, but side two is the Butterfly's claim to psychedelic/heavy-metal immortality. For seventeen minutes the band members plod along, trading off solos and taking turns carrying the melody line until they run out of ideas.

Vanilla Fudge

Vanilla Fudge proved that not all psychedelic/heavy metal came from California or England. The Fudge was from Long Island and took a unique approach, recording all rearranged standard pop hits of the day. Under the direction of producer Shadow Morton, the Fudge stripped down, slowed down, and disassembled each tune, and then restructured it with organ-heavy psychedelic fittings.

The band consisted of vocalist/keyboardist Marc Stein, drummer

Carmine Appice, bassist Tim Bogert, and guitarist Vinnie Matel. What they recorded together sounded very British. The sparse instrumentation on most of *Vanilla Fudge*, the band's debut, was closer to Procol Harum than to Mountain.

The follow-up was the concept album *The Beat Goes On*. Morton and the band attempted to chronologically trace the history of music on the LP. The record was a fiasco. The Vanilla Fudge recorded three other LPs: *Renaissance, Near the Beginning*, and *Rock 'n' Roll*. None matched the success of *Vanilla Fudge*, and in 1970 the group called it quits. Bogert and Appice had planned to form a band with Jeff Beck, but Beck was incapacitated for over a year after an auto accident. The two Fudge members went on to form Cactus and later teamed up with Beck in Beck, Bogert and Appice.

Vanilla Fudge / Atco / 1967

The big song here is "You Keep Me Hangin' On," the Holland-Dozier-Holland song done by the Supremes, which the Fudge recorded with a lethargic drag and an organ that sounds eerie, even haunting. Also on the LP are covers of the Beatles' "Ticket to Ride" and "Eleanor Rigby"; Sonny Bono's "Bang Bang"; Curtis Mayfield's "People Get Ready"; and the Zombies' "She's Not There."

Blind Faith

Blind Faith was sort of an English Crosby, Stills and Nash. Both groups were comprised of noted musicians from previously successful bands. Both made their debuts in 1969. Both were considered supergroups, a relatively new concept in rock. Blind Faith was created from the ruins of Cream and Traffic. From the former came guitarist Eric Clapton and drummer Ginger Baker. Traffic's Steve Winwood sang and handled keyboards. To play bass the group chose Rick Grech from Family.

Clapton and company made only one album (*Blind Faith*), played one major gig in England, and struggled through one U.S. tour. The band's potential, though, was staggering. Winwood's capabilities as a songwriter and vocalist matched Clapton's brilliance on guitar. Baker was one of the most compelling drummers in all of rock, and Grech, though largely unknown outside England, provided stability. By the time the album was released and the tour began, ego squabbles and a tug-of-war for artistic control caused Blind Faith to fold. Winwood then re-formed Traffic and took Rick Grech with him. Baker formed Ginger Baker's Air Force, which at one time would include *four* drummers. Clapton went off to play with American unknowns Delaney and Bonnie Bramlett.

Blind Faith / RSO / 1969

This album received somewhat mixed reviews, no doubt because the rock press expected too much. The LP is actually very good. The ballad "Can't Find My Way Home" is sung with all the clarity and soul one normally associated with Winwood. "Presence of the Lord" features Clapton's guitar; the lead work in the song is almost as good as anything he'd done with Cream. "Well All Right" is a clever and interesting version of the Buddy Holly tune. The LP cover photo of a young girl nude from the waist up, holding an airplane, caused problems when many record stores refused to display or to carry the LP. A new cover was quickly made, this one with a simple shot of the band on it, but not before considerable damage to sales had already been done.

Led Zeppelin

Led Zeppelin, very likely the greatest heavy-metal band ever, was primarily a seventies band, but its roots are in the sixties. The group evolved from the New Yardbirds. After the Yardbirds finally fell apart in 1968, guitarist Jimmy Page took the band's name and built a new group. Rather than forfeit a series of concert dates in Scandinavia, Page quickly grouped together longtime friend and bass player John Paul Jones, Robert Plant, a vocalist from Birmingham who used to be with Band of Joy, and drummer John Bonham, also of Band of Joy. Before the end of the year, the New Yardbirds rechristened themselves Led Zeppelin.

Led Zeppelin's impact was felt almost at once. Two small tours— one in England and the other in the States—got enough rave reviews to draw attention to *Led Zeppelin*, the band's debut record, and then *Led Zeppelin II*, both released in 1969. Some of the initial success enjoyed by the band came from strong management; some came from the band's ability as a live act. Led Zeppelin toured almost constantly

Courtesy of Atlantic Records

in the beginning and recorded superb albums almost as after-thoughts. But most of the success came from within. As a hard-rock, blues-based unit, Led Zeppelin *clicked.* Its music was unbelievably tight and mature, even though by the time 1970 came around the band had been together little more than a year. Page had always been a terrific guitarist, but with Led Zeppelin and the support Jones and Bonham gave him, he became an exceptional one. His solos always seemed meticulously thought out and then delivered with as much precision as those of Clapton and Hendrix. Robert Plant's vocals were far-reaching and charismatic, and onstage he was a potent frontman. John Paul Jones was as experienced a player as Page, and John Bonham rated as high as Keith Moon and Ginger Baker when it came to powerhouse drumming.

Musically the group structured much of its first album on the blues and included a couple of revamped blues standards on it. But with *Led Zeppelin II* the band was already forging its own sound: The focus was still the blues, but less noticeably so.

On both albums the sound was early heavy metal. Page's guitar dominated most tracks, and on those it didn't it competed vigorously with Plant's vocals. Such competition was healthy, as it brought out the best in both of them. The Bonham–Jones rhythm section was classically heavy and would remain that way until Bonham's death in 1980.

As Led Zeppelin became more and more popular, its influence grew accordingly. The band recorded seven mostly outstanding albums in the seventies that more or less defined the state of the art in heavy metal. After Bonham's death the band broke up, but its popularity remains quite strong.

Led Zeppelin / Atlantic / 1969

An amazing debut album, not only because of its impact on rock, but also because blues rock had never before been presented in such an engaging manner. "You Shook Me" and "I Can't Quit You Baby," two Willie Dixon tunes, are given brand new leases on life with Page's exquisite guitar licks and Plant's intimidating wails. "Communication Breakdown" is a savage rocker complete with some of the best examples of Page's solo talents heard on the record. "Babe, I'm Gonna Leave You" demonstrates the band's ability to turn ordinary tunes into dazzling rockers, and "Dazed and Confused" reveals the group's penchant for writing songs that would only serve to flex Led Zeppelin's heavy-metal muscle.

Led Zeppelin II / Atlantic / 1969

All the songs here are originals. Though a quickly recorded album, *Led Zeppelin II* shows no signs of being rushed or thrown together. The songs jell and there's a greater consistency in the instrumentation on this record. "Whole Lotta Love" is the LP's top track, but "Ramble On," "Heartbreaker," and "Moby Dick" are not far behind. Once again Page distinguishes himself on guitar and Bonham and Jones are virtually impeccable.

OTHER RECOMMENDED ALBUMS

Woodstock (soundtrack) / Cotillion / 1970

Woodstock was the high-water mark of the rock festival era (1967–69). The lineup of groups was spectacular, as were the performances in most cases. This double-record set, complete with occasional stage announcements and crowd hysteria, is as much a historical recording as a celebration of sixties rock. Classic performances by Sly and the Family Stone, the Who, Joan Baez, Santana, Ten Years After, the Jefferson Airplane, and Jimi Hendrix make this album essential listening, even if other great acts that played the fest—Creedence Clearwater Revival, Janis Joplin, the Band—are not represented.

Woodstock Two / Cotillion / 1971

A follow-up to *Woodstock*, this double-record set is not nearly as exciting or necessary as the above set. Yet there are some interesting selections by Hendrix, Jefferson Airplane, and Mountain. Recommended only for real fans of the festival or Woodstock veterans.

APPENDIX I
Top Twenty-Five Albums
of the Sixties

This is a list of twenty-five of what I consider to be the very best LPs made in the sixties. This list is presented to ignite interest and start readers thinking about their own preferences and coming up with their own lists—none of which, of course, will be more accurate or inaccurate than mine.

1. *Sgt. Pepper's Lonely Hearts Club Band,* the Beatles
2. *The Band,* the Band
3. *Beggar's Banquet,* the Rolling Stones
4. *Led Zeppelin,* Led Zeppelin
5. *Bringin' It All Back Home,* Bob Dylan
6. *Are You Experienced,* Jimi Hendrix and the Experience
7. *Meet the Beatles,* the Beatles
8. *Tommy,* the Who
9. *Live at the Apollo Volume 1,* James Brown
10. *The Doors,* the Doors
11. *Blonde on Blonde,* Bob Dylan

12. *I Never Loved a Man (The Way I Love You)*, Aretha Franklin
13. *Presenting the Fabulous Ronettes Featuring Veronica*, the Ronettes
14. *The Beatles* (the White Album), the Beatles
15. *Fresh Cream*, Cream
16. *Green River*, Creedence Clearwater Revival
17. *Going to a Go-Go*, Smokey Robinson and the Miracles
18. *Surrealistic Pillow*, Jefferson Airplane
19. *The Temptations Sing Smokey*, the Temptations
20. *Sweetheart of the Rodeo*, the Byrds
21. *Live in Europe*, Otis Redding
22. *Pet Sounds*, the Beach Boys
23. *Trout Mask Replica*, Captain Beefheart
24. *The Stand!*, Sly and the Family Stone
25. *Electric Ladyland*, Jimi Hendrix and the Experience

APPENDIX II
Periodicals
for Record Collectors

The following is a recommended list of record collecting periodicals that regularly advertise the sale of used sixties albums:

Goldmine
700 E. State St.
Iola, WI 54990

Record Auction Monthly
PO Box 758
Utica, MI 48087

Record Collector
45 St. Mary's Rd.
Ealing, London, W55 RQ
England

Record Collector's Quarterly
PO Box 6601
Falls Church, VA 22046

Record Collector's Monthly
PO Box 23
Essex Fells, NJ 07021

INDEX